Preface

S*trategic Planning: A Practical Guide for Competitive Success* shows the reader how to create strategic alternatives, test their plausibility, and argue convincingly for a preferred one. The idea for this book evolved over several years, during which I discovered that few people in small- to midsized companies knew how to do strategic planning and institutionalize the process in their company. Those individuals who could perform strategic planning, with some exceptions, did so very conservatively and tended to stay well within their comfort zone. In addition, strategic planning seems to have an aura of "mystification" about it, given the plethora of different models and approaches that exist—all promoted by their creators, cocreators, and champions and all having merit.

In writing this book, I promised myself that I would try to have something new and important to say and that it would be a short book. I have made good on my promises, and what new contributions I have made include:

- The use of an internally consistent set of terminology that clarifies the term "strategy," as well as related terms such as "strategic thinking" and "strategic planning" (Chapter 1).

- A clarification of, and several conceptual approaches to aid in, strategic thinking (Chapter 2), a major determinant of sound strategic planning and strategic decision-making.

- A rigorous method for coming up with strategic alternatives and choosing which of them to pursue (Chapter 6).

- SAM^{tw}—for a **S**trategic **A**nalysis **M**odel that **w**orks—the companion CD-ROM that accompanies this book, which is designed to help the reader *do* financial and strategic analysis using a variety of tools.

I believe that the quality of strategic decisions cannot help but improve when the complete process for performing a strategic analysis (Part 2, Chapters 4–7) is followed. This process can be adopted by a company to doing strategic planning (Chapter 8) based on the model described in Part 2 and first explained in Chapter 3. I believe that the insights I have gained from over 30 years of consulting and over 25 years of teaching are imbued in the narrative and in the process. As I state in the acknowledgements, I am in the debt of many that have gone before me and were my own teachers.

The Audience for the Book

Strategic Planning: A Practical Guide for Competitive Success has two primary audiences. One is the corporate practitioner of strategic planning, including CEOs of small- to midsize companies, their key managers, and the consultants who serve them. I believe this book will not only benefit those managers who are new to strategic planning, but also those whose current strategic-planning process is not producing desired results. Parts of the book, especially Chapter 2, Strategic Thinking, may even enhance the smoothly functioning process of those who are good at strategic planning.

The other audience, in no way less important, is MBA or executive-education students taking a course in strategic planning or strategic management. Indeed, this book benefited from over four years of experience using earlier versions of its manuscript as a course for MBA students at California State Polytechnic University, Pomona (Cal Poly Pomona). I have kept and enhanced those parts the students found most useful, and revised those parts they did not. The earlier versions of the book, CD-ROM, and course received very strong positive comments in course evaluations over that period.

Part of the audience includes those students who are now executives taking similar courses in a continuing executive education program. Both students and seasoned businesspeople will learn a skill and develop an ability that will actually be used in their future career. Knowing *how to do* a strategic analysis and *being able to do* it are, perhaps, the most useful skills one can have in the business world, especially in top management roles, whether the company is well established or emerging, small or large, manufacturing or service, public or privately held, domestic or international.

The Approach of the Book

The book's focus is narrow: It is about how to do a strategic analysis and strategic planning. It claims to do nothing else. For more information about strategic planning and other companies' experiences, I ask you to refer to the sources cited at the end of each chapter. Nevertheless, some readers will find this book an antidote to the large textbooks that give a wonderful overview of the field of strategic management and of business today, yet provide little in the way of guidance or insight as to how to *actually do* strategic planning. Even a book such as this one does not provide pat answers. Strategic planning will still be difficult to do the 20th time around because the future is still before you and unknown, and the information you need and can gather will always be incomplete, ambiguous, and uncertain. And you will never know that you made the right decision until several years later, when you can look back and see what happened. However, at least you will have the process down cold and will have the courage to ask, and grapple with, difficult questions.

The Four Focuses of the Book

1. It focuses only on "intended" strategies.

One of Henry Mintzberg's important contributions to the strategy literature was to distinguish between intended, failed, emergent, and realized strategies. While acknowledging that *emergent* strategies—those that develop by reacting or adjusting to market, competitive, and environmental changes without prior planning—are all too common in practice and often thwart *intended* (planned) strategies and produce different *realized* strategies (what actually gets implemented), this book focuses only on coming up with intended strategies. In doing so, it acknowledges that any intended strategy that is pursued could fail or even change during implementation into a different realized strategy. One can only hope that when it does change, it is for good reasons that will help the company succeed, and not because implementation has been lackadaisical.

2. It focuses only on "business-level" strategies and single-business companies.

Many strategy textbooks and companies propose and adhere to a hierarchical pattern of strategies:

- *Corporate-level* strategies, principally in conglomerates or multibusiness companies; at this level, the corporation's principal purpose is to achieve corporate financial objectives and decide which of its businesses should receive more or less resources in support of their strategic plans, or which should be divested and which others acquired.

- *Business-level* strategies, which deal with competitors—in the industry or segment in which the *strategic business unit* (SBU) is competing—and with other environmental forces. Sometimes called "grand strategies" or "master strategies" to distinguish them from functional strategies.

- *Functional-level* strategies, which I call "programs" because they are operational in nature and specify what the various functions such as marketing, R&D, engineering, production, finance, human resources, and the like, should do during the year.

Strategic Planning: A Practical Guide for Competitive Success focuses exclusively on business-level strategies, which I shall refer to as "competitive strategies," and implies that the company is in only one business. Later, in Chapter 8, where I discuss a corporate strategic-planning process, *programs* have to be designed to implement the chosen strategy or business model. In designing them, a company may have to make hard choices, for instance, how to finance a particular strategic initiative. But financing it—whether through cash, some debt, sale of stock, or other means—is a program: It is operational and concerns principally, but not exclusively, the finance department. It would not change the company's competitive position, its competitive advantage, or its chosen strategy. So it is not strategic. That is not to say it is unimportant. It may well be critical, for without such financing the company would not be able to implement its strategy.

But practice in business-level strategies can be valuable to corporate managers as well. They will learn something about crafting good strategies, something they must evaluate for their subsidiaries and divisions on an ongoing basis. However, corporate strategies *per se* are the focus of some other text.

3. It focuses only on established, for-profit companies.

A focus on established, for-profit companies means that startup or emerging companies and nonprofits are excluded. Startups have no history and need worry only about their market-entry strategy. Having a product, service, or business model already in mind, their only challenge (and a major one) is to enter the market and quickly establish themselves in their industry. They do not have time to do any strategic planning, nor do they have the same degrees of freedom of an established company. Nonprofits are an altogether different kind of organization. While strategic planning can be useful to them, this book cannot do them justice.

4. It focuses only on the "what" and "how to" of strategic planning.

This book is more about *how to do* strategic planning, and less about strategic planning. To achieve its purpose, I had to define terms that I would constantly use throughout the book and discuss *strategic thinking*—the core skill and activity of strategic planning. In doing so, I had to sacrifice the breadth of topic coverage that one finds in most books on strategic planning.

Support for the Instructor

Instructor's Manual (ISBN 0-324-23256-X) Prepared by the author, Stanley C. Abraham, the Instructor's Manual includes extensive instructions for use; sample course outlines and syllabi; criteria for choosing appropriate cases; and suggestions for in-class discussion and projects. The Instructor's Manual is available only to instructors online at **http://abraham.swlearning.com**.

PowerPoint Presentation (ISBN 0-324-31414-0) Prepared by the author, the PowerPoint slides work in tandem with the text and its Instructor's Manual to create a unique and useful instructor's package. The PowerPoint slides are available only to instructors online at **http://abraham.swlearning.com**.

Website A comprehensive website at **http://abraham.swlearning.com** is available to instructors with additional features.

Acknowledgments

As a teacher and consultant, my ideas have developed gradually over the years in the classroom and with clients. Accordingly, I owe students and clients a debt of gratitude for having helped shaped them, even unwittingly. In the same vein, I am indebted to those strategists and teachers whose ideas have also influenced me, and whom I cite with pleasure in these pages.

I am privileged to be part of a group of strategists who are contributing editors of the journal *Strategy & Leadership*. Some of them, namely Robert Allio, Stewart Early, Sam Felton, Deependra Moitra, Ian Wilson, and Robert Randall, critically reviewed the first chapters. I am grateful for their insights and wish to include among them Jim Bandrowski, who commented incisively on these chapters as well. Special thanks are due to Tiffani Argandona, a former Cal Poly Pomona MBA student, for designing, developing, and updating the SAM^tw CD-ROM that accompanies this book. She also contributed to Appendix B.

I also want to thank John Szilagyi, Executive Editor at Thomson Learning, for seeing the potential of this book, Judy O'Neill for keeping it on schedule, and James Reidel for his consummate editing of the manuscript and attention to detail.

Finally, Brenda, my wife, and Mark and Jason, my sons, have put up with many evenings without me as the book was written and revised, and I am grateful for their longsuffering and love.

Stan Abraham
Santa Monica, CA
August 10, 2004

Contents

Part One

SETTING THE STAGE

1

Defining Strategy

Of all the concepts in management, strategy is the one that attracts most attention and generates the most controversy. Almost everyone agrees that it is important. Almost no one agrees on what it is . . . But this is a concept you ignore at your peril.[1]

—Joan Magretta

S trategic planning like most disciplines has its own language or terminology. Without first defining a consistent terminology, explaining concepts or just discussing "strategy" soon becomes problematic. It makes sense, then, to begin by defining several key terms including "strategic thinking," "strategic plan," "strategic planning," "strategic management," "strategic analysis," "strategic decision," "business model," and "value proposition." As we shall see, while all are related, these terms are not interchangeable and should not be confused with each other. (A glossary of about 100 terms also appears at the end of the book.)

Influential researcher Henry Mintzberg, in discussing the topic of strategy in depth (and why strategic planning became popular and then fell out of favor), noted that people conceive of strategy in different ways: as a plan, a pattern of actions over time, as position, and as perspective.[2] Another researcher discussed the definitions of strategy by eight well-known authors in the field, and concludes:

> Some readers might go away disappointed that no final, unambiguous definition of strategy has been provided. The quick response is that there is none, that strategy is a broad, ambiguous topic. We must all come to our own understanding, definition, and meaning.[3]

This, of course, is a safe and uncontroversial conclusion—but it is not helpful. First, it reveals a reluctance to "bite the bullet" and provide a useful definition. It also suggests that there is no authoritative body of knowledge on strategy to which we can subscribe. While making strategy *real* might differ from company to company and executive to executive, we should agree on what strategy means and should possess a shared understanding of that term and other key terms.

3

Before settling on a working definition of strategy, I gathered together as many definitions of strategy that I could find. I asked a few strategists how they defined the term and looked in my personal library of strategy texts. In addition, I looked at journals such as *Strategy & Leadership* and its predecessor *Planning Review, Sloan Management Review, Harvard Business Review, Journal of Business Strategy, Strategy+Business*, and *California Management Review*. Lastly, I made a cursory search via the World Wide Web.

Appendix A contains the resulting 66 definitions that I found. These exist because of the many different frames of reference and experience with strategy. Suffice it to say, however, that this great diversity may actually do more harm than good, hampering communication among strategists and between consultants and corporate executives—not to mention students. Nevertheless, without them there can be no discourse.

Definitions of Strategy: The Persuasive Ones

There exists a bewildering variety of ways to define strategy. At the same time, there is a kind of similarity that comes from defining this same word. These definitions made use of concepts that were in vogue at various times, such as first achieving objectives, then creating a core competence and competitive advantage, and finally creating a business design and providing customer value. To the extent that you are familiar—and agree—with such concepts, then certain definitions are the ones that will most appeal to you.

Of the definitions listed in Appendix A, the following have considerable appeal, although even these have a few drawbacks. A brief commentary accompanies each:

- *"The goal of strategy is to beat the competition . . . [But] before you test yourself against the competition, strategy takes shape in the determination to create value for customer."* Kenichi Ohmae's view of strategy is persuasive because of its simplicity and directness, and because it recognizes that the way to beat the competition is to first satisfy customers. But it tries to define strategy by defining only one of its goals.

- *"A company's business design has four elements: customer selection (target), value capture (protect profit margins), strategic control (differentiation), and scope. Good strategy involves creating the right business design and reinventing it (every 3–5 years) so that it continues to keep the company successful."* Here Adrian Slywotsky and David Morrison have laid out the critical elements of a business design that will, in fact, be competitive and successful, and then add that such a business design must be reinvented for the company to remain successful, reflecting the rapid pace of change occurring all around us. (Actually, companies in high-tech industries that experience much more rapid change might be dead if they waited as long as 3–5 years to reinvent their business.)

- *"Strategy at its heart is about positioning for future competitive advantage. That is its essence. Any strategic thinking must reflect this essence. It is the purpose that drives strategy."* Stuart Wells's definition is forceful and adamant. It focuses on competitive advantage—but it also is one of the few definitions that includes the notion of strategic thinking. Positioning for future competitive advantage implies that competitive advantages erode with time unless continually developed and strengthened. Nevertheless, only a purpose—the principal purpose—for strategy is given here, that is, gaining and sustaining a competitive advantage

- *"Strategy is defining a unique market position and occupying it . . .The essence of strategy is selecting one position that a company can claim as its own. (A strategic position is the sum of the company's answers to three questions: (1) Who should the company target as customers? (2) What products or services should the company offer? (3) How can the company do this efficiently?)"* Constantinos C. Markides, taking a cue from Michael Porter's belief that strategy is about being different, sees strategy as occupying a unique market position—in other words, about finding one niche or market to dominate ("claim as its own"). That's good. But it also implies that a company that doesn't occupy a unique market position doesn't have a strategy. And is defining "strategic position" the same as defining "strategy"?

- *"Strategy at its heart [is] identifying discontinuities, determining their impact on markets of today and tomorrow, and developing new business models. [Success depends on] both strategic thinking and flawless execution."* This definition, by C. K. Prahalad and Jan P. Oosterveld states the need to continually develop business models in response to inevitable discontinuities, even though not all industries experience discontinuities. Actually, this definition is a good definition of "strategic thinking" rather than "strategy." While the part about success depending on both "strategic thinking and flawless execution" is true and important, should it be part of the definition?

- *"Within the Value Dynamics context, corporate strategy concerns the effective design and execution of a business model to create and realize value."* Taking this view of strategy, Richard E. S. Boulton, Barry D. Libert, and Steve M. Samek focus on creating an effective business design or model to create customer value. The appeal of using "business design" or "business model" in the definition is that it encompasses more than just strategy—it is the totality of what a firm does to create and deliver value to the customer, and includes programs, vision, capabilities, know-how, intent, and resource allocations. That is why it is a definition that includes the word "execution." (See definition number 17 in Appendix A, which conceives of strategy as an approach to running a business.)

- *"Strategy is a handful of decisions that drive or shape most of a company's subsequent actions, are not easily changed once made, and have the greatest impact on whether a company meets its strategic objectives . . .This handful of decisions consists of selecting the company's strategic posture, identifying the source or sources of competitive advantage, developing the business concept, and constructing tailored value-delivery systems."* Kevin P. Coyne and Somu Subramaniam see strategy in two parts. The first part, that strategy is a handful of decisions that shape a company's subsequent actions, is critical to enabling the company to meet its strategic objectives. The second part, which defines the handful of decisions, depends on knowing what "strategic posture" means and does not say how the definition would change if the company does not have a competitive advantage, which many do not. Including the design of "value-delivery systems" is good.

- *"Strategy is about uniqueness and competitive differentiation for achieving leverageable advantage in the marketplace."* Deependra Moitra's commentary on his own definition clarifies it and increases its appeal. He says that "most definitions of strategy equate it with planning. This is not quite right. While planning is needed to execute any project, you need strategy only when you have competitors and a need for competitive differentiators. Strategy is also about uniqueness, especially when you want to position and identify yourself uniquely in a competitive environment. This is also the only definition that talks about leverageable advantage, which Moitra emphasizes is essential "because competitive advantage is not sustainable in today's world."

- *"Strategy is the art of deploying resources toward market opportunities in a way that distinguishes a business from its competitors."* What is appealing about Robert Allio's definition is not so much that strategy, stripped of everything else, is about deploying resources, but that those efforts are directed at seizing market opportunities in distinctive ways.

- *"Strategy is about positioning an organization for sustainable competitive advantage. It involves making choices about which industries to participate in, what products and services to offer, and how to allocate corporate resources to achieve such a sustainable advantage. Its primary goal is to create value for shareholders and other stakeholders by providing customer value. (Value, unless constantly maintained, nourished, and improved, erodes with time.)"* Despite his need to be expansive here, Cornelis A. de Kluyver offers by far the most comprehensive and complex definition. His embraces several current concepts:

  - It involves positioning the organization for sustainable competitive advantage, even though actually sustaining a competitive advantage today is becoming more difficult than ever.

  - It involves the decision of which industry to compete in, not just taking the industry that one is in for granted.

  - It contains the notion of creating value by providing customer value and recognizing that that value, like competitive advantage, can erode over time.

Now, should strategy involve pursuing all of these different approaches and different sets of activities at the same time or even sequentially, or should one select a "best" approach?

Clearly, being better than and beating the competition is central to the concept of strategy. If it were not for competitors (or other opposing forces), companies, entrepreneurs, and the like would not need a strategy.[4] Going against other companies that are also trying to outwit you is, like overcoming an enemy in war, why you need a strategy.[5] So doing better than your competitors means, in effect, getting more customers to buy *your* product or service. This is done, of course, with the *right* strategy.

One's strategy and core competence, if possessed, *should* be embedded in a business model. *How* a company delivers value to customers and *how* a company competes are often sources of competitive advantage, and both are taken into account by one's core competence and business model.[6] Finally, it is clear that the frenetic pace of change and changing circumstances require the constant renewing of one's business model, otherwise value will flow away from it to competitors and their business models, which is another way of saying that customers will cease buying your products and buy your competitors' instead).[7]

Definitions Used in This Book

First, as a disclaimer, the definitions adopted in this book are useful for two reasons: (1) They make the book intelligible; and (2) they form an internally consistent set. But they are not the only definitions and, perhaps, not always the "right" ones in certain contexts. What this book calls a "program," someone else may call a strategy. Is that person wrong? Not really. It is all about understanding what someone means and what someone is saying. The task of understanding becomes infinitely easier with an internally consistent set. It enables one to ask questions of clarification and, if necessary, "translate" what another person is saying. Many years ago, a CEO told me that a consultant had helped his firm develop 82 strategies! On hearing some examples, it was easy to see that his firm had developed 82 *programs,* but had only one "master" strategy.

In this section, a number of very important concepts in strategic planning are defined, starting with "strategy" and including the term "strategic planning" itself. The definitions draw upon many of the concepts already discussed.

Strategy is how a company actually competes.

This definition is remarkable not only because of its simplicity, but also because it is true. It can refer to an *intended,* an *emergent,* or even a *realized* strategy. Most critically, strategy describes what an organization does, as well as what it intends to do in a plan. For example, one can infer what strategy a company is pursuing by studying what it does and where it spends its resources of capital and labor. In fact, many companies never consciously "think" about strategy, but simply act in ways that make sense to them. That does not mean that they are not following a strategy, only that one can infer from its behavior what it is. (Only the definition of business strategy by Kenneth Andrews, number 1 in Appendix A, comes close to this one.)

There are many ways of competing. For example, producing better products, targeting expanded or new markets, differentiating, low-cost leadership, vertical integration, acquisition, strategic alliances, or through superior customer service, technology, marketing, or brand management as well as combinations of these strategies. In fact, the ideal strategy should provide superior customer value and a sustainable competitive advantage.[8] Notice, however, that these desirable results are not part of the definition. We are defining the term "strategy," not "ideal strategy" or "good strategy."

All companies have a strategy, even though the strategy is not what it could be and might not achieve desirable results. People often criticize a company for not having a strategy just because its results are terrible and the company appears in disarray. A more accurate observation, however, is that it has a strategy, albeit one that has not been implemented well and is not working. Only if one could say about a company that it "isn't competing" could you also say that it therefore has no strategy.

> A **strategic decision** is any decision that affects the company's ability to compete, its position in the industry, or its viability as a going concern.

Strategic decisions differ from other types of decisions primarily in their consequences, which are more substantial for the organization. Because of this, strategic decisions tend to get made only after appreciable analysis, discussion, and debate, and typically involve a number of people in the decision. More often than not, strategic decisions are made during the strategic-planning process, whereas operational decisions are not—they are made subsequently.

Examples of strategic decisions are deciding on a strategy; which company to acquire or merge with; which technology to adopt; whether to form a strategic alliance and with whom; to franchise rather than expand with owned facilities; how to gain a competitive advantage and sustain it; which new CEO to hire; whether to sell the business; whether to enter another industry or segment; and so on.

Operational decisions include whether to upgrade the accounting system, change an advertising campaign, offer discounts or other promotional incentives, lobby for tariffs, hire anyone other than the CEO, how to reduce costs, how many and which workers to lay off, financing a particular initiative, and the like. Though these are, in all cases, very important for the organization, they are nevertheless *operational* decisions. Strategic decisions are not more important *per se* than operational decisions—they are simply more consequential.

> **Strategic analysis** is one person's or one group's attempt at arriving at a strategy, objectives, and key programs for a company, or performing an intermediate analytical task.

The major distinction between a strategic analysis and strategic planning is that there is no organizational commitment involved in doing a strategic analysis. For example, a staff analyst could do a strategic analysis of a company that the firm is considering acquiring, or a strategic analysis of the combined entity after acquisition, as a guide to the decision-makers involved in the acquisition. Similarly, MBA students could do a strategic analysis of a company for the president of the company in question, or even to demonstrate they have acquired the ability to do one. However, when a company does strategic planning—and does so seriously—then everyone involved in the process should be prepared to commit to the decisions that are jointly reached.

Strategic analysis also refers to any part of the strategic-planning process that requires analysis, for example, comparing the firm with its key competitors, assessing the attractiveness of the industry, drawing a conclusion about the firm's recent financial performance and current financial condition, whether it has a core competence, or deciding which of several strategic alternatives to choose.

> **Strategic planning** is the process by which one develops a strategy to achieve certain purposes.

First and foremost, strategic planning is a *process,* that is, a series of steps followed by a company collectively trying to agree on where it is going (i.e., *vision*) and the way it will get there (i.e., *strategy*). Those are two purposes of strategic planning. Other valid purposes include increasing the company's shareholder value, market share, or long-term profitability. Yet another purpose could be to develop a core competence and sustainable competitive advantage. Consequently, identifying the purpose or purposes to be achieved is an integral part of the process. How and whether those purposes are achieved in reality is the job of the strategy. So, choosing the right strategy is crucial. This is another answer to the question, "Why have a strategy?" It also answers the question, "Why do strategic planning?"

A critical dimension of strategic planning is who gets to participate in the process. In a few companies, only the CEO participates (whatever he or she says goes). In others, the top management team participates (which is better), and then relays what has been decided to lower management levels and employees in general. In still others, participation includes those who will help implement the plan, that is, middle managers and key other people (the best). Chapter 8 elaborates on the importance of involving the right people in the strategic-planning process. Because the outcomes of strategic planning are so dependent on who participates, on the particular process used, and on the information on which decisions are based, it is clear that doing strategic planning remains very much an art. It is a highly creative yet disciplined process that draws on the individuals' and the groups' intuition, experience, know-how, and powers of persuasion. While the strategic-planning process is relatively straightforward, actually doing it is difficult. Consider the following:

- People seldom agree on where the company stands right now and how it is performing, because people are biased, have a limited perspective, and often have personal or hidden agendas. That is, politics gets in the way of candor and truth.

- Information the company and its people possess are incomplete, dated, often inaccurate, and sometimes not useful, while the information they most need is often unavailable.

- The planning horizon is typically three to five years in the future, a future that is unknown, ambiguous, and changing before our very eyes.

Chapter 6 discusses in detail a process of coming up with a strategy and business model that fits a company's purposes, situation, and resources.

> **Strategic management** encompasses both strategic planning *and* the implementation of the strategic plan to ensure, ideally, achieving intended results.

As difficult as choosing the right strategy is, it is more difficult to implement it and achieve the desired results. This is why, in the strategic-planning process, it is imperative to include those who will be responsible for implementing it.

Why else is implementation so difficult? Because environmental, competitive, and market changes continue unabated during implementation, often requiring minor or even major adjustments to the strategy as it is implemented. If the strategy requires the company to do things it has never done before—make a new kind of product, switch to a new technology, sell to a new kind of customer, expand to a new country, and so on—then the company has to learn to do these things, develop new systems and training regimens, and even change its business model. All these things make implementation more difficult and risky—yet thankfully, not impossible. All of this is covered by the term strategic management.

Another way to think about strategic management is that this is what presidents and CEOs should be doing 100% of their time—ensuring that the strategy the company is pursuing is the right one, that it is working, and that intended results are being achieved. If intended results are not being achieved, then operational adjustments must be made. (One should first suspect that implementation is the problem, not the strategy. Chapter 7 discusses this in more detail.) If those "don't do the trick," then the higher-order strategy and objectives must be reviewed for their relevancy and a better strategy created if one can be found. The search for a better strategy, which should be an ongoing activity, uses primarily strategic-thinking skills.

> A **business model** describes the way in which a firm does what it does to deliver customer value.

A company's business model should also include its *revenue model*. That is, how it intends to sell its product or service and the assumptions on which such sales depend and how those sales will grow over time. The business model must also include the company's *strategy* or how it intends to compete and grow. For example, a supermarket's business model should explain:

- How it intends to get people to shop at its stores (e.g., provide clean and attractive interiors, have helpful staff, use "loss-leader" pricing, cultivate loyal customers with "club cards," and develop a trusted brand).

- How it will make money (e.g., efficient warehousing, distribution, and inventory control, more private-label items, and higher prices for items not advertised as specials that week).

- Whether it grows through acquisition or by building new stores in other towns or locations where the new stores can still be efficiently served by its warehousing and distribution system.

In layperson's terms, a company's business model should describe what it does, how it does it, and why. Joan Magretta's definition of business models as "stories that explain how enterprises work" is a good one,[9] except that it excludes strategy from the definition. What is called a "bundle" in Chapter 6 is, in fact, one step removed from being a business model. A *bundle* is a strategic alternative that includes elements such as the technology on which the product is based, the product, capabilities, knowledge, integration skills, systems, value-chain management, supply chain, distribution, source of financing, strategy, strategic intent, and much more. Such elements, when integrated into a cohesive "story," then become a business model. Coming up with the right business model means designing one that is not only feasible, but will also provide superior customer value (see definition of value proposition below).

> A **value proposition** is the entire set of resulting experiences—at some price—that an organization causes its customers to have.[10]

When a customer buys a product or service for a price, she or he owns and uses the product (or benefits from the service), and therefore has a net experience of the product. This experience can be instantaneous, as in a thrill ride at Six Flags Magic Mountain theme park in California, or it can endure over a substantial period, like owning a car or washing machine for over a decade. The more that the net experience or benefit is very positive compared to the price paid, the more will the customer value the proposition (purchase). In this case, the customer has received superior value (for money). The reverse is also true—a customer could receive inferior value, and think twice before buying from the same company again. A company delivers superior value when customers get more benefit or value for their money with the company's product or service than with competitor's offerings. Thus, "the value proposition is not a sideshow or one of several factors important for a business—its delivery is the whole show."[11]

From a customer's perspective, a superior value proposition means meeting all current and possibly some future needs with a product or service offered at a lower price than the customer expects or, for a given price, a greater-than-expected set of benefits. The concept of customer value changes constantly as customer expectations and perceptions change and as competitive offerings change. Coming up with or changing an organization's value proposition is a legitimate output of a strategic-planning process and, indeed, a valid subject for strategic thinking.

> **Strategic thinking** is coming up with alternative viable strategies or business models that deliver customer value.[12]

Devising a sound strategy is impossible without strategic thinking. Coming up with different, plausible strategic alternatives is both creative and conceptual, but must also be grounded in a broad knowledge of the relevant industries, competitors, markets, technologies, and other trends. And strategic thinking should not be done just when a firm engages in strategic planning, but rather all the time. It requires a deep understanding of how markets and competitors are changing and of where opportunities may lie in order to determine whether a better strategic alternative exists and what it is.

People use the term *strategic thinking* and read about it without really knowing what it means. They think it has something to do with being creative, or "thinking outside the box," or trying to outwit competitors. Of course, it is all of these things. However, does it include coming up with a vision? Does it include coming up with various scenarios to guide the planning process? Where does strategic thinking begin and where does it end? De Kluyver's definition really captures its essence. In order to come up with alternative strategies, one has to do *all* those things. One has to be creative yet knowledgeable about the industry, competitors, markets, and how they are changing. One has to be able to visualize some market space that has potential yet is still unoccupied, a niche that no one else has seen, an opportunity ripe for whoever gets there first.

Finding different strategies or business models is one thing. Strategic analysts are also expected to test them—that is, they must be feasible and implementable before recommending or arguing for their adoption. You can immediately see how companies that rely on "doing more of the same" or that simply make "operational" changes, mistakenly believing they have made a strategic change, can be rightfully accused of not doing any strategic thinking. Strategic thinking goes beyond just satisfying; it requires coming up with different and plausible strategies with good value propositions and, hopefully, that also result in a competitive advantage.[13] Interestingly, some of the definitions of strategy discussed earlier and collected in Appendix A tend to define strategic thinking, not strategy.

Strategic thinking is such a critical part of strategy formulation that Chapter 2 is devoted to it. Imagining and creating different alternative business models (or bundles) is such a difficult, conceptual, creative, and subjective endeavor that it would help if several ways of approaching it were presented to learn about it. One cannot even begin without knowing the overall purpose of the business and, therefore, about what kind of strategy or business model might help most to attain it. While it is impossible to guarantee that any business design or strategy would produce the desired outcomes—strategy-setting is affected by too many variables outside a company's control—companies have no choice but to do their best in coming up with one that is good and moves the company in the right direction.

Loizos Heracleous goes to some lengths in his book to reconcile strategic thinking and strategic planning. He casts strategic planning as "single-loop learning," where a company's actions are based on feedback without critically examining underlying assumptions, and strategic thinking as "double-loop learning," where actions are based not only on feedback, but also on the strategic parameters or assumptions themselves.[14] In contrast to sources he cites that believe that one form dominates the other, he believes

Figure 1.2   Strategic Planning vs. Strategic Management

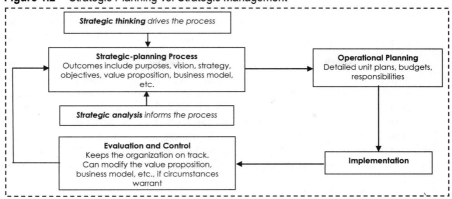

that both are necessary. "Creative, ground-breaking strategies emerging from strategic thinking still have to be operationalized through convergent and analytical thought (strategic planning) . . . ."[15].

Strategic thinking is and always will remain very much an art. In fact, the only way of knowing for certain whether a strategy or business model has been successful is by looking back three or four years hence and, with perfect hindsight, see whether and to what extent the intended results were realized.

Summary

Because it is so easy to confuse the definitions of these various terms— witness the variance in the definitions of strategy in Appendix A—the diagram shown in Figure 1.1 will show at least one consistent pattern (and even clarify any confusion that might arise from these definitions when considered together).

Figure 1.1 shows the familiar cycle of strategic planning, operational planning, implementation, and evaluation and control. While the diagram shows these as linear and sequential phases, in fact they are anything but. For example, implementation and evaluation and control occur at the same time as the next round of strategic planning. While strategic planning is defined as a process to devise a strategy to achieve certain purposes, it is also designed to make a number of other strategic decisions, such as coming up with a vision statement, setting objectives, articulating a value proposition, and clarifying its business model. Strategic analysis informs the strategic-planning process in many areas—and strategic thinking not only drives it, but is also singularly responsible for the quality of the strategic decisions and resulting strategy. (Again, strategic thinking should ideally take place all year round, not just at strategic-planning time.) Everything in the diagram comprises strategic management, the true "bailiwick" of the president or CEO and the company's board of directors.

Notes

1. Joan Magretta, with Nan Stone, *What Management Is: How It Works and Why It's Everyone's Business* (New York: Free Press, 2002), 71.

2. Henry Mintzberg, *The Rise and Fall of Strategic Planning* (New York: Basic Books, 1994), 23–29.

3. Fred Nickols, *Strategy: Definitions and Meaning*, 2000, <http://home.att.net/~nickols/strategy_definition.htm> (14 June 2004) Distance Counseling.

4. By this same logic, monopolists would have no need of a strategy. And on the surface, it would seem, nonprofits and government agencies also would not need a strategy since they do not compete. But that's not correct. Nonprofits compete ferociously for funding from a dwindling number of sources, for good people and good volunteers, and for donations from those who are aligned with their cause. Government agencies engage in their own competition for a bigger slice of the budget, as well as for good people.

5. The word "strategy" comes from the Greek *strategos,* meaning *generalship.*

6. Joan Magretta argues that business models are not the same as strategies. Business models describe, as a system, how the pieces of a business fit together; a competitive strategy explains how you will do better than—be different from—your rivals. (See her article, "Why Business Models Matter," *Harvard Business Review* 80 (May 2002): 86–92.) However, my use of the term "business model" *combines* the two notions, i.e., a business model that also enables a company to compete effectively.

7. Adrian Slywotsky, *Value Migration: How to Think Several Moves Ahead of the Competition* (New York: HBS Press, 1996).

8. Robert Allio calls strategies that have such a purpose *natural* strategies, as opposed to strategies, for example, that try to increase market share in a mature industry, which aren't natural. See Robert Allio, *The Practical Strategist: Business and Corporate Strategy for the 1990* (New York: Ballinger, 1988).

9. Joan Magretta, "Why Business Models Matter," *Harvard Business Review* 80 (May 2002): 87.

10. Michael J. Lanning, *Delivering Profitable Value: A Revolutionary Framework to Accelerate Growth, Generate Wealth, and Rediscover the Heart of Business* (New York: Perseus, 1998), 55.

11. Ibid., 57.

12. I owe this definition of strategic thinking to Cornelis de Kluyver. See definition no. 49 in Appendix A.

13. Pierre Loewe, "Developing New Business Models," presentation at the Second Annual Conference of the Association for Strategic Planning: Exploiting Strategic Alternatives, October 8, 2002, Manhattan Beach, CA.

14. Loizos Heracleous, *Strategy and Organization: Realizing Strategic Management* (New York: Cambridge University Press, 2003), 42–45.

15. Ibid., 47–48.

2

Strategic Thinking

L ike *strategy*, the term *strategic thinking* is frequently used by businesspeople who do not know what it means. A recent book *Be Your Own Strategy Consultant: Demystifying Strategic Thinking,* by two strategy professors and consultants in the United Kingdom, Tony Grundy and Laura Brown, explored the topic of strategic thinking in some depth. One chapter devoted itself to an academic perspective based on interviews with five strategy professors from the highly respected Cranfield School of Management. Another chapter revealed the managerial—or practitioner—perspective based on interviews with five senior managers from Barclays, Tesco, Hewlett-Packard, Lex, and Zurich Independent Financial Advisors. The summary of the academic perspective concluded in part:

> Respondents were not entirely clear what strategic thinking meant. This implies that, potentially, the literature itself is not so clear either, and managers may be even less clear. Strategic thinking applies to many levels, not just to the top team or to larger areas of business. Value [of strategic thinking] is frequently emergent, latent, or contingent and may thus be diluted considerably. There is value simply through linking actions and also by speeding up the decision process.[1]

> [. . .]

> A major constraint was actually the ambiguity of what "strategic thinking" actually meant. This ought to be an easy constraint to remedy, albeit one that requires extensive education throughout the management community. Perhaps strategy academics generally have some significant role in this?"[2]

Strategy academics should play a significant role in this educational process; however, they should first be clear on what it is they are teaching.

The managerial or practitioner perspective, which in length matched that of their academic counterparts, summarized the value of strategic thinking as follows:

It was discovered that the economic value (to date) has been relatively unclear. Not merely was the strategic thinking process (and its underlying influences) not very well understood by individual managers, but even the definition of strategic thinking itself was ambiguous . . . Managers were also found (largely) to be in a maze of strategic bewilderment when decision-making . . . So, whilst strategic thinking potentially might add tremendous value added [sic], because of the very partial, isolated, and fragmented way in which it is currently manifest and disseminated, much of that value was lost."[3]

As with the academics, the managers simply spoke as though they knew what they were talking about, but added little value, underscoring the tremendous confusion in concepts, terms, and processes about what strategy is and is not. Many academics and corporate managers (not to mention a few consultants) appear to be content to *guess* at what strategic thinking really means. To be sure, it implies thinking "outside the box," and that it is highly creative. Strategic thinking also has something to do with "the big picture," "to see the forest, not just the trees," and similar common sense prescriptives. Some strategy consultants use that analogy of imagining a helicopter ride that takes one up to a sufficient height to see the big picture, the road beyond the turns and the hills that, from ground level, are not visible. Some even take managers through lateral thinking and creativity exercises to "free up" people's thinking, implying that to do these things is to think strategically.[4] While these activities may be necessary, they are not sufficient and they are not strategic thinking.

Obviously, the word "strategic" is an integral part of strategic thinking. Earlier, it was noted that a company would not need a strategy if it did not have to compete—it could make do simply with a plan. But strategy implies competing and outwitting competitors. So it follows that strategic thinking has to do with finding alternative ways of competing and providing customer value. (Recall its definition from Chapter 1: Strategic thinking is coming up with alternative viable strategies or business models that deliver customer value.)

It is impossible to formulate a strategy, let alone a "best" or preferred strategy, without engaging in strategic thinking. The search for appropriate alternative strategies, often done as part of a strategic-planning process, is actually strategic thinking in action. Coming up with the "right" strategy for a company that might increase stakeholder value, make it a stronger competitor, or find a competitive arena that ensures success is done only through strategic thinking.

What about some strategies that, rather than help a company grow or become more competitive, are designed to consolidate, retrench, or even withdraw entirely from a competitive arena? Does one use strategic thinking to arrive at them? The answer is still "yes." Recall from Chapter 1 that strategic planning is defined as a process to find a strategy that will achieve certain organizational purposes. If a company is being battered in an industry, or is competitively weak in an unattractive industry, then achieving a purpose of "survival" or "finding a better opportunity" demands that the strategy selected be either retrenchment, turnaround, divestiture, or exit from the industry. The decision has to be one that is in the best interests of the organization and its stakeholders. In a similar vein, does "finding another competitive arena" come under strategic thinking? Does that mean the company is trying to run away from the competition? Not at all. It is simply searching for a way of growing and prospering where it cannot easily be beaten or impacted by its competitors, such as in a niche. So choosing the battlefield and even dictating the rules of competition, should the company be so fortunate, are legitimate aspects of strategic thinking.

But just knowing *what* strategic thinking is may not be enough; how does one *do* it? This chapter explores five principal dimensions that provide some useful ways of *stretching your thinking* about strategy, growth, providing customer value, and competing. And isn't this the central issue about strategic thinking? It is not just "thinking" or "blue-skying," but thinking specifically about different and better ways of competing, of delivering customer value, of growing, that is, thinking with some purpose in mind. Without such thinking—and absent many years of experience—actually coming up with alternative strategies or business models and choosing a preferred or "best" one become infinitely more difficult—indeed, while coming up with any kind of strategy is not difficult, coming up with alternative strategies that are worthy of a company's serious consideration is. The five principal dimensions of strategic thinking to consider are:

- How to be different
- Being entrepreneurial
- How to find more opportunities
- Being future-oriented
- Whether to be collaborative

How to Be Different

Strategy is about being different from your competitors. It is about finding your race to run and winning it. To paraphrase Michael Porter, while becoming better at what you do is desirable, it will not benefit you in the long run because it is something other competitors can also do.[5] So long as it is relatively easy for others to imitate or catch up to you, you do not have a sustainable competitive advantage, so you have not crafted a good strategy. Consider concentration, a *bona fide* strategy, where a company continues to improve its product and expand its market. If other competitors are following the same route to profits, and everyone is playing the same "game"— that is, if they have similar business models—a company might at best achieve a limited or temporary advantage (with a new product or more effective advertising). Porter insists that this is not *strategy*.[6] The exception would be if the company were to successfully differentiate itself, which is precisely what would make it difficult for competitors to imitate the strategy. Differentiating is a way of playing a *different* game or playing the same game differently, one that hopefully only your company can win. That is the point.

In the 1980s, Carmike Cinemas was the fifth largest theater chain in the United States and dominated the Southeast. It grew by acquiring failed theater chains at below market value, remodeling them at low cost, and then managing them with tight cost controls. Why did Carmike succeed and eventually become the market leader? Many other large chains had a similar business model—grow through acquisition and remodel single-screen theaters into multiplexes. How did Carmike differentiate itself? It chose to locate in small towns and villages, not urban areas. It found a niche. By so doing, it was often the only theater in town (no competition) and developed a clientele of loyal moviegoers. Yet, as it grew, it also had the buying clout of a large theater chain, ensuring that its theaters could afford to exhibit newly released films.

Casey's General Stores had a similar niche. Casey's was both a convenience store and a gasoline station at all its locations. In 1993, it had about 819 stores in seven Midwestern states (Iowa, Nebraska, Kansas, Illinois, Minnesota, Wisconsin, and South Dakota) served by a modern state-of-the-art distribution center in Ankeny, Iowa. About three-fourths of the stores were located in towns of 5,000 or fewer people; and Casey's was often the only place in town to get gas as well as convenience store items. Nationally, Casey's ranked 19th after Southland Corporation's 7-Eleven chain, Circle K, the major petroleum companies that had added convenience stores to their gas stations, and the like. Yet most of the competitors were in large urban areas and cities, which left Casey's with very little competition. Of course, Casey's had to operate very efficiently—it kept its distribution costs low by limiting its expansion to within 500 miles of its distribution center and could price its gasoline competitively by buying it on the spot market at very low prices. But *differentiating* enabled it to succeed by finding and dominating its Midwestern, small-town niche. Even Wal-Mart, on its way to becoming the world's largest retailer, also focused on rural America and smaller cities and towns partly because the large space it needed to site a store was more readily and reasonably available. Only recently has it begun to penetrate denser urban neighborhoods, such as in Southern California.

Gary Hamel and C. K. Prahalad made a similar point when they said that firms should not be too concerned about competing with their current competitors. Focusing on that could only result in making attempts to "catch up," by which time the industry leaders would have lengthened their lead again. Instead, they suggest that companies should prepare to compete in a *future* market, say, five years ahead, one which only you know about and which you have the greatest lead time preparing to serve. When you do come up with the right products to serve that market you will, by definition, be the leader and have all others scrambling to follow and keep up with you.[7] The authors are clearly on the right track, but provide little in the way of advice as to how to identify such a market together with the product to serve it.

One of the best examples of differentiation is Trader Joe's, the specialty-grocery chain. It grew from a handful of convenience stores in Southern California to 174 stores nationally and $2.4 billion in revenues in 2001. The founder, Joe Coulombe, recognized early on that he could not compete as a convenience store against the likes of the 7-Eleven chain or as a grocery store against such giants as Safeway. He knew he had to be different, so he turned his penchant for traveling to France and enjoying French food and wine into buying trips for his stores. Today, Trader Joe's differentiates itself in five ways:

- *Selective products*. It has a tight assortment of about 3,200 SKUs (stock-keeping units), a very small number for a grocery store (a large supermarket would have 50,000). The items turn over fast.

- *Private-labeled unique products.* About 70% of the items in the stores are unusual items that were found on international buying trips and immediately private-labeled with the Trader Joe's brand label. The stores do not stock commodities. Because most of the items are unique, customers can buy them only from the store.

- *Small, intimate feel of each store.* The stores are kept intentionally small (about 10,000 square feet) and very intimate. Safeway by comparison has an average store size of 55,000 square feet. If a store gets too crowded, another one is opened. Giving each location a neighborhood-store atmosphere—that is, nothing slick or chainlike—turns it into a unique social experience for the customer. The Trader Joe's brand, in fact, *is* the store.

- *Fanatical attention to customers.* Everything Trader Joe's does centers on the customer. Its whole philosophy of buying and offering products is predicated on choosing those products that customers will and do buy because the products are selected and tested with the customer in mind. This forges a bond with its customers and gets them to come back time and time again.

- *Extraordinary value.* Trader Joe's buying target is a real product with significant value, comprising taste, quality, private labeling, and price. Each product has to pass a number of tests in the tasting process. Trader Joe's thus ensures that the products taste good, meet rigorous standards of quality, and are priced competitively. That spells value from the customer's point of view. If Trader Joe's cannot find the best price for a product, the item is not carried in its stores.[8]

Trader Joe's is essentially playing its own game by its rules and winning. Its business model is inimitable. Its brand stands for something solid and unique—and is trusted by its customers. It has, in fact, loyal customers, something that few other grocery stores have. (Isn't one supermarket much like another?). Finally, Trader Joe's chooses the products it stocks and sells, whereas regular supermarkets stock brand name products from other manufacturers who have bargaining power over them. That is why it is also more profitable.

To conclude, strategic thinking finds the way a company can be different from its competitors. This means doing what it does differently or having a business model that is different from its competitors. Differentiation takes many forms such as being better than or different from the competition in certain respects that are valued by customers: better quality, more features, better performance, better reliability, easier to use, stronger, taking up less room, simpler, better looking, and so on. Done correctly, differentiation can enhance a company's brand image, create loyal customers, and help the company achieve above-industry-average profits. The best forms of differentiation are very difficult for competitors to emulate, thus creating a sustained competitive advantage.

Being Entrepreneurial

Entrepreneurs are thought by many to be "different" from everyone else. To be more precise, it is not *they* who are different, but their mindset. Aside from the fact that entrepreneurs start businesses, is it that they take more risks than most people? It might seem this way; however, research shows that entrepreneurs are actually risk-averse and not the gamblers that the popular imagination of them would suggest. In reality, it is principally the investors that furnish the initial and subsequent capital investments that take the risk. However, in their eyes, entrepreneurs bet on themselves and are, therefore, not taking any risk at all. Is it that they are more visionary than the rest of us? Not really—leaders of all kinds of organizations, for example, almost by definition are visionary and certainly as visionary as entrepreneurs. In fact, one could argue that some entrepreneurs are not at all visionary, but rather good inventors and very much preoccupied with perfecting their product or continuing to develop the technology on which it is based. Is it their determination and persistence? It is true, they are determined and persistent, but so are many people that work in established organizations and in all walks of life, from mountain climbers to athletes to political figures. Indeed, entrepreneurs are not that different from other types of people.

So what is so special about entrepreneurs and being entrepreneurial? Again, it is their mindset.

The one irrefutable difference between them and everyone else is their ability to see opportunity everywhere they look. They have an innate ability to scan the world for opportunities and look beyond the conventional. They "see" the world with different eyes. And once you get to see the world that way, you can never again see it any other way. You will have "caught the bug" and, in a very real sense, have adopted the mindset of an entrepreneur and become entrepreneurial.

What does seeing opportunities everywhere mean? It means being in a position to notice that something can be done better, quicker, cheaper, differently, more conveniently, faster, more reliably, sturdily and _____ (insert your own words). Entrepreneurs resonate with value generation and constantly try to find ways to create and deliver value. If it takes too long to do something—there has to be a shorter way. Something you use breaks down too soon—it could be made more reliable. Some problem too complex?—perhaps there is a simple solution.

The entrepreneur's ability to see opportunity depends first on a *level of dissatisfaction* with what exists today and a clear *statement of the problem*. After that, it is a matter of tinkering with ideas and possible solutions until arriving at something that would solve the problem and then developing that into a product or service with commercial potential. In every case, the level of dissatisfaction is experienced from the customer's point of view, a critical distinction. It is really a customer *need* that is being identified that the entrepreneur then tries to fill. Literally, it's "walking in the customer's shoes," spotting where value lies, and then organizing to deliver that value.

Another subliminal characteristic of entrepreneurs—*subliminal* denotes that though they may be in the throes of starting or running a business, they can no more turn off this ability to see the world the way they do than they are determined to succeed—is the ability to see something that is not there, or the world as it might be if that certain missing something was in fact in place. This characteristic is another attribute of the entrepreneurial mindset, and is critical when engaging in strategic thinking.

What entrepreneurs also do well is innovate, that is, take an idea, concept, or invention and make money with it through implementing it and bringing it to market. So with the "insight" of creating something that already has value built into it—it is better in some significant way that the customer values than what currently exists—entrepreneurs will find a way to be highly competitive and a way to bring it to market and make a profit. One strategist goes so far as to say, "Make innovation the most important core competency for your enterprise . . . [one that] will require a paradigm shift for many."[9]

Strategists, organizational leaders, and marketing people should learn to look at the world with entrepreneurial eyes. Strategic thinking is concerned not only with how to be different, but also with generating alternative possibilities of generating customer value that the organization should consider.

In high-tech industries, companies have to be eternally vigilant for upstarts that, through new products or better technology, "disrupt" them, that is, take market share from them or knock them from leadership positions. In such cases, other companies found the opportunity before you did. Of course, when it happens, it is too late—the damage is done. The solution, counterintuitively, is to come up with the opportunity *before you really need to*. Christensen, Johnson, and Rigby found that while companies overtaken or "disrupted" by other companies—such as Compaq overtaking Digital Equipment Corp. and in turn being overtaken by Dell, or Oracle overtaking IBM and having to fend off Microsoft—were innovative and had good ideas, they lacked "a robust, repeatable process for creating and nurturing new growth businesses."[10] The point is that when you need to be entrepreneurial and find a suitable opportunity or two, it is infinitely easier when you have a process for creating and nurturing new growth businesses already in place. In order for such a process to be used repeatedly, it should be the responsibility of a dedicated group that could put the acquired learning to good use.

How to Find More Opportunities

When companies are not doing well, the first area that gets attention is costs. "Let's find ways to cut costs" goes the management mantra, and that will improve the bottom line. While it may improve the bottom line, it does nothing to boost sales. So the next area that is examined is sales (which should be the first thing to look at if sales are declining rapidly). The emphasis here is purely operational:

> Do not change the strategy, do not change the target market, do not change the product, but let us in essence do more of whatever we are doing to sell more product and do it more quickly.

This may result in the advertising or promotions or price of the product changing, but essentially it is simply working harder at doing what the company was already doing.

The majority of companies wrestle for the most part with these two things: costs and getting revenues up using the *existing* business model. For some reason, their thinking does not extend to examining their revenue model. How is it that revenues are generated? Is there a better way of generating revenues? (A revenue model doesn't differ very much from a business model; certainly, the former is a major part of the latter.)

The answer is the search for opportunities, which may be related to or derive from what the company is currently doing—or it may constitute a radical departure. To be sure, identifying opportunities is an important step in a strategic analysis (certainly in the one advocated in this book). However, identifying opportunities is typically done only when a company takes the time to do strategic planning. Why not have an *opportunity-finding mechanism* operating all the time? Why not formalize it and use it to generate ideas and feasible proposals on an ongoing basis? This is what is meant by "being opportunistic."

Many companies have *new product development committees* through which they screen new product proposals. They encourage promising ones by asking for more detailed information or requiring a prototype demonstration, and giving increasing support as needed at each stage of development, for example, more time off from the regular job to work on the new project, forming a multidisciplinary team, and even actual money to build prototypes or do market research. While those new products that succeed do form the basis for a future revenue stream, the probabilities for most companies are distressingly small.

In the early 1990s, a California defense–aerospace company had such a committee; however, out of 103 product proposals, it nurtured only five of them, brought two to fruition, but sold them to other companies—not a scintillating record if the purpose was to improve revenues in a lasting way. It had, in fact, reached a point of not having any idea how it was going to survive another two years! By its very nature, the process can be likened to a funnel, where only a few of the many projects proposed are ever adopted and achieve success. Indeed, many fields experience a similar effect. An example is the criminal justice system. Of all crimes committed, only a fraction are reported, a vastly smaller number of which have a suspect apprehended, and only a fraction of those ever convicted. The statistics are depressing, yet it seems that is the best we can do.

Contrast such a system to another where the numbers of ideas are vastly increased and sifting through them is a fulltime job for several people. Why not ask customers for their suggestions? Few companies do. Why not have everyone in the company participate, instead of just the engineers? And why not broaden the suggestions to embrace any kind of improvement or innovation, not just new product ideas? This way, the ongoing focus of the company would be opportunity-recognition, and its revenue model continually refreshed.

Microsoft Corporation implements this strategy like no other company. Not only has it identified numerous opportunities to pursue, but it is also pursuing all of them. It has the rare luxury of having enough resources to do that. And the kernel of the strategy is this: In high-tech markets, where it is not clear which market will take off next, Microsoft has covered virtually all the bases. Whichever market takes off, it will be one of the leaders, having been developing products for that market longer than anyone else. Because the stakes are so high, making it big in one market will probably enable it to more than recoup *all* its earlier R&D costs pursuing multiple opportunities. Will this work for other organizations? Most companies have far fewer resources than Microsoft and are forced to be selective. Being selective is akin to choosing the best strategy to pursue and forces the use and application of strategic thinking.

High-tech markets, called *hypercompetitive environments* by Richard D'Aveni, are especially susceptible to sudden technological innovation.[11] That is why it is so difficult to sustain market leadership. However, it does allow smaller companies with a technological edge to leapfrog industry leaders, however temporarily. That is the point. New technology, or more accurately *newer* technology brought to market faster, is a rich source of new opportunities. It is a risky business, though, especially when the pace of technological change is very fast. The key thing that separates the good opportunities from the bad ones is how well margins can be maintained over time—or how well the resulting product can resist obsolescence over time. D'Aveni found that, in general, a sustainable competitive advantage in a hypercompetitive industry is almost impossible to attain; companies could expect only temporary advantages at best.

Adherents of Breakthrough Thinking™ have a wonderful name for a particular opportunity an organization decides to implement—the Solution-After-Next.[12] Once the organization's purpose is established, an act of synthesis and choice from suggestions given by employees and management, the organization ponders how it can best attain that purpose. This gives rise to a process of exploring opportunities, but with the following peculiar twist. Say that the purpose of the organization would be met by developing and producing "Product A." The managers are then asked to imagine what competitors would do if the firm were to introduce Product A. Why, the managers reply, they would produce Product B which would be superior to A in certain respects. They were then asked, "What would you do next?" "Well, we would have to top that and probably come up with Product C," they replied. Well, why not set out to produce Product C *now?* This is not easy to do, as you can imagine, but you can also see why it is called the "solution-after-next." It is a way to leapfrog competitors.

When many small to midsized companies do strategic planning, they undertake a SWOT analysis—meaning **S**trengths, **W**eaknesses, **O**pportunities, and **T**hreats—as part of that process. In most cases, however, the opportunities they list are mundane, predictable, and "safe." It is the one area in the whole strategic analysis that, to do it justice, requires thinking "outside the box." The following six opportunity-seeking questions may serve to get an *out-of-the-box* brainstorming process underway for coming up with possible opportunities:

- *What other type of customer could benefit from our product, even if used in a different way?* Hughes Aircraft was a major defense contractor for many years until defense budgets began declining in the early 1990s. One of its divisions focused on selling and servicing satellites for government and industrial clients. To reduce its dependence on governmental contracts, it created a different business model, one directed at a *consumer* market, of beaming cable channels and movies off satellites to home-mounted satellite dish receivers. By 2001, the division, now called DirecTV (and the main piece of the old Hughes Aircraft that sold its remaining defense businesses to Raytheon), accounted for 77% of Hughes' profits.[13]

- *What other products could we produce for the same customers?* A good example is Tyson Foods. In 1967, it was doing very well, with $53 million in annual revenues from selling raw chickens mainly to grocery stores in Arkansas and neighboring states. Growth options at the time involved either trucking the chickens to more states or coming up with new products. The first new product was a chicken patty for sandwiches. In due course, as a result of trying to figure out how to "do more with chicken" (its motto), it began offering chicken pieces, marinated chicken, frozen prepared chicken dinners, chicken tenders, chicken nuggets, and ready-to-eat chicken "buffalo wings." Along with these product innovations, Tyson explored different distribution channels. Instead of reaching housewives through grocery stores, it tried to reach consumers even when they went out to eat, and began selling to fast-food outlets, restaurants, airlines, and hospitals. In the early 1980s, it worked with McDonald's to add chicken to its menu, resulting in a seven-fold increase in revenues and 19-fold increase in EPS in the decade that followed as Chicken McNuggets became popular.[14]

- *What other products could we produce, for any customers, that use the skills, techniques, technologies, and know-how that we have?* Matsushita Corporation is a conglomerate that produces products for many markets worldwide. At one point, it was faced with the maturing of its rice cooker, oven toaster, and food processor product lines. Using technologies contained in each of them (computer-controlled heating from the rice cooker, heating devices from the toaster, and motors from food processors), it created a new consumer product, a bread machine, that produced a variety of breads reliably and simply every single time. The product produced record-setting sales the first year it was introduced.[15]

- *Is there a way of reinventing our business model that would give us a competitive edge?* The late 1980s was a bad time for the auto insurance industry in California. Voters passed Proposition 103, mandating auto insurance premium rollbacks and other reforms. Massive rebates to consumers left the industry awash in red ink. One company took this as a wake-up call. Progressive Insurance made up its mind that if anything it did was not good for the consumer, it was not going to do it. For example, instead of the weeks it took to settle claims, Progressive settled claims on the spot, 24/7, before other companies were aware that there had been an accident. To potential customers, it quotes competing rates as well, even if they turn out to be lower. Also, it bases its rates more on where and when a car is driven than on age, driver's record, and other established criteria. Progressive is growing six times faster than the industry and enjoys a profit margin of 8%, whereas the rest of the industry has run at an underwriting loss the past five years.[16]

- *What unmet needs do people or companies have that we could meet, even if it means acquiring the necessary know-how and expertise?* Computer server manufacturer Sun Microsystems found itself in a tailspin, with its stock price plummeting 92% from a peak of $64 in 2000 to less than $5 as of July 2002. Dell Computer Corporation hit hard at the low end with its under-$10,000 servers, and IBM at the high end by offering its large corporate customers complete, easy-to-use e-business systems with hardware, software, and everything else they may need. Sun is changing its strategy to focus on software development. Its new strategy, called ONE (Open Net Environment), is designed to spur sales across the company's product lines. By giving away its entry-level application server software that it once sold for $3,000 (for Linux, UNIX, and Windows operating systems), it hopes that companies will be tempted to buy other enterprise products such as software that controls employee access to networks. Observers are not sure the strategy will work, even though Sun is "betting the farm" on it. (Its former free-spending Internet customers have disappeared, so it has virtually no choice.) Since 1983, Sun tried to beef up its software business, but time and again it failed. However, if this time around the strategy includes acquiring the necessary strategic and software expertise, and if the customer value proposition is a powerful one (this means coming up with the right products when the customers most need them), then the strategy could work.[17]

- *What are the highest-growth industries now and in the foreseeable future?* This is a variant of the previous topic, involving possibly diversifying into a business in which the company has little experience or know-how. Right away, some people would say that doing such a thing would be irresponsible and a recipe for disaster. But there is a way of doing it intelligently and also minimizing the inherent risk of a diversification strategy. A company could always hire someone to head up the effort with a great amount of experience and know-how in the proposed industry. It could also acquire a company already in that business whose management had the necessary experience and expertise. Assuming, then, that these steps could take care of the inherent (initial) risk, the issue here is which are the high-growth industries?

As a final note, it goes without saying that a company should never forget its present business even while it is looking for elusive opportunities that will be its next blockbuster. The corporate graveyard is littered with companies that have allowed themselves to become distracted from their main business, sometimes through an acquisition, integrating vertically backwards, diversifying, or searching for other opportunities. The two must be done simultaneously. Once the current business stops growing, two things happen; pressure to maintain profits and the stock price lead to cost-cutting, including programs for new-product development, and the cash available for developing new sources of revenue dries up.[18] Putting someone or a small group permanently in charge of the opportunity-finding process will enable the company to keep its focus on its present business (whose growth must also be maintained). Losing that focus can be fatal to a business.[19]

Figure 2.1   Some Strategic Frontiers

Company-Specific	Company-Generic	Marketplace
New product	Franchising	Artificial intelligence
New product category	Globalization	Biotechnology
New distribution channel	JIT manufacturing	Genomics
New manufacturing process	Mass customization	Internet
New positioning	Outsourcing	Nanotechnology
New sourcing strategy	Partnerships	Smart materials
New technology	Patent exploration	Wireless communications
	Services	Automation

Source: Robert E. Johnston Jr. and J. Douglas Bate, *The Power of Strategy Innovation: A New Way of Linking Creativity and Strategic Planning to Discover Great Business Opportunities* (New York: AMACOM, 2003), 117.

A recent book, *The Power of Strategy Innovation: A New Way of Linking Creativity and Strategic Planning to Discover Great Business Opportunities*, proposes that companies adopt a process called "strategy innovation."[20] The authors Robert E. Johnston Jr. and J. Douglas Bate describe a process that you will recognize from this chapter: strategic thinking. In particular, one important concept is exploring a "strategic frontier" that is essentially anything a company might do in the future that it is not currently doing (not an extension or version of its current strategy), be it targeting a new market, entering another business, merging with another company, forming strategic alliances, broadening the product line, adopting a new technology, and so on—the list can be long. The authors define it as "that unexplored area of potential growth that lies between today's business and tomorrow's opportunities"—this unexplored territory is given the Latin name, terra incognito. Figure 2.1 presents some examples of strategic frontiers.

Their method advocates first getting top management agreement (or alignment) as to which strategic frontier is to be explored, but this unnecessarily limits the person or group and runs the risk of the chosen frontier not being the correct one. It is better for the exploration to be open-ended and to *inform* it with information about how industries, competitors, and markets change.

One of the best models for sustained growth that embodies some concepts discussed earlier comes from a book written by three McKinsey partners that lead the firm's global growth practice: Mehrdad Baghai, Stephen Coley, and David White. They call it the "three horizons of growth":

- *Horizon 1* constitutes the company's core business, and accounts for the lion's share of profits and cash flow. Unless the Horizon 1 business is successful, initiatives in Horizons 2 and 3 stagnate and die.

- *Horizon 2* comprises businesses or lines of business on the rise, the emerging stars of the company that could transform the company, but not without considerable investment. Though profits are still several years away, they show strong revenue growth and a growing customer base. They are entrepreneurial in nature and single-mindedly seek to increase revenues and market share. They could be extensions of the firm's current business or moves into new directions. Horizon 2 is about building new streams of revenue for the firm and, in time, will become Horizon 1 ("cash cow") businesses.

- *Horizon 3* businesses are options on future opportunities, but they are not just ideas. Rather, they are *real activities and investments,* however small, such as research projects, minority stakes, pilot projects, etc. These may either not amount to anything (i.e., never ever showing a profit) or could eventually end up as Horizon 1 businesses.[21]

The key is to manage all three horizons concurrently. Putting off Horizon 2 or 3 businesses is tantamount to closing down the company's future. While these may be new terms for short-, medium-, and long-range projects, the principle is the same—to ensure long-term growth, the company has to "fill the pipeline" (difficult to do) and then nurture Horizon 2 and 3 projects into Horizon 1 successes (another level of difficulty). A company's vision has to encompass *all three horizons,* not just Horizon 1. Using earlier constructs, this is a great description of a formal opportunity-finding mechanism operating all the time, producing a "portfolio" of products or businesses with potential that then have to be managed and brought into the mainstream of what the company does (Horizon 1 businesses). Identifying and starting Horizon 3 businesses, for example, takes a very different (entrepreneurial) mindset and approach from managing the current core Horizon 1 business successfully. The difference? Opportunity-finding and strategic thinking.

Another idea is to think of—and run—the fledgling business (the new opportunity) as a separate enterprise. Doing so may require a business model very different from the company's current one. Trying to create and implement a new business model while operating the existing one is difficult at best. Christensen discusses companies coming up with a disruptive strategy, that is, one that will disrupt the market but, at the same time, broaden the customer base and help the company grow. He cites the example of Teradyne, a company that made sophisticated integrated circuit testing equipment. In the mid-1990s, it sensed that competitors were about to introduce a cheaper, simpler version of the product that could test simple circuits at the low end of the market. Rather than wait, Teradyne decided to beat them to it. But creating such a product would also disrupt Teradyne's current product, and so needed to be handled by an independent group within the company. By keeping very tight control on costs and a *separate* focus, the venture achieved $150 million in annual sales within 18 months of its release in 1998.[22]

Being Future-Oriented

The consequences of any decision made today play out in the future. Likewise, every decision made during the strategic-planning process, including the strategy itself, happens in the future. It is no wonder then that strategists and key organizational managers should feel comfortable in thinking about the future, because that is where they are going to live and work, implement plans and achieve results, and take the company to where it is going. It is not the present but rather the future.

But by and large, managers are not comfortable thinking about or dealing with the future. Many view it as beyond their control. They feel that nothing they can do can change the inexorable momentum that carries us into the future. It is a fatalistic attitude. Others believe simplistically that the future is going to be very much like the past and blithely extrapolate everything in a straight line. This sounds naïve and it is.

Perhaps the most appropriate view is something in between. People can control certain things and not others very much like their personal behavior. One cannot change other people or their behavior (beyond one's control), but one can control how one responds to other people and what one does oneself. Most of all, it is a deep down belief that what you do does make a difference and can affect how things turn out in the future. This is called a *normative attitude*. Similarly, people with a normative attitude do not extrapolate everything. While certain industries that are stable for a number of years lend themselves to short-term extrapolation, others are more volatile or unstable and are likely to be discontinuous—the future is unlike the past.

How does thinking about the future relate to strategic thinking? Is it a form of strategic thinking? Not at all. Can it enhance strategic thinking? Absolutely. First, any kind of strategic thinking you do is going to be set in the future. So learning some ways of forecasting or anticipating the future can serve you very well. Secondly, trying to do strategic thinking with a fatalistic or naïve attitude about the future will adversely affect the results you achieve; you need to have a normative attitude, one that asks, of all possible futures, what you might do to bring about a desired future. Finally, being comfortable about the future means being comfortable with ambiguity, uncertainty, incompleteness, and subjectivity . . . easier said than done. For example, most accountants, used to dealing only with historical information, find dealing with the future very difficult. In fact, they have resisted auditing forecast information for public companies for years, unwilling to take responsibility because of the uncertainty.

Methods of looking at or analyzing the future are called *futures research methods*. The two most relevant ones that would enhance strategic thinking are *scenario planning* and *future mapping*. Neither is easy to do, and neither can be done quickly. They demand facilitation by experts, the involvement and education of many individuals, and a time period of from weeks to months. Yet despite the difficulty, companies that use them benefit as much from the educational process and shared learning as they do from the output that helps to hone, direct, or change their thinking.

Scenario Planning[23]

The value of doing scenario planning is high if there is an issue deemed critical to the future of the company and about which sufficient information is unavailable to determine how the issue will turn out. For example, a critical issue for the automobile industry in the United States might be energy—and more specifically gasoline—prices. (In another country, the critical issue might well be infrastructure such as roads, highways, and gas stations.) For the housing, construction, and lumber industry, as well as homebuyers, the critical issue is interest rates, a principal driver and inhibitor of demand. A critical issue for the movie theater industry and its suppliers today is digital cinema—in what form and when will digital transmission and projection systems be introduced; and what will persuade movie theaters to invest in and switch to that technology? It is around such a critical issue that a scenario is devised—or, more accurately, two to three scenarios so that they may be compared and contrasted. Potential strategies are not only possible responses to a scenario about the future, but also to what different players are likely to face and do within each scenario. These actions in turn may influence which strategy might be more appropriate.[24]

To begin to form scenarios, one needs to collect information about key forces impinging on that critical issue and driving forces in the macroenvironment. This is very research-intensive, and could cover markets, new technology, political factors, economic trends, demographic changes, and so on. Schwartz says that in this phase one should look for major trends and trend breaks—both difficult to do. Next, the key factors and driving forces are ranked on the basis of two criteria: (1) how important they are in determining the success or outcome of the critical issue identified in the beginning and (2) the degree of uncertainty surrounding them. One is looking for the most important and the most uncertain. The factors that are most important and most uncertain will now form the axes along which the eventual scenarios will differ. The purpose is to end up with just a few scenarios whose differences make a real difference to decision-makers. These sets of issues must be reshaped and regrouped in such a way that a logic for each one emerges and a story (the scenario) can be told. As Stuart Wells says, "the essence of this process is writing stories about the future as if we were viewing the past."[25]

Perhaps a benefit of equal importance to the value of the insights gained from developing scenarios is the learning that takes place during the process, which should be integrated into the strategic-thinking and decision-making processes. Liam Fahey suggests the following scenario-learning principles:

- Scenarios are only a means to an end. They have value only to the extent that they inform decision-makers and influence decision-making. Scenarios cannot be allowed to become irrelevant to the key issues facing the company and the decisions corporate leaders must contemplate and make.

- Scenarios only add value to decision making when managers and others use them to systematically shape questions about the present and the future, and to guide how they go about answering them.

- In each step of developing scenarios, the emphasis must be on identifying, challenging, and refining the substance of managers' mindsets and knowledge—what lies between their ears—and not on refining and perfecting scenario content.

- Alternative projections about some future must challenge managers' current mental models by creating tension about ideas, hypotheses, perspectives, and assumptions.

- The dialog and discussion spawned by consideration of alternative futures directly affects managers' tacit knowledge.

- Scenarios are not a one-time event. They generate indicators that allow managers to track how the future is evolving. Thus, learning induced by scenarios never ends.[26]

Scenarios can be used in other ways besides creating a context for making decisions, such as helping to decide among alternative strategies. The Computer Information Systems (CIS) Department in the College of Business Administration at Cal Poly Pomona went through a strategic-planning process in 2003. The CIS department came up with four strategic alternatives. One was quickly discarded, but the department could not decide among the other three. To break the deadlock, volunteers were requested to lobby for each strategic alternative and try to persuade others to vote for the one each recommended. They did this by creating a *miniscenario*—a description of how things might turn out in five years' time—which they presented at a department meeting (see Appendix C, Figure C.2). The scenarios and their champions succeeded in breaking the deadlock and enabled the department to pick one strategy that it decided to implement. These particular scenarios required some thought, but not a lot of research, and some effort, but no cost.

Future Mapping[27]

Future mapping is defined as a set of tools to sort and prioritize possible events that influence the way the future develops. With such information, strategies or actions could be taken to increase the likelihood of some events rather than others occurring, presumably those events that favor the company in question. In layperson's terms, it is something one can do to influence the future to one's own advantage.

Managers and others, over time, become accustomed to making decisions based on their experience. The mental models that explain to them how the world works are developed over a long period of time, are deeply trusted, rarely shared or articulated with anyone, and underlie their decisions and actions. While truly serving these managers well, such deeply ingrained mental models also inhibit change and learning. As C. K. Prahalad points out:

> The problem with change or adopting new technology is not "how fast can one get on the learning curve," but rather "how fast can one forget old methods or assumptions" that get in the way. The "forgetting curve" for most organizations is flat. That is, they cannot forget, and so have real difficulty changing and moving into new spaces.[28]

One of the real tasks of planning and strategic thinking is to adjust experience-based mental models to reflect rapid changes in the competitive environment, and to adjust to grasping opportunities that such mental models do not even see.

Building a scenario using future-mapping tools requires developing "endstates," a snapshot of future industry conditions. This snapshot itself requires a set of events, an *event* being a specific, concrete manifestation—it happened—of a trend or issue influenced by industry participants; several likely scenarios, a list of events leading to an endstate; and doing "cross-futures analysis" that compares the lists of events leading to each scenario. Event sets could be technical, business/industry, regulatory, or socio-cultural. Examples are: "AT&T drops out of computers, 1993," and "Amgen reaches $1.0 billion in sales, 1995." At least two types of scenarios are created—one reflecting conventional wisdom and another that is very different from or unlike it. The purpose of the former is to show people how they think, that is, their existing decision-making context. The latter, called "endstate-driven scenarios," contains events that the group could label as "must happen" or "must not happen." At this stage, the group going through this process begins to understand what it should be paying attention to and what it could safely put on a back burner. It finds that the process quickly boils down to a list of specific actions to take, thus making strategic discussions concrete.

Typical questions about particular events include:

- Is the event a threat or opportunity for the company?

- What is the desired outcome?

- What can we do to support a desired outcome?

- Do we have sufficient resources to support a desired outcome?

- Which part of the organization or who should be responsible for implementing these tactics?

Future mapping is keyed specifically to how an industry develops or could develop. It provides participants with a holistic, cross-functional understanding of how their industry works. It is directed externally primarily on customers, markets, and competitors. In essence, it could be thought of as contingency-based planning that forces the selection of the best endstate from the viewpoint of the company while still exploring implications of other endstates. In the process, participants have a unique opportunity of changing, or updating, their mental models and enabling necessary changes and action with less resistance and with more speed.

Both scenario planning and future mapping stretch participants' thinking, introduce new possibilities, challenge long-held assumptions, update mental models, form valuable vehicles for learning and shared understanding, and often become the basis for strategic decision-making. Most managers and companies, however, lack the skill and experience to use the methods; they should avail themselves of outside expert consulting.

Whether to Be Collaborative

Strategic Alliances, Acquisitions, and Mergers

The complexity of change and the imperative of competing more effectively or differently have led firms to consider a number of other opportunities and ways of growing and competing, ones that are collaborative to varying degrees, even with competitors. Such opportunities lie on a continuum that is minimally collaborative (and not at all integrative) at one end, to the other, in stages of increasing collaboration and integration, which is an acquisition (total integration) of another company. The continuum and principal stages, developed by the late Dr. Peter Pekár Jr., are shown in Figure 2.2.

Meant here are the various strategic alliances, joint ventures (a highly committed strategic alliance), and mergers and acquisitions. While the various forms of strategic alliance and acquisition do not constitute strategic thinking *per se*, they often form the *output* of strategic thinking: coming up with strategic alternatives that involve forming strategic alliances or acquiring another company. For this reason, a brief discussion about them will enable the strategist to think about such alternatives while engaged in strategic thinking.

Outsourcing   Companies, such as Nike, often outsource their entire production and manufacturing to another company, their R&D to a university or R&D firm, their marketing and sales function, their financial function, their distribution, and so on. Do these have strategic benefits? Yes, if they make the company a stronger competitor, but not otherwise, say, to reduce costs. (See Outsourcing as a Strategic Alliance.)

Licensing (nonequity)   This includes licensing the use of another company's technology—or licensing one's own technology to other companies, licensing the use of a trademark or logo such as Harley-Davidson does on clothing, mugs, telephones, and the like, or licensing the use of proprietary characters such as Spiderman, Superman, and Mickey Mouse. The motivation here is to increase sales, although from Harley-Davidson's perspective, it would be to strengthen its brand image and make a little extra money as well.

Shared resources and competencies (nonequity)   This includes, for example, sharing the cost of R&D—the way a consortium of semiconductor manufacturers did in the 1980–90s when they created Sematech, or as large defense/aerospace companies have been doing for the last decade to spread skyrocketing costs—or exclusive cross-distribution agreements whereby a company in one country exclusively sells the complementary products of a foreign company, and the foreign company undertakes to sell the products of the first company in that foreign country. Some companies also do cer-

Figure 2.2   Continuum of Strategic Alliances

Source: Peter Pekár Jr., "The Value of Strategic Alliances," presentation at the Association for Strategic Planning's first annual conference, *New Strategies for a Rapidly Changing World*, LAX Airport Crowne Plaza Hotel, October 9, 2001.

Outsourcing as a Strategic Alliance

Donna Dubinsky, founder and CEO of Handspring: "Our company outsources as much as it possibly can—all manufacturing and distribution, for example, gets done elsewhere—in order to keep its innovative core as small as possible. When I joined Apple in 1981, I was employee #2,588, and we were doing over $200 million in annual sales. At Handspring, we hit $200 million in annual sales with about 250 employees . . . Today, you can do the same business with one-tenth of the staff."[30]

Other examples of outsourcing as a strategic alliance include:

- **The Marketing and Sales Function.** Innovative Technology Licensing LLC, a wholly owned subsidiary of Rockwell Scientific Company LLC, has retained Ventis Group LLC to pursue licensing opportunities for certain patents and intellectual property developed by Rockwell Scientific and its two owners, Rockwell Collins and Rockwell Automation. In addition, Ventis Group will be responsible for business development, including sales and marketing activities targeting the printing industry." Press release from Ventis Group LLC dated September 16, 2002, emailed to me by Ventis Group partner Nelson Dodge the same day.

- **The Financial Function.** Gene Siciliano has a business in which he does this for small companies. See **www.cfoforrent.com**.

- **The Distribution Function.** Dell Computers has Ingram Micro seamlessly handle its packing and distribution of computer equipment to end-users.

---

tain manufacturing jobs for other companies. Ford and Mazda formed a strategic alliance after they decided that Mazda had the advantage over Ford in developing the new transmission for the Ford Probe.

Partial acquisition, noncontrolling (< 50%)   This is the first of the alliances that involve more integration and commitment (equity) than just a contract. In its most common form, large companies, seeking an edge in their industry, look around for a startup or emerging company that has a new technology or innovation but that needs capital to develop it and grow. The large company will typically infuse capital into the small one by acquiring a noncontrolling interest in the company. In addition, the investment allows it representation on the board of the small company and first rights to the technology or innovation being developed. The large company may or may not later acquire a controlling share of the small company with an additional investment. (Some companies use such partial acquisitions as Horizon 3 projects that, in time, could become Horizon 1 winners.)

Joint ventures   This is a special class of strategic alliance with a high degree of commitment; yet it keeps the two companies that are forming the alliance separate companies. The high degree of commitment comes in the formation of a separate corporate entity (referred in the literature as "two parents giving birth to a child") through a complex and encompassing agreement between the two parents. The agreement covers the ownership split (50–50, 60–40, etc.), what each parent is contributing to the child such as technology and patents, money, management, distribution, facilities, and the like, the purpose and objectives of the child, the management team for the child, how long the agreement will endure and on what terms either party can terminate the agreement and the joint venture, as well as other legal considerations. Research has shown that joint ventures in which the management team comes from one parent—typically the dominant one— are more likely to succeed than those in which both parents supply managers, especially with international joint ventures in developed countries.[29] For example, Coca Cola formed a joint venture with Nestlé S.A. in 2000 called Beverage Partners Worldwide that will offer new products in the growing "rejuvenation" category of ready-to-drink coffees, teas, and herbal drinks.[31]

Acquisitions   This is when one company buys a controlling interest in another (it does not have to be 100% although it often is). When this happens, the acquirer calls the shots. Its board of directors survives (the other's does not); its management stays in place (the other's typically doesn't); and its people survive cuts where there are redundancies (the other's do not). Most importantly, it gets to set the strategy for the consolidated company and, in all likelihood, retains its corporate culture. Is acquiring another company a strategic move? Yes, if it makes the company a stronger competitor, gives it a competitive advantage it never had before, or enables it to enter another industry or country (if that were a part of the strategy).

But all too often, acquisitions are not strategic, do not accomplish intended purposes, and were never part of a strategy in the first place. The success rate for acquisitions has been abysmal—20% is a common figure cited by many professionals. A recent study of 30 acquisitions made during 1990–2000 found that 24—80%—failed. Over 70% of the sample deals failed because the acquirer paid too much (the most common reason).[32] Yet despite the staggering failure rate, acquisition deals have been increasing at a very rapid pace until recent years (see Table 2.1).

Acquisitions fail for the following key reasons:

- *The acquirer overpaid* and the overpayment could never be recouped or the debt paid down. (See Mattel Overpays.)

- *The intended synergy was never realized* (and, in retrospect, could never have been), so the performance of the combination was less than expected.

- *The purpose of the acquisition was never strategic* in the first place, but rather financial or to satisfy the CEO's ego, that is, it distracted management from running its core business.

- *The different cultures could never be properly integrated,* primarily because integrating them was never perceived as an important facet of making the acquisition work.

Table 2.1   Value of Acquisition Deals Worldwide, 1980–2001

1980....................... $40 billion	(1,880 deals)	
1990....................... $108 billion		
1997....................... $657 billion		
1998....................... $1.2 trillion		
2000....................... $1.3 trillion	(9,600 deals)	
2001....................... $800 billion		

Source: From a classroom presentation given at Cal Poly Pomona, October 24, 2001 by Thomas R. Korzenecki, Managing Partner, Parsons, Korzenecki & Co, Investment Bankers, Pasadena, CA.

- *Key people leave (management turnover).* Curiously, many acquisitions are made principally for particular people and their expertise so, when they leave, much of the potential value of the deal is destroyed.

- *The company is operating outside of its core competence* and knows little about the business it has just acquired or the industry it is in.

Yet alliances and acquisitions work when they are part of an overall strategy. Whirlpool Corporation, in pursuit of a global strategy, moved from a purely domestic manufacturer of major home appliances in 1987 to a leading worldwide manufacturer largely through acquisitions and strategic alliances. By 1995, it was the leader in its home U.S. market, #3 in Europe, #1 in South America, and pushing to enter China and other Asian markets.[33]

Mergers result in combining two companies (also 100% integration), although no one company "calls the shots" as in an acquisition. The resulting board of directors comprises representatives from both boards; the chairperson is usually from one company, the CEO from the other, with other positions going to the best people from both companies. Sometimes, a new name for the combination is created such as *Verizon* being created from the merger of GTE and Bell Atlantic or *Cingular* from the merger of Pacific Bell and Southwest Bell. Sometimes the name of one of the pre-

Mattel Overpays

A classic example is Mattel's acquisition of The Learning Company (TLC) for $3.6 billion in May 1999. Instead of increasing Mattel's profits by $50 million, it reduced it by $206 million. Mattel subsequently incurred $300 million in losses and lopped $7 billion off the company's valuation (a 61% plunge of its stock price). The debacle cost CEO Jill Barad her job. TLC was divested (many said "given away") in October 2000—Mattel took an "after-tax loss from discontinued operations of $441 million related to its write-off of its investment in The Learning Company" in its third quarter 10Q report.[34]

merger companies is retained for the combination as in the name *Bank of America* being retained after it merged with NationsBank. Sometimes the names are fused from parts of the premerger names, as in *DaimlerChrysler*.

The rate at which alliances are created is growing at about 25%/yr.[35] Over 10,000 alliances were formed worldwide in 2000, over 3,500 in the United States in 2000, of which almost 1,000 were equity alliances or joint ventures. Incredibly, half of all recent alliances were among competitors, especially in the healthcare, airlines, and energy industries. Acquisitions and alliances generate nearly 40% of all corporate revenue. The lesson here is that more companies are forming alliances and participating in acquisitions, even though it is still very difficult to make them succeed.

In conclusion, the strategic questions for which a strategic alliance or acquisition might be the solution—or output of strategic thinking—include:

- Will we become a stronger competitor?

- Does it fit with our existing strategy?

- How will it improve our situation?

- What competitive edge will it give us? Will it give us a competency we lack?

- What is the risk, and is it worth taking?

Collaborating with Customers

The Internet is responsible for the profound changes experienced by organizations in virtually every kind of customer interaction over the past decade. Consumers have become more knowledgeable and more active in purchase decisions. In some cases, such as in healthcare, that is a good thing, as patients are now seeking independent information about their health issues from sports injuries to cancer, more aggressively taking charge of their own health and, in fact, becoming informed consumers of healthcare services and products from their doctors and other professionals and pharmaceuticals. In other cases, some retailers are being forced to play price games, as price information on many consumer items can readily be found on the Internet. Without a reason for higher prices, consumers will not pay them.

The power of consumers, then, is growing, because they are "armed" by information. They are able to make choices that suit them and make them more quickly. Is the business world ready for this? Have business models changed to reflect "the new consumer?" C. K. Prahalad and V. Ramaswamy characterize consumers as going from "isolated to connected, from unaware to informed, from passive to active."[36] These consumers have access to enormous amounts of information, are developing a global view, are developing "thematic consumer communities" (witness the book reviews and favorite-book lists available for potential consumers on Amazon.com), experimenting (as with MP3 and file-sharing), and becoming politically and socially active.

The future of competition will be a race as to who can cocreate value with the consumer first, and in how inimitable a way, because companies are no longer the sole creators of customer value. This is where the field of strategy and the power of consumers are heading. Competition will increasingly require firms to be collaborative, not only with other companies by way of strategic alliances, mergers, or acquisitions, but also through increasing collaboration with customers. Products and services are increasingly becoming only parts of an "experience environment" for the consumer. Companies are going to be part of an experience network with other firms and customer communities—for example, sailboat manufacturers, sailboat trade shows, accessory producers, marinas, weather networks, yacht clubs, owners of other sailboats, and the like. You can see how someone intent on buying a sailboat or customizing an existing one can get information from a variety of sources, virtually "experiencing" the product or upgrade before buying it, or buying it because of the satisfying experience. It is not just about price. Such experience environments existing in book retailing, medical care, software creation—Linux was created almost entirely by a consumer community—and GM's OnStar, to name a few.

What are some ways of collaborating with customers? Consider the following:

- *In the R&D arena* About 600,000 people tested the beta version of Windows NT. That translates to $600 million of R&D done by consumers—free. It was also consumers, in another example, that codeveloped Sony's PlayStation2. In a similar vein, consumers give and have given feedback to many high-tech manufacturers about products such as networking software and cellular phones, and communicate their expectations of value and what they are looking for. In so doing, they are cocreating value.

- *In operations* At one point, FedEx's call center was overloaded with tracking inquiries, resulting in irate customers. Now, customers can check the status of their own packages. FedEx got the customers to take the initiative. Its call-center costs dropped dramatically, and customer satisfaction went way up. It succeeded because it made its system transparent and gave customers easy access. In effect, it became its customers' transportation partner.

- *In creating experiences* Rather than just providing pacemakers for people with heart problems that need them, medical-equipment manufacturer Medtronic creates value to the patient with the pacemaker *and the experience*. While the pacemaker itself no doubt has value in extending the patient's life, it has even greater value in that it can be corrected periodically, or monitored all the time, by his or her doctor, or in an emergency could allow the patient's history to be shared with a local hospital enabling a conference call to take place with the primary doctor so the patient could get the best care when most needed.

- *In adding value to the experience of using the product* Consider OnStar, the advanced automotive-communications system of General Motors. For a fee it can help make reservations, find a place to eat, get weather reports, contact emergency services, get messages to your family, and supply a host of other services. OnStar enables GM to sell a differentiated "experience" rather than just an automobile loaded with features.[37]

To be successful in cocreating value, firms must focus on a new set of "building blocks," which Prahalad and Ramaswamy call DART, namely, in-depth **D**ialog with customers, new kinds of **A**ccess to information, the freedom to exchange information to conduct **R**isk assessments, and **T**ransparency to facilitate the interaction. When such building blocks are combined in different combinations, the opportunities for customer collaboration skyrocket. Consider:

- Access *and* transparency—as in getting the right kinds of accurate information for stock investment decisions.

- Dialogue *and* risk assessment—as in the public's increasing ability to influence policy with regard to cigarette smoking.

- Access *and* dialogue—as in New Line Cinema reaching out to the more than 400 unofficial fan Web sites, giving them insider tips, and seeking their feedback on details of, the *Lord of the Rings* film trilogy.

- Transparency *and* risk assessment—as in automobile and tire manufacturers disclosing information to the public about the risks associated with vehicle design, tire pressures, and driving conditions, which they are reluctant to do.[38]

The challenge is to find innovative ways of cocreating value with customers.[38]

Manifestations of Strategic Thinking

Strategic thinking clearly benefits a company and its strategic-planning process. Yet not all companies do strategic thinking. Those that do tend to keep that fact to themselves. So how can one tell whether strategic thinking is going on in a company? Most of the time one cannot. But if one knows what to look for and asks a few questions, it is possible to discern whether strategic thinking is being done. The following sections illustrate the signs or indications of strategic thinking and by no means constitute a definitive list. However, they may be helpful in recognizing the existence of strategic thinking in an organization. They are arranged in roughly descending order of strategic benefit for the company.

Strategic conversations   A strategic conversation is a free-ranging discussion on a topic of strategic interest to an organization. Because of its characteristic "no-holds-barred" freedom to say whatever needs to be said, it invariably produces ideas and thinking that are ultimately useful in the strategic-planning process and that might not be captured in any formal process.

All major strategic planning, according to Peter Schwartz (and stated at a major conference in 2002), does not take place during the strategic-planning process.[39] What goes on in a formal process is almost always a ratification of what has already happened. A strategic conversation is an attempt to understand the *real* strategic-planning process, often entirely informally. Schwartz's friends at Bell South used to call it the "HERs" process—hallways, elevators, and restrooms—because that's where the most interesting conversations take place. While real decisions got made, real issues got confronted, real knowledge was developed, and so on, almost all of it took place in this *conversational* mode. And that is how real learning takes place. If you are going to have good strategy, it involves good learning, learning about new realities, new facts, new competition, new opportunities, new directions, and challenging old knowledge. Simply doing a strategic plan as an act of coming up with a set of new plans for the coming year as if nothing had changed is pointless. The problem is that if *everything* has changed and you need to come up with a plan, how are you going to learn about those changes?

Furthermore, again paraphrasing Schwartz, it is one thing to do this for an individual, but how do you get a *group* of decision-makers, who almost always have to act together, to acquire that knowledge and to develop and implement strategic plans? The only way you learn together is through conversations. Whether formal or informal, a strategic conversation is the learning vehicle whereby the group adjusts to a new worldview to enable strategic plans to be developed and implemented. The sequence is: shared conversations, shared learning, change one's mental maps, and then develop better strategic plans. Toney Manning, in an article, echoes Schwartz in ways that are particularly pertinent:

> Strategic conversation is far more than just an occasional practice that can be adopted or abandoned at will: it is without doubt the central and most important executive tool.
>
> [. . .]
>
> What senior managers talk about—clearly, passionately, and consistently—tells me what they pay attention to and how sure they are of what they must do.[40]

Are there strategic conversations going on in your company? Have you participated in any? What mechanism does your company use to learn about, share, and assess the changes going on around it and their implications?

Membership in Schwarz' group   Peter Schwartz, one of the world's leading futurists, is chairman of Business Global Network (**www.gbn.com**), an international think tank and consulting firm. One of the firm's activities involves a dues-paying membership of companies around the world, whose executives periodically attend meetings on topics of strategic interest (e.g., technology, biology, digital futures, terrorism, political alliances, etc.) that are undergoing sometimes profound change. Experts on the subject matter as well as the executives engage in free-flowing conversations around the topic, during which much learning and shifting of one's views takes place (unfreezing and shifting of frames of reference). The result is a much greater awareness of changes taking place around the world and a renewed commitment to share similar experiences with others in the organization. Do you know of anyone in your organization that has even heard of a company like Global Business Network, let alone joined a strategic conversation there?

Management meetings that discuss strategic issues   Most companies engage in strategic planning once a year and they are way ahead of others that do not do any. Some companies, however, such as QLogic Corporation, have weekly management meetings at which topics are discussed that are relevant to the company's business such the economy, demographic changes, new technologies, political and legislative trends, competitive moves, and so on. (See QLogic.) While there is no specific strategic-planning agenda, the meetings serve to keep people abreast of changes going on around them, provide an opportunity for questions and shared learning, and give the management more time to prepare strategic responses if the changes hit too close to home. Does your management team hold regular meetings during the year to discuss strategic topics relevant to the firm?

A wonderful description of management meetings is given by George Conrades, CEO of Akamai:

> Every Monday the entire management team gathers together, and we argue about the key challenges we face . . . We're intellectually ruthless, and we all cherish that ruthlessness. It's the cornerstone of our culture, really . . . We never let it get personal. It's always constructive—aimed at ripping a question apart so we can be as sure as possible that we come to the best decision . . . I can tell you one thing: everyone here is committed to open communication. The give-and-take is incredibly valuable in ensuring that we do smart things and do them fast. Plus, it's a lot of fun.[41]

Attendance at strategy conferences   A number of strategic planning and management conferences are held every year, organized by professional associations such as the Association for Strategic Planning, the Strategic Management Society, the Strategic Leadership Forum, the Conference Board, and the Academy of Management, to name just a few. Such conferences help expand the intellectual and perceptual horizons of their participants, see the world from others' viewpoints, interact with people outside of one's industry and, of course, network. For a short time, it is like breathing in fresh air—suddenly invigorating and energizing.

Casual conversations about strategic issues   Depending on the kinds of managers and people in a company, several of them might chat casually over lunch, or in the coffee room, or on a plane/taxi on the way to a meeting, or wherever and whenever the opportunity presents itself. These conversations are not planned. They are, however, often substantive and always energizing. Participants often follow up by doing more research or emailing each other.

Membership in industry and strategic organizations   Many professional organizations provide intellectual, experiential, and methodological insights to their members by way of regular monthly meetings, invited dinner speakers, and just interaction among the members. The organizations listed above that organize annual conferences are five such organizations, but the list of organizations one can join is simply huge. Some that come readily to mind include the Association for Corporate Growth, the American Marketing Association, the Society for Competitive Intelligence Profes-

---

QLogic

QLogic Corporation shared the Association for Strategic Planning's 2002 Excellence in Strategic Planning Award. Frank Calderoni, Senior Vice President and CFO, discussed its "process" during a speech at ASP's annual conference on October 8, 2002.

sionals, and the Young Presidents' Organization. Again, while speakers and events provide ideas and useful information, perhaps what people remember most is the conversation they had over dinner with several people on interesting (business) topics.

Management Club with invited speakers   Some larger companies, like Boeing Satellite Systems in Los Angeles, have a "management club" that invites speakers and experts on a variety of topics germane to the company's broader environment. They serve to broaden the perspective and keep the managers current on a variety of topics. Some speakers become consultants to the company and continue to "infect" managers with new thinking and methods. (Small companies cannot do this because of the considerable cost.)

Sharing of strategic and environmental information   Some companies do the "data collection" part of strategic planning all year round. Certain people are selected to be the "gatekeepers" for particular kinds of information of interest to the company such as economic, demographic, political, regulatory, technological, sociocultural data, information on particular countries, competitive information, and the like. Everyone knows who these individuals are, so if anyone comes across some information (a book, an article, a speech, a conference, a Web site) pertaining to that topic, he or she alerts that individual and sends along whatever information was found. In this way, everyone's consciousness is raised about issues *external* to the company. Periodically, either monthly or quarterly depending on the rapidity of changes in that particular area, the gatekeeper summarizes all the material gathered that month or quarter, and ruminates "out loud" about the implications of those changes or events on the company—typically via memo or email.

Authoring and sharing position papers   For companies that can afford to employ high-level staff people (or even lucky enough to have managers that like to think and write about issues), generating "think pieces" about important issues is extremely provoking and often strongly influences the organization's strategic decisions. Often, the top consulting firms have such people, and publishing such articles (either internally or more often externally for PR reasons) serves to keep the consulting firm in the public eye and can generate for it a lot of business.

Reading strategic journals, books, and magazines   Finally, reading and keeping up with articles and books on strategy and related subjects can be a fulltime job for anyone.[42] The top-six strategic journals are (in my opinion, and listed alphabetically):

- *Long Range Planning* has a strong European flavor
- *McKinsey Quarterly*, which is available online too
- *Sloan Management Review*
- *Strategy+Business*
- *Strategy & Leadership*
- *Strategic Management Journal*

Summary

This chapter discussed five principal ways of stretching your thinking about how to provide better customer value and how to compete more effectively. Because the world is continually changing, often at an alarming pace, the task of looking for and coming up with better ways of providing customer value and competing—the task of strategic thinking—never ends.

- Are there ways the company can differentiate itself or its products and achieve a competitive advantage? Can it create its own game and rules, and win?

- By "walking in the customers' shoes"—as entrepreneurs do— are there products or services currently offered that one could improve upon? What are some customers' dissatisfactions, and could the company provide the solution?

- Is the company's search for opportunities wide-ranging enough? Has it examined every combination of customer needs, current capabilities, and technological advances? Are there opportunities in other growth industries? What about ways of reinventing its business model? Has it explored all its strategic frontiers, including those parts that are "terra incognito?" Is the company investing in R&D and experiments now that will, in time, become one of its core businesses?

- What steps is the company taking to address uncertainty in the future? Has it mapped out a number of likely futures? Does it assume a certain future will happen, but has contingencies in case things turn out differently? Is the company dependent on "whatever" the future will bring, or is it trying to "define and design its own future?" Is there a preferred future it should be enabling?

- Has the company explored taking advantage of opportunities that become feasible only through forming a strategic alliance or acquiring/merging with another company? Has it looked at ways in which it could cocreate value with its customers?

Unfortunately, the definition of strategic thinking does not tell you how to do it or even how to get better at it. But this chapter has tried to suggest ways of doing so.

Strategic thinking, clearly, is not performed in a vacuum. It presupposes a basic level of understanding and familiarity about the company and its industry, competitors, markets, and environment. And it assumes that a company's managers, for example, understand the company's business model and current business strategy. But such a "basic level of understanding" by itself will not necessarily produce good strategic thinking or yield a strategy worth pursuing. Strategic thinking goes beyond that. It is both a skill and activity that, for a while, diverges—that is, explores an ever-increasing array of options and choices—and then converges—that is, continually sifts through those myriad choices, discarding some, refining others, and narrowing down the choices to a few that can be seriously considered and debated with others in the strategic-planning team.

In its divergent phase, strategic thinking often takes place in a social context with others. Parts of the strategic-planning process that allow questioning and that debate issues stimulate new ideas and challenge long-held beliefs and assumptions, yielding new information and insights that ultimately shape or alter the course of the strategic debate. A consultant could stimulate strategic thinking by posing hard questions for the management group to wrestle with. Some companies go further and organize strategic conversations that include not only those involved in the strategic-planning process, but select outsiders invited for their expertise and possibly opposing viewpoints.

As a skill, strategic thinking requires a future orientation and a normative attitude ("we *can* affect the future, we can design our own future"), an ability to cope with rapid change and ambiguity, wide-ranging knowledge of the business world (many industries and technologies besides the ones in which the company is engaged), and the conceptual ability to imagine futures that don't currently exist. The ability to communicate complex ideas and changes clearly and argue for certain options (perhaps even in a strategic conversation) is absolutely critical.

Notes

1. Tony Grundy and Laura Brown, *Be Your Own Strategy Consultant: Demystifying Strategic Thinking* (Cincinnati, OH: Thomson Learning, 2002), 186.

2. Ibid., 188

3. Ibid., 225

4. For a good introduction and survey of lateral thinking, see Edward De Bono's *Lateral Thinking: Creativity Step by Step* (Harper & Row, 1970); *Lateral Thinking for Management* (McGraw-Hill, 1970 and Pelican, 1971); and *Serious Creativity: Using the Power of Lateral Thinking to Create New Ideas* (HarperBusiness, 1992).

5. Michael Porter, "What Is Strategy?" *Harvard Business Review* 74 (November–December 1996): 61–78

6. Ibid.

7. Gary Hamel and C. K. Prahalad, *Competing for the Future* (Cambridge, MA: Harvard Business School Press, 1994).

8. Stan Abraham, "Talking Strategy: Dan Bane, CEO of Trader Joe's," *Strategy and Leadership* 30, no. 6 (2002): 30–32.

9. Dennis A. Black, "Creating Strategic Plans with the Power to Win," *Strategy and Leadership* 29, no. 1 (2001): 31.

10. Clayton M. Christensen, Mark W. Johnson, and Darrell K. Rigby, "Foundations for Growth: How to Identify and Build Disruptive New Businesses," *MIT Sloan Management Review* 43 (Spring 2002): 30.

11. Richard D'Aveni, *Hypercompetitive Rivalries: Competing in Highly Dynamic Environments* (New York: Free Press, 1995).

12. Gerald Nadler and Shozo Hibino, *Breakthrough Thinking: The Seven Principles of Creative Problem Solving* (New York: Prima Publishing/St. Martin's Press, 1994).

13. Robert B. Tucker, "Strategy Innovation Takes Imagination," *Journal of Business Strategy* 22, no. 3 (May–June 2001): 24.

14. Ibid., 24.

15. Jay L. Abraham and Daniel J. Knight, "Strategic Innovation: Leveraging Creative Action for More Profitable Growth," *Strategy and Leadership* 29, no. 1 (2001): 26.

16. Ibid., 27.

17. Jim Kerstetter, "Can Software Stop Sun's Slide?" *BusinessWeek Online,* 15 July 2002, <http://www.businessweek.com/magazine/content/02_28/b3791096.htm> (17 June 2004).

18. Lawrence M. Fisher, "Clayton M. Christensen, the Thought Leader Interview," *Strategy+Business* no. 25, (Fourth Quarter 2001): 121–122.

19. Al Ries, *Focus: The Future of Your Company Depends on It* (New York: HarperBusiness, 1996).

20. Robert E. Johnston Jr. and J. Douglas Bate, The Power of Strategy Innovation: A New Way of Linking Creativity and Strategic Planning to Discover Great Business Opportunities (New York: AMACOM, 2003).

21. Mehrdad Baghai, Stephen Coley, and David White, *The Alchemy of Growth: Practical Insights for Building the Enduring Enterprise* (New York: Perseus, 2000).

22. Clayton M. Christensen, Mark W. Johnson, and Darrell K. Rigby, "Foundations for Growth: How to Identify and Build Disruptive New Businesses," *MIT Sloan Management Review* 43 (Spring 2002): 29.

23. Peter Schwartz, *The Art of the Long View: Planning for the Future in an Uncertain World,* rev. ed. (New York: Currency Doubleday, 1996), 241–248.

24. Stuart Wells, *Choosing the Future: The Power of Strategic Thinking* (London: Butterworth-Heinemann, 1998), 108.

25. Ibid., 104.

26. Liam Fahey, "How Corporations Learn from Scenarios," *Strategy & Leadership* 31, no. 2 (2003): 9. See also these other excellent articles on scenarios in the same issue of *Strategy & Leadership*: Stephen M. Millett, "The Future of Scenarios: Challenges and Opportunities," 16–24; David Mason, "Tailoring Scenario Planning to the Company Culture, 25–28; and Betty S. Flowers, "The Art and Strategy of Scenario Writing, 29–33.

27. Robert G. Wilson, "Future Mapping: Comments on Our Experience with a Scenario-Building Technique," presentation at the *Planning Forum Annual International Conference,* Toronto, April 30, 1991. Robert Wilson is president of Northeast Consulting Resources, Inc., Boston, MA.

28. Stan Abraham, "The Association for Strategic Planning: Strategy is Still Management's Core Challenge," *Strategy & Leadership* 30, no. 2 (2002): 39.

29. Frank Lekanne Deprez and René Tissen, *Zero Space: Moving Beyond Organizational Limits* (San Francisco: Berrett-Koehler, 2002), x.

30. Matthew Schifrin, "Partner or Perish," *Forbe.com,* 21 May 2001, <http://www.forbes.com/best/2001/0521/026.html> (17 June 2004).

31. J. Peter Killing, *Strategies for Joint Venture Success* (New York: Praeger, 1983), 124.

32. Carol Ackatcherian, *Mergers and Acquisitions: Why Do They Fail?* Unpublished MBA Project Final Report, Cal Poly Pomona, May 2001, 34.

33. Arthur A. Thompson and Bryan Fuller, "Whirlpool Corporation," in Arthur A. Thompson and A. J. Strickland III, *Strategic Management: Concepts and Cases,* 10th ed. (New York: Irwin McGraw-Hill, 1998).

34. Mattel, Inc., *Mattel Reports Third Quarter Results—Earnings per Share in Line with Market Expectations,* 10 October 2000, <www.shareholder.com/mattel/news/20001019-43141.cfm> (17 June 2004).

35. The data in this paragraph come from Peter Pekár, "The Value of Strategic Alliances," presentation at the Association for Strategic Planning's

first annual conference, *New Strategies for a Rapidly Changing World,* LAX Airport Crowne Plaza Hotel, October 9, 2001.

36. C. K. Prahalad and Venkat Ramaswamy, *The Future of Competition: Co-Creating Unique Value with Customers* (New York: HBS, 2004), 2–5.

37. C. K. Prahalad, Keynote address at the *Third Annual Conference of the Association for Strategic Planning* on October 14, 2003, in Stan Abraham, "Cocreating unique value with customers: C.K. Prahalad introduces a novel approach to competitive advantage," *Strategy & Leadership,* in press.

38. Ibid.

39. Stan Abraham, "Conference Report: Experiencing Strategic Conversations about the Central Forces of Our Time," *Strategy & Leadership* 3, no 2 (2003): 61–62. Peter Schwartz helped to organize the conference, and his remarks are cited in the article.

40. Toney Manning, "Strategic Conversation as a Tool for Change," *Strategy & Leadership* 30, no. 5 (2002), 35–37.

41. N. G. Carr, "On the edge: An Interview with Akamai's George Conrades," *Harvard Business Review* 78 (May–June 2000), 118-125.

42. The *Journal of Business Strategy* was "going downhill" until acquired by Emerald Publishing Ltd. in 2002. The *Harvard Business Review* is preeminent for general, not strategic, management. Likewise, the *California Management Review* is good for general management. *Strategic Management Journal* is very theoretical.

3

Strategic-Planning Models

A strategic-planning model serves many purposes. The most important is *planning the process* of doing strategic planning, also referred to as "planning to plan" or metaplanning. Another purpose is to *lay out the process* of strategic planning so that everyone involved understands what is going to happen. Another is to *explain the process* of strategic planning to those who may not understand it, as trainers do to new organizational hires or professors to students. Another is to *change the process* from what the organization used to do to a better one, taking the opportunity to justify and explain the changes to the organization at the same time. Finally, the model can *set out a timeline,* during which the planning process is accomplished.

Though strategic-planning models all differ in some respect, they are similar in approach. They begin with a situation analysis, followed by strategic analysis and choice among alternatives, and end with recommendations, implementation, and evaluation. This chapter discusses some existing models to illustrate their differences and similarities—and the model that is introduced in this book (and its companion CD-ROM).

Other Strategic-Planning Models

James F. Bandrowski advocates a five-step "creative planning" process that includes steps for analysis, creativity, judgment, planning, and, ultimately, action:

- *Step 1, Analysis,* involves evaluating a company from six different angles—profitability, markets, competitors, technologies, operations, and organization. It also involves developing creative insights into the company and its industry such as what are the company's major issues, the blocks to increasing profitability, and the traditions in the company or industry that no longer make sense.

- *Step 2, Creativity,* involves creative leaps and imagination, a time to generate ideas about any aspect of the company-ways to increase profitability and productivity, reduce costs, beat the competition, and the like. This step is to inject fresh thinking into the process.

- *Step 3, Judgment,* takes the "wild" ideas generated in Step 2 and prunes out the infeasible ones, modifies or combines some of the others, and produces usable strategic concepts. These are refined further until they become feasible and prioritized. The strategy you will pursue will start to come into focus here.

- *Step 4, Planning,* allows you to stand back and articulate the company's mission, vision, positioning, and values or guiding principles. Also in this step, the company sets the quantitative objectives it will try to achieve over the next several years and the strategy it will use to achieve them. Finally, to work out the details—the action programs, budgets, financial forecast, and contingency plans—that have to be in place for implementation to proceed smoothly

- *Step 5, Action,* is the step where the plans and strategies are implemented. The plan becomes a framework for decision-making and control throughout implementation. Each operational unit should also create its own plans, replete with objectives, resource allocations, assignments, and timetable.[1]

Roger Kaufman proposes a different model. First, you must choose the appropriate planning level (mega-, macro-, or microplanning): "mega" for the corporation, "macro" for the division, and "micro" for operational planning. Steps 2–5 involve collecting data about the organization's beliefs and values, its vision—focusing on ends and not means, that is: what is, what should be, what could be—its current mission, and its needs (i.e., the gap between what is and desired results). Steps 6–12 involve planning, where matches and mismatches are identified, and visions, values, needs, and current missions are integrated. In these steps, differences are reconciled (try for what is "right," not just acceptable), needs are prioritized, and a preferred future is selected. Finally, after doing a SWOT analysis and deriving decision rules, strategic action plans are developed. In the final phase (Step 13), the plan is implemented.[2]

Another five-step strategic-planning model by Kerry Napuk provides stages represented by a series of "simple" questions that facilitate the complexities of modeling. These, in turn, generate objectives, urgent issues, and best opportunities for which Napuk says to set one or more strategies and the actions to achieve them (as well as assigning a person, priority, and resources to each action).

1. How did we get here? What has accounted for our success or lack thereof?

2. Where do we want to go? Is our vision real? Does it build on things we do really well? What are the company's strengths and weaknesses? Do the strengths support the vision?

3. What are the objectives, in order of importance? Are they all achievable? What are the goals (quantitative indicators)? How do they compare to competitors and the industry?

Customer Value Package

Albrecht describes the *customer value package* as multidimensional architecture for managing the customer's experience with the enterprise, and with the value it creates. The customer value package must be right if the organization hopes to build in the customer's mind an impression of quality and value for money.[5]

4. How do we get to where we want to go? What and where are the best business opportunities, which may require market research? What strategies are needed to realize these opportunities? What market plans are needed to realize the business opportunities?

5. How do we make the plan work? What resources are needed to convert the opportunities such as people, funds, and technology? How will these resources be obtained? What are the critical risks, threats, and responses to strategies? What actions need to be taken?[3]

Karl Albrecht describes a strategy formulation process that begins with environmental, opportunity, and organizational scanning akin to situation analysis. This leads into a model-building stage that comprises what he calls a *Strategic Success Model*. The strategy formulation process ends with successive stages of gap-analysis and action planning—choosing *key result areas* (KRAs)—setting objectives that will close the gaps, and strategy-deployment, which is the necessary communication that precedes implementation. Albrecht's Strategic Success Model comprises five levels:

1. *Creating a vision statement*—a shared image of what the leaders want the company to become, an answer to how the organization would like those it cares about to perceive it.

2. *Creating a mission statement* that is a simple, compelling statement about how the enterprise does business, a customer value model that is value defined from the customer's perspective, and a statement of core values essential to accomplishing the mission—not motherhood statements.

3. *Defining the strategic concept*, which requires knowledge of the operating environment, the logic of the business and strategy, and the customer value package, also referred to as the firm's value proposition. (See Customer Value Package.)

4. *Defining strategic initiatives*, both KRAs and business targets (objectives).

5. This last level includes not only outcomes, but also *adaptive goals*—not the business targets of the previous step, but new problems and challenges noticed during implementation that deserve the organization's attention.[4]

In yet another five-step model, Kenichi Ohmae advocates:

1. Clearly defining the business domain.

2. Analyzing the basic forces and trends in the environment, extrapolating into the future, and describing the most logical and succinct scenario in which the company will mostly likely find itself competing.

3. Choosing only a few strategic options and deploying resources boldly and aggressively.

4. Regulating the strategy according to available resources.

5. Staying with the strategy unless basic assumptions change.[6]

Michele Bechtell uses Hoshin planning as the basis for strategic planning. As the preface to her book *The Management Compass: Steering the Corporation Using Hoshin Planning* states, "*Hoshin kanri* is a management methodology to reliably execute strategic breakthroughs."[7] Developed in Japan, *Hoshin kanri* is rapidly gaining favor in the United States and around the world. "HP, Intel, Milliken, TI, Zytec, and P&G are among the world-class corporations using Hoshin management to link daily activity with strategic objectives."[8]

The model used in Hoshin management starts with creating a long-term vision and aligning the organization's goals with changes in its environment. Next, management must select and define a vital few breakthrough objectives—or gaps that need to be closed—to sharpen the organization's future focus. Management then must create a companywide plan of attack, aligning people, activities, and resources behind those things that matter most to the organization. The rest is implementation. Daily activities must be aligned with the plan and progress tightly controlled. Changes in the environment may spark changes in the organization's priorities, requiring operational plans to be modified and the organization to become more flexible. Hoshin management can be summed up in two words: focus and alignment.

Timothy Nolan, Leonard Goodstein, and J. William Pfeiffer in their book, *Plan or Die,* suggest an *applied* strategic-planning model as follows:

1. *Planning to plan*—setting up the planning process, deciding how to involve the organization's principal stakeholders, and deciding who to involve and what data to collect.

2. *Values scan*—identifying the underlying and real values of the people in the company and how the company intends to do business.

3. *Mission formulation*—must include *what* function the organization serves, *for whom* it serves this function, *how* it goes about fulfilling this function, and *why* it exists.

4. *Strategic business modeling*—the process by which the organization specifically defines success in the context of the business it wants to be in, how that success will be measured, what will be done to achieve it, and with what organizational culture. This includes topics such as proactive futuring, the organization's approach to innovation, its orientation to risk, and its competitive stance.

5. *Performance audit*—how well the organization has been doing, which includes a SWOT analysis.

6. *Gap analysis*—represents the difference between the outcome— what is desired—and the performance audit—where the company is now. If the disparity is too great, the strategic business model has to be reworked and the process repeated iteratively until the gap is within the capabilities and resources of the organization to close.

7. *Integrating action plans*—of each business and functional unit within the organization into a comprehensive whole.

8. *Contingency Planning*—focuses on the low-probability events that would have a high impact—positive and negative—on the organization if they were to occur.[9]

Dave Francis has proposed a ten-step competitive-strategy process. The first nine steps are the strategy-planning model, with the final step being the strategy's implementation:

1. *Exploring industry scenarios*—assessing opportunities and threats for similar firms.

2. *Assessing market dynamics*—defining customer groupings.

3. *Evaluating structural profitability*—answering the question, "Can we make money?"

4. *Analyzing competitors*—helping you know your enemy.

5. Collecting external perceptions—challenging your assumptions.

6. *Clarifying values*—clarifying what you believe in.

7. *Generating ideas*—exploring all the things you could do.

8. *Developing strategic options*—clarifying alternative futures.

9. *Defining a competitive strategy*—identifying your formula for gaining superiority.[10]

These steps, as you will see, bear considerable similarity to those presented in this book.

William Finnie outlines a three-cycle process for strategy development and implementation:

- *Cycle 1, Strategy Development* (primarily qualitative and top-down)—includes defining the business and setting strategic objectives, including *big, hairy, achievable goals* (BHAG); developing generic strategies and customer-driven, competitor-driven, and people-driven strategies; developing the vision and mission statements, key moves, and broad action plans; and getting bottom-up commitment.

- *Cycle 2, Strategy Implementation* (primarily quantitative and bottom-up—includes forming departmental strategies and SMART goals.

- *Cycle 3, Strategy Implementation*—further includes creating performance measures and detailed action plans.[11]

Robert E. Johnston Jr. and J. Douglas Bate, while proposing a model for strategic thinking—or "strategy innovation" to use their term, actually incorporate aspects of strategic planning that go beyond just strategic thinking. Their strategy innovation or "Discovery" process is divided into the following five phases:

1. *Staging Phase*—where the Discovery team is selected, key roles identified, and objectives of the initiative are set.

2. *Aligning Phase*—where the Discovery team and senior management align themselves as to the focus and scope of the initiative, agreeing on the "strategic frontier(s)" to be explored, for example, new markets, new ways of providing customer value, new products, or a new business model entirely.

3. *Exploring Phase*—where the Discovery team collects new insights on the strategic frontier that lead to identifying new opportunities for the company.

4. *Creating Phase*—where the Discovery team creates and refines a portfolio of new business opportunities using the insights gained in the preceding phase.

5. *Mapping Phase*—where the Discovery team creates a strategic road map outlining key events, trends, milestones, and the like to move the company into its strategic future.[12]

Cornelis De Kluyver proposes a more traditional model, integrated by three questions:

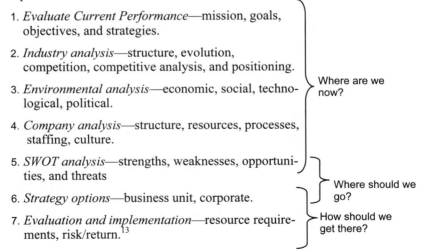

1. *Evaluate Current Performance*—mission, goals, objectives, and strategies.

2. *Industry analysis*—structure, evolution, competition, competitive analysis, and positioning.

3. *Environmental analysis*—economic, social, technological, political.

4. *Company analysis*—structure, resources, processes, staffing, culture.

} Where are we now?

5. *SWOT analysis*—strengths, weaknesses, opportunities, and threats

6. *Strategy options*—business unit, corporate.

} Where should we go?

7. *Evaluation and implementation*—resource requirements, risk/return.[13]

} How should we get there?

Finally, Bill Birnbaum, in *Reinventing Strategic Planning,* proposes an update of the traditional strategic-planning process that he calls the *Strategy 21 ™ Process*:

1. *Examining the current business model*—including whether the company has a competitive advantage, what it is, and whether it

is eroding; how competitive the company is; whether it has a core competence; how its industry, market, and environment are changing; and what the weakest link is in its business model.

2. *Beyond the current business model*—including scanning the environment outside the business model for potential new competitors, threats from substitutes, other distribution channels, and so on.

3. *Designing the "grand strategy"*—choosing from among three options such as continuing or improving on the current business model; changing to a new business model; or diversifying so as to manage multiple business models.

4. *Developing a compelling vision*—creating an exciting vision of the company's future that everyone in the company can get behind.

5. *Assuring enablers of strategy*—these include intellectual capacity (creating a learning organization), processes, organizational structure, technologies, external relationships, and capital resources.

6. *Setting objectives to measure success*—including measures from the following categories: financial, marketing/sales, products/services, operations, human resources, and community.

7. *Designing a monitoring process*—checking over time that both the set objectives and the strategy are being achieved. [14]

Unlike other authors on strategy, Birnbaum focuses on *strategic thinking* and, in turn, business-unit strategy, corporate strategy, and global strategy. However, he does not instruct the reader on how to do a strategic analysis.

The variety of the models briefly described represent consulting industry's approaches as opposed to the strictly academic, and for that reason have some validity as to their usefulness in the real world. All of them differ to some degree and emphasize different aspects of the strategic-planning process. Notice, however, that with the exception of Bandrowski and, to a lesser extent, Francis and Johnston and Bate, none of the other authors discuss how to generate and choose strategic alternatives. Perhaps somewhere in the process strategic alternatives are considered and addressed, but this step is clearly not important enough to be labeled as a major step in the process in its own right.

For this reason, a model that includes the steps of identifying strategic issues, creating strategic alternatives, and arguing for a preferred choice could well be called "new." (These are introduced in the next section and explained in greater detail in Chapter 6.) It is the principal rationale for this book. Part II covers a description of the entire strategic analysis process that includes strategic alternatives and choice at its core.

A Strategic Analysis Model That Works

Virtually every college textbook on strategic management presents a model of the strategic management process around which the book is organized. [15] The models are all-encompassing and inclusive. They are based

SAM^{tw}

The companion CD-ROM to this book—SAM^{tw}, Strategic
Analysis Model that works—contains worksheets that conform
to this model for doing a strategic analysis as well as possess-
ing full financial analysis capability. Guidelines for using it are
contained in Appendix B as well as on the CD-ROM itself.

on research and, in turn, account for as many real-world examples as possible. While each such model is different in some way from all the others,
they are for the most part similar. Yet, while they provide a template for
anyone wanting to learn about strategic planning, they provide little or no
help as to *how* to do it.

This book, not surprisingly, also proposes a model. In many respects it
is similar to those advocated by others. However, its purpose is different.
The purpose of this model is to show how to actually perform a strategic
analysis that can be used by an organization for making decisions or recommendations. This model can be used by a company to do a strategic
analysis and strategic planning as well as by graduate students learning this
skill. Like the models surveyed in the previous section, it has also been
used, refined, and proven and covers only the process of doing a strategic
analysis. Though it can be adapted to a strategic-planning process, it is not
intended for strategic management (see Figure 1.1). The latter includes the
all-important phases of implementation, evaluation, and control, whereas
this model goes only as far as deciding the direction and strategy for the
company, setting short- and long-term objectives, and coming up with principal programs. (See SAM^{tw}.)

Figure 3.1 presents a diagram of the model, which is divided into
three unequal phases: situation analysis, alternatives and choice, and recommendations. *Phase I, Situation Analysis,* involves understanding the
external environment and how it is changing as well as the internal environment of the company and how it is changing. Phase I involves much
data collection, which is necessary if the analyst is unfamiliar with the
company, its technology, or its industry. It also involves *perception* of a
high order. (At one time, this phase was called the "Perception Phase.")

No person is an accurate or comprehensive observer of facts and
events, especially if more facts and events are happening than one has the
capability to know about or process. There is no such thing as "facts" or
"truth," but only what we *perceive* as facts or truth. This observation has
been demonstrated many times in consulting engagements and classrooms
when people, confronted with essentially the same data, make such different sense of those data.

People's perceptions differ because everyone has a different frame of
reference against which new data are compared and contrasted in order to
make sense of them. For this reason, many companies form special
groups, like a top-management group, to do strategic planning. The
group's shared perceptions bring a useful dimension to the task.

Thus, we have to rely on our own perception of what is going on
around us, on what others tell us, and on what we read in the newspapers,
the business press, and the Internet. While some people believe everything
they are told or read, others are skeptical. While some really try to make

Figure 3.1 A Strategic-Analysis Model—That Works (SAMᵗʷ)

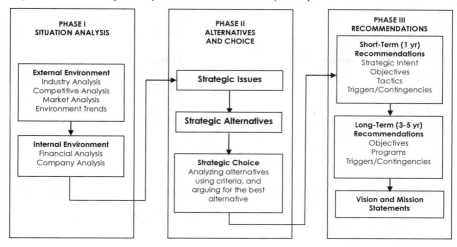

sense of events and forces, others simply go through the motions. While some bother to look around them only when they are forced to, others try to decipher what is going on all the time, searching for opportunities and different ways of competing. While some will be content to accept the data they collect, others will question the relevance, timeliness, and timeframe of those data.

Books, including this one, can only tell you what to do in the situation-analysis phase. But you are not doing it well unless you acquire a thorough understanding of how the company and its external environment have changed and are changing, where the problems and pitfalls lie, and where future opportunities beckon. That is the key. Set your sights on understanding the data collected, for example, know where the market is going and not routinely collect data. Peter Schwartz asserts that the principal purpose of doing strategic planning is to develop a shared understanding of the implications of the changes going on in the world so that the company has a basis for deciding what to do.

That *gestalt* understanding (the "big picture") is crucial to performing the other two phases well. Experienced managers will have an easier time of doing this for their own company and environment, as opposed to learning about an unfamiliar company and its environment, as managers must do who are studying potential acquisition candidates or students must do when studying cases. It is from such an understanding that the key strategic issues facing a company are derived.

Phase II, Alternatives and Choice, involves two kinds of skills—*synthesis* and *strategic thinking*. Synthesis is needed to formulate the key strategic issues facing the company. Strategic thinking is needed to develop strategic alternatives—the most difficult part of the entire process. Choosing a preferred alternative is never easy, especially if the alternatives are really good ones.

Some strategy scholars, however, maintain that strategic decisions do not get made "to order," or made as a result of a systematic and analytical process, as these are. Rather, they maintain, the firm tends to adopt strategies that emerge (called "incremental strategies") and cannot predict when such decisions actually get made—they just "happen." It is true that in some companies decisions are made almost without being made. The company remains so flexible that it is able to "experiment" with new strategies whenever the need arises and seamlessly adopts the one that finally wins consensus. Would that all companies could manage themselves like that. Yet many companies are more traditional or do very little strategic planning. Becoming one of the flexible ones overnight is out of the question. For these companies—the rest of us—this model is the next best thing. At a very minimum, it forces a serious reexamination of the current strategy, whether it's working, and whether it should be changed and to what.

Phase III, Recommendations, tackles the question of how—and how fast—the chosen strategy should be implemented. In this phase, the firm decides on its strategic intent, short- and long-term objectives, programs (actions that help achieve the objectives—called "tactics" if they occur within the next year), and contingencies if certain assumptions prove wrong, unforeseen events occur, or the company's performance fails to meet expectations.

Lastly, the model gives the analyst the opportunity to review or revise the company's mission and vision statements. While the mission and, especially, the vision statement should guide what a company does in the future, it often takes a complete strategic analysis to realize whether they need to be changed or not. For this reason, examining or changing them is done at the end of the process.

Normally, all this would not be enough to run a company. Strategic planning without implementation is useless. The model does not include implementation because it covers only strategic planning, not strategic management's implementation and control factors. Nevertheless, operational planning and implementation are briefly addressed in Chapter 9. But there is no question that implementation becomes a joy if it turns your organization into a stronger competitor and helps it realize its strategic intent and vision, increase its shareholder value, or helps it become the best in the world at what it does. Those outcomes turn on the strategic thinking, analysis, and planning that were done.

While managers and students can learn to use this model and understand the rationale behind the process in a relatively short time, it nevertheless takes great skill, industry experience, creativity, a "strategic mindset," and discipline to become good at it. For this reason, it helps to have patience and practice from analyzing many companies or cases. Managers of companies do not typically have access to cases, nor do they have the time to practice. Instead, they have to hone their skills on the job, getting involved in doing strategic analyses whenever they can, especially in a team and, ideally, with the guidance of a skilled consultant. Doing a strategic analysis in a group is particularly beneficial, the more so if the group is diverse in its composition—different functional areas, different levels (strategic and operational), men and women, and senior, experienced people along with new, younger, and intelligent associates. Only over time will a manager in a corporate setting be able to hone his or her skills doing strategic planning.

Summary

This chapter has outlined the principal steps or phases of eleven strategic-planning models that form the basis of the books written by their authors, and there may well be others. All of them make sense and have been used "in the field" to help organizations of various kinds. The purpose for doing so was to demonstrate that while each one was different, they exhibited more similarities than differences.

The chapter also introduced the strategic-planning model used and explained in this book and companion CD-ROM. While it many ways resembling the other models, the distinguishing feature of this one is its guidance in using strategic thinking to come up with strategic alternatives and choosing a preferred one using criteria meaningful to the organization. After all, without persuasive arguments for pursuing a different strategic direction or business model, the organization would never change. While some of the other models also included the step of developing strategic alternatives, this book's focus is on how to do it, and even provides computer-based templates and instructions in the companion CD-ROM that make it much easier.

Notes

1. James F. Bandrowski, *Corporate Imagination Plus: Five Steps to Translating Innovative Strategies into Action* (New York: Free Press, 1990).

2. Roger Kaufman, *Strategic Planning Plus: An Organizational Guide* (Newbury Park, CA: Sage, 1992).

3. Kerry Napuk, *The Strategy-Led Business: Step-by-Step Strategic Planning for Small- and Medium-Sized Companies* (New York: McGraw-Hill, 1996), 223.

4. Karl Albrecht, *The Northbound Train: Finding the Purpose, Setting the Direction, Shaping the Destiny of Your Corporation* (New York: AMACOM, 1994).

5. Ibid., 175.

6. Kenichi Ohmae, *The Mind of the Strategist: Business Planning for Competitive Advantage* (New York: Penguin, 1983).

7. Michele L. Bechtell, *The Management Compass: Steering the Corporation Using Hoshin Planning* (New York: AMA, 1995), 5.

8. Ibid., 5.

9. Timothy Nolan, Leonard Goodstein, and J. William Pfeiffer, *Plan or Die! 101 Keys to Organizational Success* (San Diego, CA: Pfeiffer, 1993), 124–149.

10. Dave Francis, *Step-by-Step Competitive Strategy* (London: Routledge, 1994), 10.

11. William C. Finnie, *Hands-On Strategy: The Guide to Crafting Your Company's Future,* 2nd ed. (New York: Grace Advisors, 2000), 23.

12. Robert E. Johnston, Jr. and J. Douglas Bate, *The Power of Strategy Innovation* (New York: AMACOM, 2003), 40–41.

13. Cornelis A. de Kluyver, Strategic *Thinking: An Executive Perspective* (Upper Saddle River, NJ: Prentice Hall, 2000), 8.

14. Bill Birnbaum, *Strategic Thinking: A Four Piece Puzzle* (Costa Mesa, CA: Douglas Mountain Publishing, 2004), 189–206.

15. See Michael A. Hitt, R. Duane Ireland, and Robert E. Hoskisson, *Strategic Management: Competitiveness and Globalization,* 6th ed. (Mason, OH: Thomson South-Western, 2005), 6; Arthur A. Thompson, Jr., John E. Gamble, and A. J. Strickland III, *Strategy: Winning in the Marketplace— Core Concepts, Analytical Tools, Cases* (New York: McGraw-Hill, 2004), 11, 37; Charles W. L. Hill and Gareth R. Jones, *Strategic Management: An Integrated Approach,* (Boston: Houghton Mifflin, 2001), 6; and Thomas L. Wheelen and J. David Hunger, *Strategic Management and Business Policy,* 9th ed. (Upper Saddle River, NJ: Pearson Prentice Hall, 2004), 10, 20–21.

Part Two

THE STRATEGIC ANALYSIS PROCESS

4

Analyzing the External Environment

The strategic-planning model proposed in this and the following chapters can be used for a strategic analysis of a real company—and for a strategic management case study that has "real world" relevance for an MBA or executive-education course. The model can be used for a public or private company, a manufacturing or service company, a large or small company, or an industry leader or follower. However, as stated in the Preface, it cannot be used for the following three kinds of company or organization:

- A conglomerate or multibusiness company.

- A nonprofit organization.[1]

- A startup company with neither a history nor strategic alternatives.

While this model is proven, it may not represent the *best* way to do a strategic analysis—there are as many models as there are consultants, strategic analysts, and teachers—and there is no way of knowing which ones are better than others. This book does not "reinvent the wheel" and, as explained in Chapter 3, most strategic-planning models are similar. But this model is one that is relatively easy to explain, easy to learn and use (though it does takes a lot of practice to do well), and one that works. Above all, it incorporates a unique method for coming up with worthwhile strategic alternative "bundles" from which a preferred course of action can be chosen. This part of the model can even be abstracted and used in conjunction with other strategic-planning models or methods, which means it could readily be incorporated and customized into a company's particular process.

The next four chapters together describe the three phases of the model. This chapter and Chapter 5 describe the first phase: *Situation Analysis*.

An analysis of the external environment covers the industry or segment in which the company competes, its competitors, markets, and other relevant environmental trends and changes. The purpose is to understand how the company's relevant environment is changing and might change in the future—in this sense, "relevant" means anything the company might affect or could be affected by. Without such an understanding, doing strategic planning becomes much more difficult. (Recall that Chapter 2 discussed *strategic conversations*, a free-ranging discussion activity to help those involved in strategic planning understand how the environment has changed and how those changes might impact the company's future.)

Industry Analysis

An *industry* is the collection of competitors that produces similar or substitute products or services to a defined market. The word "industry" in industry analysis can mean a segment of a larger industry or the industry itself. If a company manufactures disk drives for personal computers, for example, it could say that it competes in the disk drive industry for purposes of doing a strategic analysis, even though that is really a segment of the personal computer (PC) industry, which itself is a segment of the computer industry. What we are really analyzing is the arena in which the company competes.

One thing to keep in mind when you do an industry analysis is to write down what you believe is true for the industry, *not* for the company under analysis. Sometimes industry data are easy to obtain because they are regularly published or because trade groups or consulting firms keep tabs on industry statistics. However, many industries are not tracked by any group, or they consist of privately held firms for the most part. This makes getting industry data and completing an industry analysis difficult. If you find yourself guessing a lot—or guessing at everything—your knowledge of the industry is minimal or nonexistent.

To minimize errors when using inadequate data or relying on one person's estimates, assemble a group of people to share perspectives and use shared estimates in the analysis. If the group is fairly knowledgeable about the industry, the perceptions you record about the industry will be more accurate and make your understanding more complete. Group members who have differing estimates and opinions will be forced to explain their views and, in the process, either convince others they are correct or be persuaded to change their own views or estimates. In this way, a shared perspective leads to greater understanding, and can be achieved.

The purpose of doing an industry analysis is to answer the following kinds of questions:

- What are the industry's dominant economic characteristics?

- How is the industry changing? What is causing it to change?

- Do buyers and/or suppliers have more bargaining power?

- How high are entry barriers?

- Is the industry concentrated (some industry power) or fragmented?

- What does one have to do well in this industry in order to succeed?

- How attractive is the industry?

What are the industry's dominant economic characteristics?   The industry's dominant economic characteristics include the following:

- *Industry size*—total dollar sales of all firms in the industry.

- *Industry growth rate*—percentage increase or decrease over the previous year.

- *Scope of competitive rivalry*—local, regional, national, international.

- *Number of competitors*—if known.

- *Stage in the industry's lifecycle:*

  - Emerging—must be a brand new industry with total industry sales less than 5%.

  - Growth—total industry sales growing at over 5% per year.

  - Shakeout—a transitional period between growth and maturity where some competitors fail and others are acquired by larger ones and the number of competitors shrinks.

  - Mature—total industry sales of between 0–5%.

  - Declining—the growth rate must be negative for several years in a row.

- *The customers or buyers*—Who and where are they, and roughly how many?

- *Degree of vertical integration*—How many or what percentage of firms in the industry are vertically integrated forwards? How are many vertically integrated backwards? How many are vertically integrated in both directions?

- *Rate of technological innovation*—How dependent is the industry on technological innovation? How much innovation is taking place?

- *Product characteristics*—Are they commodity-like or differentiated? High- or low-tech?

- *Economies of scale*—for example in purchasing, production, shipping, distribution, or advertising.

- *Capacity utilization*—High or low? How sensitive are variations in capacity utilization to profits?

- *Industry profitability*—If not high, what are some causes?

How is the industry changing?   To understand how an industry is changing, identify the driving forces causing those changes. Examples of driving forces include:

- Changes in the industry growth rate.

- Changes in who buys the product and how customers use it.

- Product or marketing innovations.

- Technological change.

- Entry or exit of major firms.

- Diffusion of technical know-how.

- Increasing globalization of the industry.

- Changes in cost and efficiency, for example, in process innovations.

- Emerging buyer preferences for differentiation.

- Changes in governmental or economic policy.

- Deregulation or increasing regulation of an industry.

- Changing societal concerns, attitudes, lifestyles.

- Reductions or increases in uncertainty and business risk.

- Likelihood that this and one or more other industries will "merge" or converge (see Convergence).

It is one thing to ascertain that an industry has been and is changing, but quite another to gauge the way it will change in the future. Unfortunately, that is what is really needed here. If you can come to understand how an industry is changing and what is causing it to change, chances are good that you can predict how it might change in the future. In many industries today, rapidly advancing technology is changing everything about the industry—the product itself, how it is made, how it is distributed, and how it is used. (Chapter 2 mentioned that companies are increasingly cocreating value with their customers, which also changes industry dynamics.) This short list should get you or your group thinking about your industry—and depending on that industry, other factors besides these may be important and should be considered.

Do buyers and/or suppliers have more bargaining power? If both buyers and suppliers do, chances are that industry has low profitability, the product is viewed as a commodity, rivalry among competitors is fierce, and innovation is relatively low. On the other hand, if the industry has more bargaining power than both buyers and suppliers, chances are that it is profitable, the products and competitors are differentiated, competition is controlled as it is in monopolistic competition, and innovation may be fairly

Convergence

The merging or coming together of industries as new companies, cooperative ventures, or even as new ways to compete with each other is a relatively recent phenomenon, for example, the convergence of the PC, graphics, digital audio and video, and software industries into what is now called "multimedia," or the convergence of the telecommunications, cable-TV, television, and computer industries into something as yet unnamed that will bring entertainment into our homes in a brand new way.

rapid. These considerations are key aspects of Michael Porter's Five-Forces Model of Competitive Threats and, as you will see, the companion SAM^tw CD-ROM helps you construct and analyze a five-forces model for your industry.[2]

What exactly is bargaining power? In simple terms, it comes down to who dictates the terms—price, delivery, quality, and the like—in a trading negotiation. For example, consider someone trying to sell a used car to a buyer. There is a certain "Blue Book" price that pertains to a car of a certain model, age, mileage, condition, and options. However, if it is a make and model that is in high demand, with low mileage and in good condition, the price will be higher. In fact, it is possible that several potential buyers may actually bid up the price. The seller could demand full payment in cash and other conditions and would probably get them. In this case, the seller has bargaining power and will end up making a deal strongly in his favor. On the other hand, if the seller is desperate to sell the car, or it is not in very good condition—perhaps even needing major work done on the engine— and the seller has to advertise extensively to sell it, raising his costs, he may have to accept the first offer that comes along, probably at some fraction of his asking price. In this case, the buyer would have all the bargaining power and the seller none. (Later, strategies that are effective in regaining lost bargaining power from either a buyer or a supplier will be discussed.)

For another example of bargaining power, consider the unfortunate predicament of a California tool manufacturer. About 90% of its production goes to one OEM (original equipment manufacturer) customer. Profit margin is understandably low. Now, the customer is demanding a price reduction of 10% and delivery in small quantities at frequent intervals, forcing the tool manufacturer to carry even more inventory and increase its costs. If the company were not so dependent on this one customer, it could refuse to supply it. But it cannot. Instead, it gets squeezed. Who has the bargaining power here?

This example is true and, while unfortunate, it illustrates how short-sighted companies can be. Unlike Toyota and other companies that practice *Kaizen*, where independent suppliers sign long-term agreements with the manufacturer, virtually collocate with the manufacturer, earn fair profits, and are given help and training to supply products and parts at the desired level of quality and delivery, this customer is intent on running one of its principal suppliers into the ground. Wal-Mart is another example of a company that, because of its size and influence with its customers, retains the bargaining power when negotiating with its suppliers. It, too, appears to run many of its suppliers into the ground and out of business in its drive for ever-lower costs.[3]

If a company has many suppliers all competing for the contract to supply it, the company has bargaining power. If it has to purchase a component, however, and only one company can supply it, that company will have bargaining power. One strategy suppliers have for retaining bargaining power is to raise the switching costs of the buyer, that is, it will cost so much for a buyer to switch to a competing supplier that it will not do so. Consider a supplier that gives its customer—and all the people in the customer's organization who do any ordering—computer terminals that are tied in with its own system, enabling the customer to order at any time, track the status of delivery of any order, and so on. The service is so convenient, and the purchasing company's people so well trained and comfortable in using

Figure 4.1 Porter's Five-Forces Model of Competitive Threats

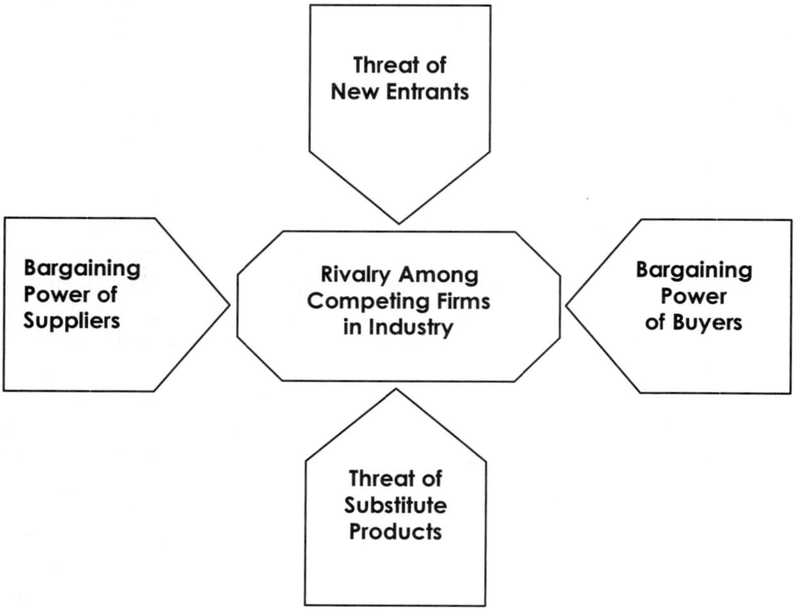

the ordering system, that it might not change suppliers even if a lower-cost competitor came along.

The elements of industry structure are shown in Figure 4.1.

How high are entry barriers? We need to estimate this because high entry barriers keep potential entrants out of an industry. This is a good thing if your company is already in the industry; but a bad thing if your company is trying to enter an industry. Barriers to entry could take any or several of the following forms:

- High capital investment to enter.

- Expertise in a certain technology or manufacturing process, a core competence, or proprietary technology, which could cost a lot or take a long time to develop.

- An established brand name and customer loyalty, both of which take time to develop.

- Distribution channels all tied up.

- Competitors with significant market share and market power.

- Competitors with low costs, including significant economies of scale.

When estimating barriers to entry, it is easier to imagine potential entrants like yourself and then assess whether barriers to entry are sufficiently high to deter entry. However, what if the potential entrant is a much larger corporation with more than adequate financial resources, and possibly also a strong brand identity in a related market? The results of this assessment might turn out quite differently. The issue is to try to imagine (1) who the likely potential entrant might be; (2) why it might want to enter this industry now; and (3) make as best an assessment as you can.

Also, in some industries, it may be easy to enter the industry, but practically impossible to compete effectively once having entered. For example, in the donut industry, anyone can open a single donut shop that serves local customers ("easy to enter"). Yet such an entrant would unlikely compete with the large national chains like Dunkin' Donuts, Winchell's, and Krispy Kreme, and so would not present a threat at all ("hard to compete with").

Is the industry concentrated or fragmented?   A *concentrated* industry is one in which a few firms in the industry account for a large portion of total industry sales. Examples are commercial aircraft manufacturing, in which only two firms compete (Boeing and Airbus), or the business of auditing public companies in the United States, in which 96% of the work is shared among the "Big Four" certified public accounting (CPA) firms. Even six to eight firms, accounting for upwards of 40% of an industry's sales, would qualify to be called *concentrated*. In fact, industry concentration is really a continuum—an industry could be extremely, very, fairly, or somewhat concentrated and, at the other end, extremely, very, fairly, or somewhat fragmented. Where exactly an industry lies is purely subjective.

A *fragmented* industry is one in which no one firm has more than a fraction of a percent in market share. Examples are beauty salons and the auditing of privately held businesses. Bookstores and fast-food restaurants used to be fragmented industries, but now are fairly concentrated due to franchising and the emergence of dominant chains.

Making an accurate assessment directly influences your likely future strategy. If you are in a concentrated industry, but not one of the major players, you will have to tread very carefully—you could get stomped on if you make a wrong move or antagonize one of the big competitors. If you are in a fragmented industry, it is very difficult to increase market share unless you can clone or standardize your business and duplicate or franchise it.[4] This is what some fast-food companies did and what enabled them to become global giants such as McDonald's, KFC, Burger King, and so on.

What must a company do well in order to succeed in the industry? These are called *key* or *critical success factors* (CSFs). Think of them as constituting the rules of the industry. Just as every sport has its own set of unique rules, there is no way that one can "play" in an industry let alone dominate it without knowing and playing by those rules. CSFs attach to an industry, not to a company, and every industry has a different set. Do you know the CSFs for your industry?

Ideally, you should be able to identify six to eight CSFs. One way is to first come up with a much larger number, say 15 CSFs, and then edit them down to those that are really essential to succeeding in your industry rather than in any industry. In the next section, the value of identifying the industry's CSFs become evident because they are used to compare your company to its key competitors.

How attractive is the industry? Can one measure this, and is it important? Yes and yes—but the "measurement" is highly subjective, and the result is more useful in some situations than others.

Because the notion of attractiveness is inherently subjective, not only what is perceived matters but also who is doing the perceiving; that is, from what vantage point an industry is viewed. Having said this, it might put people off entirely from trying to ascertain an industry's attractiveness. But the purpose is not to get widespread agreement on your assessment, just agreement among your strategic team. So measuring an industry's attractiveness is worth doing, and the subjectivity is minimized when a group does the assessment and their perceptions are shared.

"Attractiveness" is made up of a number of attributes or characteristics. To discover them, imagine what an ideal industry would look like. It would have, for example, a huge market (potential customer base), be growing rapidly, be hugely profitable, have few competitors, not be regulated at all, have high entry barriers (i.e., the degree to which companies are prevented from entering an industry in which yours is established), and no need for technological expertise that the company could not handle. This would yield the following initial list of factors for an industry-attractiveness analysis:

- Size of potential market
- Industry growth rate
- Degree/intensity of competition
- Degree of regulation
- Entry barriers
- Degree of technological innovation

These factors, of course, constitute a good but incomplete list; they may be changed or amplified.

The analysis takes the form shown in the example in Table 4.1. First assign a weight to each of these factors according to their perceived importance (SAM^{tw} makes sure the weights add up to 100), then rate each factor from the point of view of the company doing the analysis on a scale of 0–1.0, 1.0 being

Table 4.1 Industry-Attractiveness Example

Factor	Weighting	Rating	Product
Industry growth rate	24	0.8	19.2
Profitability	20	0.8	16.0
Size of potential market	16	0.9	14.4
Degree of technological innovation	14	0.6	8.4
Degree/intensity of competition	13	0.5	6.5
Entry barriers	8	0.8	6.4
Degree of regulation	5	1.0	5.0
Totals	**100**	—	**75.9**

highest, and finally multiply the weight by the rating for each factor (SAM^{tw} also does this). Be careful in two instances—if degree of competition is high, your rating should be low; and if degree of regulation is low, your rating should be high. If you remember that the rating should be high for any factor that makes the industry more attractive, and low if the opposite, you will not go wrong. Add up the products to yield a percentage figure.

The index of 75.9 in the example in Table 4.1 shows this to be an attractive industry, attractive enough to stay in it and invest in improving the company's position in it.

It is when such an analysis yields a result of less than 50% that the company might well ask the fateful question: "Should we continue to be in this industry, or should we exit?" The answer will also depend on a similar analysis assessing competitive strength (discussed in the next section) and yielding another index. The two indices are then plotted on a grid called the General Electric or G.E. Matrix, also discussed in that section.

Strategic Group Map

In industries that contain disparate competitors, a strategic group map is a useful technique to cluster strategically similar competitors. Competitors can show differences—and similarities—to each other in market segments, breadth of product line, degree of specialization, brand identification, distribution channel selection, product quality, technological leadership, degree of vertical integration, cost position (if known), provision of services, positioning, pricing policy, relationship to home and host government as well as other factors.[5] Those that are similar to each other belong to the same strategic group. The more distant one strategic group is from another reflects the extent to which they are dissimilar.

An industry often consists of a small number of distinct strategic groups. A strategic group map is a two-dimensional representation of an industry's strategic groups. To create one, choose two strategic dimensions that are not correlated with each other such as price and quality and that have the capacity to separate the competitors in the industry. For example, if all companies in the industry have broad product lines, choosing this dimension as one of the axes will not work—all the competitors would be bunched up at one end. On the other hand, positioning might be a useful dimension to use if there are some companies at the high end, some at the midlevel, and some at the low end of the industry. Other than the two guidelines given above, there is no rule for choosing strategic dimensions that would serve as axes for the strategic group map. (Nevertheless, the dimensions chosen as axes for a strategic group map should embody strategic variables, not performance.) Try several and see which two separate the competitors or rivals into clusters on the map. When you have several clusters that make sense and can articulate the strategy of each cluster, you have a useful strategic group map. Naturally, using the technique presupposes a good working knowledge of competitors in a particular industry.

Figures 4.2 and 4.3 show examples of strategic group maps. Figure 4.2 is a simple strategic group map that represents the pharmaceutical industry. Figure 4.3 shows a slightly more complex strategic group map of the wholesale lumber industry. (SAM^{tw} has strategic group map templates for four, five, and six groups; choose an appropriate one.) You can see different strategic dimensions in use, and can appreciate the fact that companies in

Figure 4.2   Strategic Group Map of the Pharmaceutical Industry

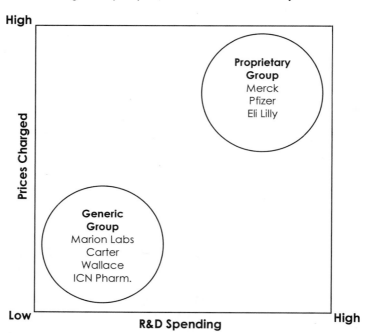

Source: Charles W. L. Hill and Gareth R. Jones, *Strategic Management: An Integrated Approach,* 5th ed. (Boston: Houghton Mifflin, 2001), 96. Copyright © 2001 by Houghton Mifflin Company. Adapted with permission.

the same strategic group compete more intensely with each other, while competition between distant groups is virtually nonexistent. Typically, the size of each strategic group in a strategic group map is proportional to the market share represented by that group, though the circles in the maps shown in Figures 4.2 and 4.3 do not signify market share.

What can we tell from a strategic group map? First, the fact that the companies in a particular strategic group are strategically similar and constitute the group's key competitors. Those in a nearby group form the next tier of competitors. In all likelihood, companies in a distant strategic group are not really competitors although they are in the same industry. For example, in the U.S. beer industry, Anheuser Busch competes with Miller Brewing in the same strategic group, but not with the many microbrewers and some of the imported high-end beers, which are in distant strategic groups. In another example, this time in the hospitality industry, Days Inn (low end) does not compete with Ritz Carlton (high end) because they are strategically dissimilar and in different strategic groups—their markets are quite different.

Secondly, the implications of Porter's Five-Forces Model are different for different strategic groups. Entry barriers vary among the groups, as do bargaining power with suppliers and customers, the threat of substitutes, and the intensity of intragroup rivalry. Thus, it could be more desirable to be in one strategic group than another: There could be more oppor-

Figure 4.3   Strategic Group Map of the Wholesale Lumber Industry

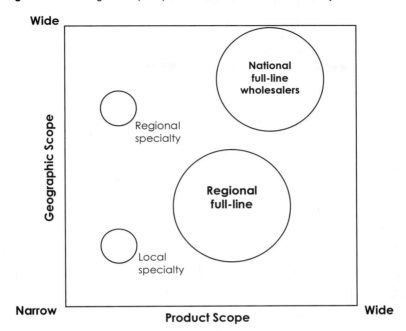

Source: Stewart C. Malone, Simons Lumber Company (1990) Case. *Case Research Journal*, 1992. Reprinted by permission from the Case Research Journal, Copyright © 1992 by the North American Case Research Association and the author(s)

tunities and fewer threats.[6] For example, in retailing, a recession would adversely affect high-end department stores but actually increase demand for discounters and mass merchandisers. Because of such differences, it may be worthwhile for a company to move consciously from one strategic group to another. The ease of doing so depends on the size of mobility barriers between the groups (factors that inhibit both entry into and exit from a group). For example, in Figure 4.1, Marion Labs is a generic pharmaceutical company that competes with others in its strategic group; it would find it very difficult to move into the proprietary strategic group with companies like Merck and Eli Lilly, for example—it lacks the necessary R&D skills and resources that would take time and a great deal of capital to acquire.[7]

Thirdly, one could discover some unserved demand in an area of a strategic group map not occupied by any strategic group. In creating a strategic group map of the automobile industry, using pricing and safety as the two strategic dimensions, a group of business students found that no company was offering a low-priced, high-safety automobile. Such a car might appeal to parents with teenagers and possibly older drivers.[8]

Finally, it is possible for a company to belong to more than one strategic group such as Hilton Hotels and Marriott competing in both the high end and affordable ends, through the lower-rate Hampton Inns and Courtyards by Marriott respectively, in the hospitality industry. In this illustration, each company, rather than surmount mobility barriers by moving to

Market vs. Industry Shares

Technically, this means *industry shares*—the percentage of total industry sales each company has—because that is what is actually measured. However, the term "market" share is so universally recognized to denote industry share that this same convention will be used here.

another strategic group, has penetrated another strategic group through internal diversification and acquisition.

Competitive Analysis

Strategy began as a military concept.[9] Before going into battle—and during the battle itself—generals try to find out everything they can about the enemy: their strength in numbers, their weaponry, supplies, communications capability, precise locations, intents, and strategies. To go into a battle with no information about the enemy is to put you and your troops at considerable risk and your chances of success at virtually zero. It is only with good intelligence about the enemy—their movements, resources, and strategies—that a general or leader can plan his or her own strategy and deploy his or her own resources to win the battle or achieve a military objective.

The same imperative exists in business today. In virtually every business, companies must be aware of and know how to deal with their competitors. The first step is to ask yourself: "How much do I know about my competitors?" One should know—or try to obtain—at least the following information about one's competitors:

- *Market share*—Sometimes these are published and widely known because they are tracked by industry trade associations or consulting firms. Sometimes, however, they are difficult to discover, and you may have to guess at these. In any case, be sure that you are focused on the industry or segment in which your company competes, and get market shares only for that arena. Be particularly careful when using industry data derived from SIC (Standard Industry Classification) codes to compare "apples" with "apples." (See Market vs. Industry Shares.)

- *Geographic scope*—Are your competitors local, regional, national, or international/global competitors? Foreign diversified international or global competitors may be among the most difficult competitors you may face. Their entry into your territory or arena is cross-subsidized by profits from operations in other countries. So they can afford many years of losses and *not* go out of business and *not* go away. They compete for the long haul, and can indulge in pricing strategies designed to secure greater market share.

- *Whether diversified*—Are your competitors conglomerates with a portfolio of businesses in unrelated industries, companies with many related businesses, companies with many strategic alliances, or companies in only one business?

- *Whether vertically integrated*—The degree to which competitors are vertically integrated, especially backwards along the supply chain, may give them cost and competitive advantages that can be difficult to overcome.

- *Competitive advantage*—Do your competitors possess a competitive advantage? What is it? How large is it? How long has it endured? How have they sustained it? How hard are they working at extending it? Are they unwittingly letting it erode?

- *Core competence*—What are the core competences that underlie your competitors' strategies? Which ones have a core competence and which ones don't?

- *Strategic intent*—How are your competitors trying to position themselves in the industry? Are they aggressively trying to overtake rivals on their way to market dominance, or are they more concerned with defending their ranking and maintaining market share? Do they have their sights on one particular competitor such as Pepsi does on Coke, or Ford on GM, and AMD on Intel?

- *Generic strategy*—Are your competitors following a cost-leadership, differentiation, focus, or best-value strategy to increase their profitability?

- *Strategy*—What strategies are your competitors following? In most cases, they can be inferred from other information known about the companies and what they are actually doing. Have the strategies been working or are they about to be changed? Are mergers among key competitors likely? Are any of them looking to be acquired? If in a high-tech industry, what is their investment in R&D as a percent of sales?

- *Resources and capabilities*—How strong financially and technologically are each of your competitors? How flexible are they to adapting to the changing environment? How well managed? How fast do they bring new products to market? Do they have innovative cultures and a record of innovation? Which one just got a new CEO?

- *Assessment on the industry CSFs*—For each key competitor, how does it rate on the industry's CSFs? In other words, in your opinion, how *strong* a competitor is it? How does it compare with you, again on the industry's CSFs? This analysis takes a form similar to that shown in Table 4.1. Instead of competing alternatives, use one column for your own company and the rest for your key competitors, perhaps limiting these to about three to four companies. An illustrative analysis is shown in Table 4.2.

With respect to the CSFs, first choose them and then rank them in order of importance, that is, in the order of assigned weights (generally a group decision). Then rate your company along the dimensions of the listed CSFs, again on a scale of 0–1.0, with 1.0 being highest, compute the product, and then add up the products to yield a competitive index at the bottom. Do the same for each competitor in the table, using your best judgment.

Table 4.2 Illustrative Critical-Success-Factor-Weighted Analysis

CSF Prods	Weighting	Company		Competitor A		Company B		Competitor C		Competitor D	
		Rating	Prods	Rating	Prods	Rating	Prods	Rating	Prods	Rating	Prods
Strength of brand	25	1.0	25.0	0.8	20.0	0.9	22.5	0.8	20.0	1.0	25.0
Distribution channels	20	0.6	12.0	1.0	20.0	0.9	18.0	0.8	16.0	0.7	14.0
Rate of new prods	15	0.8	12.0	0.5	7.5	1.0	15.0	0.7	10.5	0.8	12.0
Financial strength	15	0.9	13.5	0.6	9.0	1.0	15.0	0.8	12.0	0.9	13.5
Customer service	13	0.8	10.4	0.7	9.1	0.8	10.4	0.9	11.7	0.5	6.5
Low costs	12	0.5	6.0	0.6	7.2	0.5	6.0	0.6	7.2	0.8	9.6
Totals 100		—	78.9	—	72.8	—	86.9	—	77.4	—	80.6

In the example shown, the company under analysis scored 78.9. Comparing the scores will give you a rough idea of how your company "stacks up" against its competitors, as well as how each of your key competitors stacks up against the others. To the extent that your ratings of your own company and those of your competitors are fairly accurate or realistic, the analysis gives you useful information of two kinds:

- It points out where you may have a competitive advantage or competitive vulnerability. In Table 4.2, your company's strong brand may constitute a competitive advantage. Competitor A may have one in its extensive distribution system, and Competitor B may have one in its ability to generate new products rapidly. Any 0.5 rating in the table would signify a competitive vulnerability, something that should be addressed in that company's short-term plans (like your company's costs).

- It identifies which competitors are more dangerous than others. In the table, judging from the totals at the bottom, your company lies in the middle of the pack, with Competitor B and Competitor D to be more feared than the other two competitors.

Completing this kind of analysis about your key competitors is another good test of how much or how little you know about them.

Market Analysis

This section focuses on the company's *customers*, which could be companies in another industry, for example, defense, or individuals, commonly called "consumers." While it is relatively straightforward to get information about a customer industry, getting useful information about consumers is more difficult. The demographic or socioeconomic groups of some consumers make them harder to analyze and understand. Here are some considerations you should know about your customers as a group (whether corporations or individuals) and about your market:

- *Target market*—For example, if banks buy your product, your market is banks. But are you targeting all banks worldwide, only the large banks, only neighborhood banks, only banks with over $2.0 billion in deposits or over 500 branches, or middle-market banks nationally? Very few companies can target the entire population of their markets (exceptions are Coca-Cola, Microsoft, etc.). So how would you define your target market—what is it, how large is it, and how fast is it growing?

- *Degree of penetration*—How far is the market penetrated by all the companies in the industry? In other words, what proportion of the target market has bought a product/service from this industry? If the answer is 60%, the market is 60% penetrated. So there is 40% left that is unserved or underserved among them. When a market is 100% penetrated, it is considered saturated. (See Degree of Penetration: Complexities.)

- *Customers' current needs*—From your knowledge of your customers and industry, can you infer what these are? And can you assess the degree to which such needs are currently satisfied?

Degree of Penetration: Complexities

The *degree of penetration* is more complex than the illustration discussed here. For example, not all of the target market may purchase a product from the industry for various reasons:—they cannot afford to, don't need to, and the like. So the target market is often reduced to what is called a *served market* made up of viable customers who could buy the product or service. Also, though rare, it is possible for markets to be more than 100% penetrated, as when households own more than one TV or car.

When we speak of "needs," we mean *benefits* or what we now term *value propositions.*

- *Customers' future* needs—This is a chicken-and-egg situation. New products and services often affect customers and satisfy needs they never knew they had, and sometimes unsatisfied needs are the spark that causes new products and services to be introduced. Try to address the question: *How are customers' needs changing?* To the extent that you find this difficult to answer, it means you are not in touch with your customers

- *Distribution channels*—How do the industry's products reach this market? This does not mean exclusively by delivery truck, but rather are wholesalers and distributors involved? Retail outlets? Are salespersons used to make direct sales calls? Does the company use catalogs and direct mail? To what extent is the Internet now used as a distribution channel? Note the difference between what distribution channels your company uses and those used by the industry in general.

- *Channel markups*—what are the channel markups at each stage? That is, if your distribution channel uses all these stages, what price do you sell to the wholesaler, what price to the distributor, what price to the retailer, and what price to the final customer? What volume discounts are expected and offered at each stage? While your profits depend on the price *you* get for the product, your competitiveness depends on what the customer will pay

- *Price-sensitivity*—How price-sensitive are customers in your target market? This is critical with respect to how you set and change your prices and, indeed, which distribution channel you use. The example illustrates the importance of knowing how price-sensitive your customers are. (See Price-sensitivity and a Law Firm)

- *Current trends*—In what ways is your target market changing? Are customers buying differently? Are they becoming more demanding? ("Changing needs" was covered above.) Any other aspect of your customers not covered elsewhere should be covered here.

Price-sensitivity and a Law Firm

A patent law firm once held a retreat to go through a strategic-planning process. During the process, of course, the firm maintained that it was the best firm of its kind in the area. However, its billings (i.e., its sales) were flat, a situation that led to the retreat in the first place. During the competitive analysis, it turned out that the firm had about five principal competitors, *all* of which charged higher hourly rates than this firm did. It took a while, but the partners finally admitted that hourly rates generally corresponded to reputation—the higher the fee charged the better the firm was perceived to be. Worse, it turned out that several partners were offering discounted rates to clients for fear that they would not even get their business. They all wailed that if they raised their rates, the firm would suffer a drastic decline in business. They felt hamstrung. The answer, of course, was that either they were serving the wrong kinds of clients, or they were not as good as they claimed to be, which perhaps was closer to the truth given their discounting behavior. Certainly, the market was not *nearly* as price-sensitive as they thought it was, given the fees its competitors were charging—and getting.

To the extent that the company does business in several markets (e.g., different countries), this kind of analysis should be completed for each of those markets.

Environmental Trend Analysis[10]

Much has been written about the dizzying pace of change going on around us, and clearly, any planner worth his or her salt has to take such change into account. But how? One way is to divide the environment into categories or manageable pieces and, in each category, try to articulate (1) what is changing and in which direction and (2) with what impact on the company. If the change has no relevance for the company or for what it might do in the future, then ignore it.

People who engage in environmental scanning, a common name given to identifying and analyzing trends that are external to the business, have found that it is easy to get caught up in what they are discovering. Before they know it, they are collecting information for its own sake. Most companies cannot afford that luxury—and most students cannot afford the time. Again, confine the search to trends that are relevant to the company, that is, any trend that affects the company or that may affect it in the future.

Another important point that people doing environmental scanning often lose sight of is the currentness of collected data. Typically, one can find information on trends using historical data. However, the milieu in which strategic planning takes place, or the period during which the consequences of present decisions play out, is the *future*. So a trend noticed during the 1996–2000 timeframe, for example, may have limited value or even none at all in the 2004–2007 timeframe. However, if you can extrapolate or extend the trend in a justifiable manner to the future timeframe in question, then you have something of value. Nevertheless, be careful here, because some trends are *discontinuous,* that is, behavior in the future is different from behavior in the past. While simple extrapolations can be performed by almost anyone, more complex forecasting such as technological forecasting must be done by an expert and often constitutes an in-house or consulting project depending on where the expertise lies. For such projects, it goes without saying that the organization must have the requisite time and resources. The tradeoff between spending resources doing something properly and taking educated guesses when such resources—time and money—are unavailable can be vexing. There is no right or wrong answer here save that one must always make the most of the present situation.

In many cases, rather than doing the forecasting yourself, you can find estimated or projected data on trends to fit your future timeframe. For example, demographic data taken from census data contain projections for at least 30 years into the future. Whenever using such projections, you need to know how reliable the source is and, preferably, how the projections were derived. The more critical such data are to your company, the more pains you should take to ensure that you are using reliable data and a reliable forecast or analysis. Economic forecasts, for example, are particularly difficult to verify as to quality—economists can be notoriously wrong even for short-term forecasts.

Finally, the environmental scan should cover a geographic scope that matches the arena in which the company competes. For example, a distribution company operating and competing only in Southern California should pay more attention to what is happening in the Southern California economy rather than what may be happening nationally. A large multinational company would have to extend its scan into every country in which it does business (buying, manufacturing, or selling) as well as include exchange rates between those countries and how events or trends in one of the countries might affect any of the others. The international environment is far more complex than dealing with just one country. For example, managers in each country are typically asked to complete an environmental analysis in their own country along with other analyses and projections required for strategic planning.

Listed below are six categories that correspond to those in the SAM^{tw} CD-ROM and, for each one, a number of variables are given that can merit scanning:

- **Economic**

  - *Structural shifts*—the trend from an industrial economy to a service economy, or from a predominantly manufacturing to a knowledge-based economy.

  - *Structural variables*—such as energy costs rising faster than raw material costs, or general or minimum wage rates changing.

  - *Inflation and unemployment rates*—as one goes up, the other typically goes down, and vice versa. Both are affected by fiscal policy controlled by the government and monetary policy controlled by the Federal Reserve Board, which also controls interest rates.

- *Interest rates*—deserve a separate listing and are the most watched economic indicator anywhere. These reflect the cost of loans, mortgages, and credit, as well as how much savings and certificate of deposits (CDs) can earn.

- *The consumer price index (CPI)*—a relative indicator of how far and how fast prices have risen compared to a base year.

- *Housing starts*—a leading indicator of whether the economy might turn down or up.

- *Balance of trade*—wherein the relative levels of imports and exports as a percentage of gross national product (GNP) are changing, giving rise to trade surpluses or deficits (the latter perennially indicative of the United States).

- *Exchange rates*—which reflect the value of one country's currency against another. A declining value of the U.S. dollar, for example, means that U.S. exports will be more competitive in world markets and imports more expensive, while a rising value of the dollar means that imports will become cheaper and U.S. goods in world markets more expensive.

- *Personal disposable income*—often associated with income data (demographic), and very useful when combined with demographic data such as geographic data, age, and ethnicity.

- **Regulatory/Legislative** Regulations differ from rules because they are made and enforced by state and federal regulatory agencies. Legislation refers to laws enacted by state assemblies and Congress. For both types, precursors to impending changes can be discerned by close observation of the political process at the appropriate level of government. Also, rules are made according to well defined processes that include opportunities for rebuttals by industry or interested parties. Scannable variables include:

  - *Volume of regulations*—enacted each year as reflected in the number of pages in the *Federal Register* devoted to them (which keeps increasing).

  - *Regulations governing the industry*—in which you compete. Some industries are so heavily regulated that they are called "regulated industries, such as railroads and airlines."

  - *Regulations that cut across all industries*—which include tax regulations, workplace safety, insider trading, bargaining in good faith in labor negotiations, anticompetitive practices, and price-fixing. All industries encounter some form of regulation even though not considered "regulated."

  - *Deregulation of an industry*—such as telecommunications and electric power, or some degree of deregulation such as airlines, banking, and transportation.

  - *Merging industries*—such as banking, insurance, and brokerage industries into what is now called *financial services*.

- *Changes in standards*—by which regulations are enforced such as crash resistance, fuel economy, and exhaust emissions in automobiles, allowable concentrations of contaminants or impurities in air and water, labeling in practically everything, and the like.

- *Trade regulations*—including tariffs or quotas to limit imports into a country or make importing more costly, prohibition of certain imports (e.g., agricultural products into California), quarantining of animals, and the like.

- *All the above*—at both state and federal levels.

- **Political/Legal**

  - *Increasing influence, activism, and power of interest groups*—such as the American Medical Association, the U.S. Chamber of Commerce, the Business Roundtable, the National Association of Manufacturers, and the American Association of Retired Persons (AARP); corporate political action committees (PACs); single-cause groups such as antinuclear or antiabortion (prolife) groups, women's groups, environmentalists, Mothers Against Drunk Driving (MADD), and the National Rifle Association (the "gun lobby").

  - *Fighting against or demanding enforcement of regulations or laws*—which is now a courtroom trend.

  - *Increased litigation in the United States*—that is, the propensity for people to sue at the "drop of a hat."

- **Demographic**

  - *Population growth*—that is, in the general population.

  - *Growth rate of a particular group*—such as the 25–39 or over-65 age group, which gives clues as to whether the population of a country is aging or getting younger, or has a "baby boom" or "bulge" moving through it.

  - *Geographic distribution*—which reveals migration patterns.

  - *Ethnic mix*—which reveals the extent to which regions or cities are growing more diverse, or becoming dominated by one ethnicity.

  - *Income levels*—which reveal patterns of wealth distribution and indicate relative purchasing power, especially when combined with geographic data that can monitor average individual income as well as household income.

  - *Literacy rates*—reflecting the extent to which a population has received basic education and can read its own language.

- **Attitude/Lifestyle**

  - *Household formation*—includes the family structure one chooses to establish such as married-couple families, one-parent families with either female or male head of household, couples with no children, and gay or lesbian couples. Also of interest is the average number of persons per household.

- *Type of work and who is working*—this includes what one does as a professional, technical, hourly, volunteer, part-time, or other kind of worker and who is doing it. For example, the rise of women in the workforce, especially in professional and technical jobs; two-income households in which both husband and wife work; and more elderly people continuing to work and delaying retirement, while others take early retirement to start their own business.

- *Type and level of education achieved*—more useful when combined with ethnicity, race, and sex demographic variables. This also includes the extent of taking continuing education classes or seminars.

- *Consumption patterns of goods and services*—especially homes, durable goods, furnishings, automobiles, clothes, beverages, and personal services and shifts in patterns within each category.

- *Leisure activities*—including all types of sports and physical-fitness activities, cultural events, movie attendance, travel, and home-centered activities such as watching network and cable television and videos, reading, gardening, and cooking as well as shifts in patterns among each category.

- **Sociocultural**

  - *Changes in social regulations*—such as increases in consumer and environmental protection, changes in Supreme Court rulings, trend of the courts deciding issues that the political process cannot.

  - *Changing social expectations*—such as attitudes towards work, rising consumer demands, greater acceptance of sex and violence in the movies and on television, public campaigns against smoking, migration towards greater personal health and physical fitness, and the growing activism among women and minority groups.

  - *Changes in economic values*—less acceptance of economic growth as an unqualified benefit to society, increasing concern with how economic benefits are distributed in society (e.g., how people are taxed).

  - *Changes in political priorities*—for example, defense versus nondefense appropriations.

- **Technological**

  - *Pace of change*—of basic science or research as manifest in the number and nature of new patents applied for and issued.

  - *New companies*—formed to exploit new technologies and products based on new technologies.

- *R&D spending*— changes in the average percentage of sales spent on research and development (R&D) in a particular high-technology industry.

- *Technology diffusion*—which means the changes in the time required for a new technology to become accepted in general use.

- *Innovation lag*—changes in the period between when the scientific solution to a technological need is first recognized and the emergence of the first viable product using the solution technology and its successor.

- **Other trends**—anything noticed but not included in the above categories.

From this analysis, assuming reasonable accuracy, you will have the beginnings of opportunities—these are trends that have a strong positive impact on the company—and threats—those that have a strong negative impact on the company.

Environmental scanning should not be done during the two weeks leading up to a strategic-planning session. Students, for example, doing a class project are unusually constrained by the time available to complete a project during a quarter or semester and can only do a cursory job of identifying environmental trends and "guessing" at the impact they may have on the company. Instead, environmental scanning should be an ongoing, year-round activity done by many people throughout the organization. (See The Environmental Scanner.) However, someone on the strategic-planning staff needs to coordinate this activity. If done year-round, it would be unlikely that the company would be blindsided by any changes in its environment—and it would also be one of the first to notice opportunities as they open up. This last point is worth emphasizing, because the earlier an opportunity is noticed, the more lead time the company would have to exploit the opportunity.

Some ideas for sources of data to do environmental scanning include the following:

- Experts or leaders in the field, including professors at universities, authors of books or articles in major journals, opinion leaders who give speeches (e.g., Alan Greenspan), staff of specialized magazines, well-known consulting firms, research insti-

---

The Environmental "Scanner"

One simple way is to put an individual in charge of each category of environmental scanning, and anyone finding a trend in that category should send or email the reference or article to that person. Every month or quarter, the category leader should review the accumulated trends and write a monthly or quarterly report for management. When the time comes to do strategic planning again, all the relevant information should be at hand and already reviewed and summarized.

tutes, security or financial analysts, and officers or members in the professional association in question.

- Specialized and technical journals and trade magazines relating to the product, technology, or industry in question, as well as those specializing in different fields (e.g., strategy) and different countries.

- The reference desk at most university and major city libraries.

- Conferences, symposia, and conventions covering the latest ideas relating to the trends in question (economics, regulation, technology, demographics, etc.).

- Major federal government regulating agencies, U.S. Census Bureau, state and local agencies that maintain databases for public use.

- The Internet and the major search engines such as Google and Yahoo!

As you scan, bear in mind the future timeframe in which you are interested—that is, the period from now until the planning horizon, typically a three-year timeframe, possibly longer, depending on the business or industry you are in. Clearly, trends that have an immediate impact within the planning horizon—whether the impact is positive or negative—should occupy your highest priority. Trends that require a longer period of time to impact the company beyond the planning horizon are correspondingly less important, but should nevertheless be noted and monitored. Trends that have no impact on the company should be ignored. However, trends that could have a significant impact on the company, but which would have that effect only in the very distant future (say, in a decade), should be monitored on a backburner without spending too much time or effort on them.

Summary

This chapter covered the external situation analysis and what it entails. It is virtually impossible to do strategic planning without knowing how a company's relevant world is changing. In particular:

- The economic characteristics of the industry in which the company competes.

- How the industry is changing.

- Who the company is really competing with, how tough the competition is, and how the company compares with its chief competitors.

- Who the company's target market is, how much the company knows about its customers, and how its customers are changing.

- What else is changing that could affect the company either negatively (a threat) or positively (an opportunity), in the economic, regulatory/legislative, demographic, sociocultural, or technological environments

The chapter also presented several analytical methods useful in doing an external analysis: Porter's Five-Forces model, industry attractiveness, the strategic group map, and critical-success-factor analysis. While using these techniques is subjective for the most part and, therefore, possibly not rigorous or accurate enough for some, the ultimate purpose of doing such analyses should not be lost—to understand the external environment of the company and in what critical ways it is changing, and how those changes could affect it.

Notes

1. This is not exactly true. The model can be adapted for a nonprofit organization, although it takes considerable skill. This was done recently with the Computer Information Systems Department, an academic department in the College of Business Administration at the California State Polytechnic University, Pomona. Not only did this department perform strategic planning for the very first time, it also used the model described in this book. It became the winner of the Association for Strategic Planning's Excellence in Strategic Planning Award in 2003. Appropriate parts of its application for that award, which details the process it used, are presented in Appendix C.

2. Michael E. Porter, *Competitive Strategy* (New York: Free Press, 1982).

3. See Abigail Goldman and Nancy Cleeland, "An Empire Built on Bargains Remakes the Working World" (first of three parts on the "Wal-Mart Effect"), *Los Angeles Times,* November 23, 2003, A1; and Nancy Cleeland, Evelyn Iritani, and Tyler Marshall, "Scouring the Globe to Give Shoppers an $8.63 Polo Shirt" (second of three parts on the "Wal-Mart Effect"), *Los Angeles Times,* November 24, 2003, A1.

4. See also Michael E. Porter, "Chapter 9, Competitive Strategy in Fragmented Industries," *Competitive Strategy: Techniques for Analyzing Industries and Competitors* (New York: Free Press, 1982), 191–214.

5. Ibid., 127–129. See also Porter, "Chapter 7, Structural Analysis Within Industries," 126–155.

6. Charles W. L. Hill and Gareth R. Jones, *Strategic Management: An Integrated Approach,* 5th ed. (Boston: Houghton Mifflin Company, 2001), 95–96.

7. Ibid., 97.

8. Jeffrey S. Harrison, *Strategic Management of Resources and Relationships: Concepts and Cases* (Hoboken, NJ: John Wiley & Sons, 2003), 176.

9. For example, Sun Tzu, *The Art of War*, James Clavell, ed. (New York: Delacorte, 1983).

10. The following section is based on Liam Fahey and V.K. Narayanan, *Macroenvironmental Analysis for Strategic Management* (St. Paul, MN: West, 1986).

5

Assessing the Company Itself

A nalyzing and assessing the internal environment of the company has several purposes. The most important pieces of information about this internal environment that must be identified are the company's:

- Recent-past financial performance and current financial condition.

- Strengths and weaknesses.

- Opportunities and threats.

- Capabilities—and determining which, if any of them, are core competencies that would give the company a competitive advantage.

- Competitive strength.

- Current strategy—and determining whether it is working or needs to be changed.

- Corporate culture.

- Management and leadership capabilities

Company Analysis

If a company analysis and assessment had been performed in the previous year, then all that is necessary is to review what has changed since that time. Top managers of a company, for example, would probably have an ongoing grasp of change and would be able to complete the company analysis very rapidly. However, companies that have undergone significant change such as a new CEO and new top managers, a reorganization, embarking on a new strategy, using new technology or production processes, and the like, may have a harder time assessing itself.

Recent past financial performance and current financial condition You need three to five years of the firm's historical financial data—income statements and balance sheets—including the most recent year for

Z- and Z$_2$-Scores

Z- and Z$_2$-scores are bankruptcy predictors or indicators developed by Edward Altman. The formulas are presented in the SAM^{tw} CD-ROM. The Z-score for manufacturing companies come from Edward L Altman and James K. LaFleur's paper, "Managing a Return to Financial Health," in *Journal of Business Strategy*, Summer 1981. In that article, the coefficients or weights of the various terms in the linear regression equation are different from those that appeared in Altman's original paper, "Financial Ratios Discriminant Analysis and the Prediction of Corporate Bankruptcy," in *Journal of Finance*, September 1968. The Z$_2$-score for nonmanufacturing companies came from a conversation between the author and Dr. Altman in 1997.

which complete data are available. A thorough financial analysis of multiyear data consists of the following elements:

- Computing all liquidity, activity, leverage, and profitability ratios for all years.

- Computing year-to-year changes for all line items (in both the income statement and balance sheet) and all ratios for all years.

- Computing average annual changes over all five years for certain items.

- Computing common-size income statements for all years (everything on the income statement expressed as a percent of revenues).

- Computing a Z- or Z$_2$-score for each year, but only if the company is suspected of performing poorly or increasingly poorly over time. This computation involves financial ratios, so it is easy to compute. (See Z- and Z$_2$-Scores.)

- Summarizing what all the numbers mean, that is, forming a conclusion about how the company has been performing financially and about its current financial condition.

These computations are automatically done for you in the SAM^{tw} CD-ROM if you input three to five years of financial data about the company. (There is a separate worksheet for three years' worth of data, four years' worth, and five years' worth; choose the appropriate one.) It bears repeating that you should enter the company data carefully without making a mistake (check and double-check it against the original income statements and balance sheets) and without altering the structure of the template.

The last step in the analysis is the most important one. What can you make of the numbers? What picture do they paint of the company's performance over the past several years? You could draw any one of the following five conclusions:

1. The company is very well managed, has been performing extremely well, and is in strong financial condition.

2. The company is very well managed, has been performing extremely well, and is in strong financial condition *except for one major bad thing*. For example, the one year that it had problems or a major problem in one area such as very high debt, both of which would need to be explained.

3. The company had its ups and downs and turned in a mixed performance over this period. That is, one cannot say it has been well managed and performing well, and one cannot say it is in serious trouble either. The results are, in fact, inconclusive. So explain what the company did well, what problems it had, and why it is not "back on track."

4. The company's performance was poor and key result indicators were declining steadily (or precipitously) over time; the company is or should be in serious financial trouble *except for one major good thing* such as increasing revenues.

5. The company's performance was poor and key result indicators were declining steadily (or precipitously) over time; the company has not been managed well and is in serious financial trouble.

In each case, support the conclusion with selected statistics, and also summarize the current financial condition of the company.

SWOT Analysis

Identifying Strengths and Weaknesses

Strengths and weaknesses are the "internal" aspects of the traditional SWOT analysis. They are two sides of the same coin. Whenever something—or someone—is reviewed or assessed, it makes sense to point out the good points or what was done well, as well as the areas that need improvement. This assessment is easy to do superficially, which is more often the case, but difficult to do candidly and realistically. It is nearly always subjective—but less so if done by a group with multiple perspectives—and should be done in the following two ways:

- *Compare the firm to itself*—at some previous point in its history: What is it doing better? What has not improved, and what is it doing worse?

- *Compare the firm with others in its industry*—a more difficult but more useful comparison: What does it do better than—and not as well as—other firms?

The typical strengths that companies have might be:

- Adequate financial resources to implement any likely strategy

- Strong cash flow

- Strong brand recognition

- Effective advertising and promotion
- Consistent high quality in products/services
- Effective distribution
- Access to economies of scale
- Insulation from competition
- Proprietary technology and patents
- Cost advantages
- Low-cost leader
- Product innovation skills
- Proven management
- Ahead on the experience curve
- Visionary CEO, strong leader
- Productive corporate culture that supports the strategy

The problem is that it is so easy to classify what you do as "good," and therefore a strength. However, what is "good"? It depends on how high a company's internal standards are and how widely held. For this reason, it should always compare strengths (and weaknesses) with its closest competitors. (See Strengths vs. Baseline Skills.) Consider the story of a printing company in northern San Diego County during the boom years of the 1980s. Every company was growing except this one. When the company asked its customers why they came to it for printing, the customers proudly showed off four-color brochures and posters and said: Every company was growing except this one. At a planning retreat, the company's salespeople were asked why its customers came to it for printing. Proudly showing off four-color brochures and posters, one of the salespeople said, "It's because of our quality." Upon further questioning, none of it to the liking of the company's managers and salespeople, it turned out that other print shops in the area also offered superb quality, otherwise they would have had no customers. So what this company had was simply a *baseline skill* that enabled it to compete—but not a strength. When further asked which competitor seemed to be doing the best and why, the consensus was that the leader not only offered superb quality, but had the lowest prices (and probably lowest costs), offered free pickup and delivery of orders, and offered design services. Of these, low cost, if true, was a strength for the competitor as well as its customer service. Possibly aggressive management and good marketing and promotion played a part, too. After its analysis, this company came to the conclusion that it had no strengths, which is also why it was not doing well in a growing market. Perhaps this criticism is too harsh: Good printing capability may have been a strength. However, it was clearly negated by the company's competitors. This is a good illustration of the value of comparing your strengths with your competitors.

With respect to weaknesses, managers often have no problem admitting to weaknesses because they are self-evident. Others find them hard to own up to because doing so casts them in a bad light as an ineffective manager. Sometimes, if a company is having problems, and the top management team is meeting to discuss them, it is quite common for one department to find a way of blaming another department for the company problems. The production manager might blame human resources for inadequate training resulting in low quality. Marketing might complain that engineering and R&D never acted on its good market intelligence to create new products. Or R&D could complain about a cut in its budget for something far less important. In all these examples, grappling with weaknesses is not about finding who is at fault or who is to blame. It is about gaining a realistic understanding of the company's weaknesses so that steps can be taken to alleviate or correct them.

Weaknesses can take myriad forms. Some examples include:

- No clear strategy, vision, or direction

- Obsolete facilities

- Sub-par profitability because of high costs, inappropriate pricing, and the like

- Lack of managerial depth, experience, and talent

- Key skills and competencies missing or obsolete

- No core competency

- No competitive advantage

- Internal operating problems and inefficiencies

- Too narrow a product line

- Falling behind in R&D and innovation

- Poor marketing skills

- Unable to finance needed strategic initiatives

- Weak or inadequate distribution network

- Weak or no brand image

- Poor or negative cash flow from operations, unable to service debt

- Low Z- or Z_2-score, which indicates that bankruptcy is imminent

- Long cycle time to get product out

Again, the weaknesses become real when compared to other companies in the industry. For example, you might think your company has low costs—and list that as a strength—and then discover that your costs are among the highest in the industry. Suddenly, that so-called strength becomes a weakness. Take another example. A firm has been doing fairly well for several years and suddenly gets a new CEO. The new CEO looks around him and sees nothing but weaknesses and wonders aloud how this firm ever survived. (This happened when Ford executives first toured the Jaguar plant in the United Kingdom before acquiring the company.)

These illustrations show that when making any assessment, even a seemingly "casual" one like identifying a strength or weakness, you are using an implicit standard or reference in making it. More experienced people will tend to be more critical because they have probably worked in organizations where virtually everything was done better, thus raising their own standards or frame of reference. Again, the goal here is not to be "right" at the expense of someone else being "wrong." Rather, it is to reach consensus on what is real and problematic, so that it can be attended to and the firm's future prospects improved.[1]

Opportunities

Opportunities and threats are viewed as the "external" components of the SWOT analysis. Certainly, opportunities are sought outside the company, but cannot be identified without a thorough understanding of the company's strengths, capabilities, core competence, and the like, if they are to be considered "real." For that reason, it is included in the internal company analysis portion of the situation analysis.

Change produces both threats and opportunities. Many companies, however, worry only about the threats, and do not undertake systematic or frequent enough searches for opportunities. When an opportunity is found, it can take several years to take advantage of it, especially if it requires acquiring and adapting to new technology, understanding a new market, or changing the corporate culture to do it. So the earlier it is found the better. Hence the search for one should ideally be ongoing and, at a minimum, once a year. (Recall the discussion about finding opportunities in Chapter 2.)

An opportunity has a specific technical definition: a *product market issue.* It must include a product or service the firm offers, even an existing one, and a defined customer group at which that product or service is targeted, even an existing one. Figure 5.1 shows a matrix of products against markets. All companies in business are, by definition, in the top-left cell, selling existing products or services to an existing market.

The following represent real opportunities:

- Staying with an existing product and existing market and penetrating the market further (i.e., staying in the original top-left cell).

- Improving the product for an existing market, implementing a product-development strategy. Examples include automobile companies, with their annual models, and software companies, with new versions of existing software.

- Creating a new product for an existing market, also a product-development strategy. Examples include Nike offering athletic apparel in addition to athletic shoes for the same market; Microsoft offering just about everything it can for existing computer users; and Calvin Klein designing and selling clothes as well as perfumes.

- Expanding the market for an existing product, implementing a market development strategy such as getting the product to appeal to young adults instead of just teenagers or lowering the price so that more people can afford to buy the product.

- Finding a new market for an existing product, also a market-development strategy. Examples abound everywhere—companies going regional from being just local or a regional company going national or entering a new country, all without changing the product or service.

The bottom-right cell—coming up with a new product for a new market—is not common because of the huge risk such a move entails. Its technical term is "conglomerate diversification." No examples come to mind to illustrate this strategy; it is rarely discussed in strategic management literature for good reason and will not be here. Companies that must enter a brand new market with a brand new product should do so either through acquisition or one or more strategic alliances if they are to reduce the extremely high risk.

Product or market development strategies are seldom implemented by changing only one of the components, that is, improving the product without expanding the market or expanding the market without improving the product. The truth is that improving or modifying the product often attracts new customers (e.g., creating a convertible from a sedan, or making a sedan sportier), and markets are usually expanded by modifying the product in some way (e.g., selling cars in the United Kingdom requires putting the steering wheel and driver controls on the right-hand side). Nevertheless, even if both products and markets change, the strategy that dominates is the one where the intent is either product or market development.

Ideas for opportunities should ideally come directly from customers and potential customers. This means that the company must be in tune with its customers and be talking to them constantly. Consider this example with an industrial customer. Your firm supplies it with a component or OEM part it uses in its product. You have missed an opportunity if you are suddenly told that the customer has redesigned its product and no longer needs the product you used to supply. You have been negligent in terms of knowing what is going on with your customer. Had you found this out the moment the customer contemplated redesigning its product, you could have sent one of your engineers to serve on its design team (free of charge, of course). His job would have been to find something in that new design your company could supply better and cheaper than the customer could and then coach you in your bid to win that contract.

In terms of improving the product or introducing a new one, where do ideas come from besides the customer? This is another crucial phase in

Figure 5.1 Product Market Grid of Opportunities

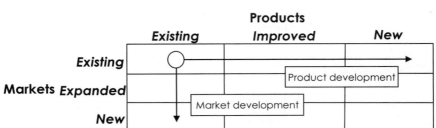

strategic planning, where creativity as well as knowledge about your external environment plays a pivotal role. In addition to those discussed in Chapter 2, the following two approaches might be helpful:

- *System for innovation*—This is most useful for coming up with new product ideas rather than changes to an existing product line. In its most basic form, this involves an announcement to all employees to submit ideas for new products to a special committee (sometimes called the *New Product Development Committee*), preferably on a standard form for the purpose. The form would ask for just enough information to enable the committee to determine whether it should follow up on the idea or not. If the idea has some merit, the person making the proposal is asked to do more research and fill out another set of forms that ask for more detailed information, such as market demand and likely customers, manufacturing process, costs, additional development needed, and likely volume. If the committee still believes that the idea has merit and market potential, then at this stage it could decide to allocate resources to develop the concept or idea further, possibly to a prototype stage, along with detailed market and competitive analyses. This would continue until the product was approved for full-scale manufacturing and marketing. With such a system in place, the committee would meet as often as there were projects to consider. Employees should be given guidelines and some incentive to propose projects, and should always have their efforts acknowledged.

- *Abell's scheme.* Derek Abell proposed a three-dimensional concept for defining the mission of a corporation, shown diagrammatically in Figure 5.2. Abell maintained that mission statements should contain all three elements. Such a scheme, however, could also be used to search for new opportunities.

    First, brainstorm different kinds of customers or customer

Figure 5.2 Abell's Scheme

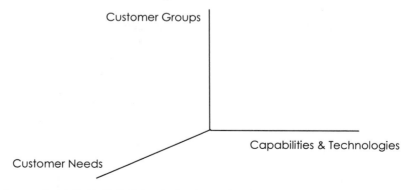

Source: Derek F. Abell, *Defining the Business: The Starting Point of Strategic Planning*, 1st ed. (Englewood Cliffs, NJ: Prentice-Hall, 1980) 29-30. © 1980. Reprinted by permission of Pearson Education, Inc., Upper Saddle River, NJ.

groups that might use or buy the product. Then, brainstorm different products that could be made using the company's skills, capabilities, and technologies. For example, a furniture company, which makes the upholstery for all its furniture and whose business was declining, produced an idea in a brainstorming session to manufacture sails for boats—the same skills are used as in making upholstery, though using different designs and different materials. Lastly, brainstorm other products your customers need or buy that you can also provide. With respect to this last dimension, consider Reader's Digest Association, publisher of *Reader's Digest,* the largest-circulation magazine in the world (around 28 million readers in 1992). As famous and as popular as its magazine and brand are, the real value to the company is the huge database of subscribers that it has (about 50 million households in the United States and an equal number spread across other countries). It has used that database to sell a variety of products such as condensed books and other publications, videos, CDs, and so on. In 1992, 66.7% of its revenues and 91.8% of its operating profits came from selling products through mail order (its "database distribution channel"), far higher percentages than its flagship magazine.[3] Using Abell's scheme, what other products could it send down this distribution channel (that would be amenable to mail order and that would appeal to its subscription customers)?

Also, remember that what you are doing is drawing up a menu of opportunities, not the final ones you are going to adopt. Thus, you might think of it as creating a wish list, without regard to how many items get on that list. At this point, do not be judgmental, especially when a number of them are the result of a brainstorming process. Later, prune the list down to those that appear feasible and relevant to the company's business. You will now have a much smaller number but, in all likelihood, still too many for you to adopt. As a guideline, you should have no more than ten real opportunities, with four to six as a more typical range. (Investigating the feasibility of more than a handful of opportunities becomes prohibitively expensive for all but the largest companies.) Most, if not all, of these will appear later as strategic issues, asking in effect if it makes sense for the company to pursue them.

In 1997, a multidisciplinary team of students undertook a yearlong project to identify commercial opportunities for a large aerospace company in the Los Angeles area. The company had a system for innovation, which in the past three years or so had yielded over 80 ideas, but only three of which had been pursued and implemented. All three had since been sold to other companies (the company did not consider it was "in" those other businesses). So, in terms of ongoing products and revenue streams, the company was still searching for opportunities to pursue. Furthermore, finding new opportunities took on particular significance because the defense industry was in long-term decline. In explaining how it went about the process of seeking opportunities, the company showed the team a triangular diagram (see Figure 5.3) and used it to define the project, which was essentially to find a number of concrete opportunities the company could pursue.

Figure 5.3 Opportunity-Search Method

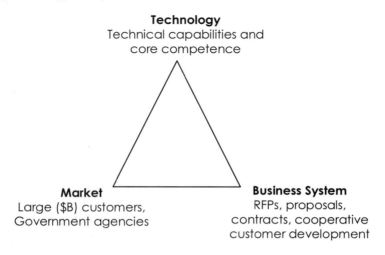

Technology
Technical capabilities and
core competence

Market
Large ($B) customers,
Government agencies

Business System
RFPs, proposals,
contracts, cooperative
customer development

This triangle in Figure 5.3 represents the company's strategic options. For example, it could try to find new customers without changing either its technical capabilities or its business system—this constraint limited it to very large billion-dollar companies or the federal government. Or it could update its technical capabilities without changing the other two, or its business system, while keeping the others constant. Or it could change any two sets of variables while keeping the third constant. Or it could change all three at once. Clearly, the more variables that are changed simultaneously, the riskier the strategy. Initially, the team was asked to confine its search for opportunities by finding new customers while keeping the other two variables constant. Later, because the charter was too restrictive, the constraint was relaxed to include acquiring a new technology or core capability if the opportunity in question was significantly large and worth pursuing, and even include changing its business system.

The actual method this team used was a combination inside-outside approach. The inside-out part involved first gaining an understanding of the company's technologies, capabilities, products, and business systems, and then trying to find new markets and applications that might fit the company. The outside-in part involved first looking at competitors, markets, industries, and application areas to find opportunities, and then checking to see which of them matched the company's technical capabilities and business process, that is were feasible for the company. The project came up with 28 ideas, but quickly discarded about half of them because of obvious deficiencies or mismatches with the company's capabilities. The remaining ideas were then pruned to seven candidates from which the company selected four for further study. The team finally recommended three solid opportunities that met all criteria. Clearly, the company's system for innovation was not working. The project showed that to "gear up" to find opportunities is time-consuming and costly. This company and any other company should be looking for opportunities all the time and acting on those it finds that are "good bets."

Opportunities are the lifeblood of any organization and one of the primary sources for key strategic issues for the company. Many strategic issues focus on whether the company should pursue this or that opportunity, and in fact the key opportunities find their way into one strategic alternative or another. That is when the decision is made as to which opportunity or opportunities should be pursued, particularly in the typical case where the company cannot afford to pursue more than one at a time.

Threats

Threats are *external* to the company. (An "internal" threat is classified as a weakness.) Left unaddressed or even ignored, threats can wipe out a company. Consider this partial list:

- Low-cost foreign competition
- Growth in sales of substitute products
- Slower industry growth
- Costly regulatory requirements
- Adverse effects of a recession or business cycle
- Growing bargaining power of customers and suppliers
- Changing buyer tastes and needs
- Demographic changes with adverse effects on the company
- Increasing interest rates
- Increasing supply prices
- Raw material shortages
- Adverse exchange rates
- Impending legislation with possible adverse consequences for the company

Implicit in recognizing a threat is the fact that it is a trend moving in a certain direction. Even if you identified some threats when you were doing the environmental analysis earlier, put them down again in this section. Yet at what point—at what value of a trend—does a particular threat become real? For example, if your company is in the real estate industry, and interest rates are inching upwards, is that a threat? Probably not. But if they pass 12%, pass 15%, and sit at 18%, is that a threat? By then, it is probably too late! Or if the price of a critical raw material rises, precisely when does it begin to threaten the company and prompt it to take offsetting action?

One way to deal with this problem is to classify threats on a two-dimensional grid as shown in Figure 5.4. The purpose of doing so is to sort out which threats to pay attention to and do something about, and which to continue monitoring. Plot each threat on the grid as best you can. To do so, you will have to decide on the severity of the likely impact of the threat on the company. Using the interest rate example above, a just-rising interest rate would not have a high negative impact on the company; it would go into the short-term *low*-impact quadrant. However, a

Figure 5.4 Classifying Threats Grid

		Time (years)	
		Short Term (< 3 yrs)	**Long Term (> 3 yrs)**
Severity of Negative Impact	**High**		
	Low		

fast-rising, high-interest rate would (i.e., a short-term *high*-impact quadrant). It is a judgment call; but again, if done by a group of people, the assessment will be more reliable.

Those threats in the top-left quadrant (high negative impact in the short term) should receive priority attention by the company. Those in the top-right and bottom-left quadrants should both receive second priority, with individual threats being handled in appropriate priority order. The least pressing group is that in the bottom-right quadrant, which may need just steady monitoring but no action.

For high-priority threats, gather more data about them, assign a committee or task force to track, study, and report on them and, most importantly, come up with contingency plans for dealing with them. These threats, along with selected threats from the top-right quadrant, should probably be treated as strategic issues.

The TOWS Matrix integrates the SWOT analysis—it is an opportunity to come up with strategies that take advantage of strengths and opportunities, minimize or downplay weaknesses, and counter threats. The strategy ideas it produces should be carefully considered later as strategic issues and as potential strategic-alternative "bundles." (SAM[tw] makes this easy to do.) Figure 5.5 illustrates the use of the method based on an analysis of Winnebago Industries, Inc., the largest manufacturer of recreational vehicles in the world, as it was in the 1970s.

Core Competence and Competitive Advantage

Core competence and competitive advantage are becoming increasingly important concepts in the strategy literature. Because considerable confusion surrounds these and terms related by context, it makes sense to define them:

- *Capability*—the capacity for a set of resources to integratively perform a task or activity.[4]

- *Core competence or strategic capability*—a capability that is simultaneously valuable, rare, costly to imitate, and nonsubstitutable, and one that underpins a company's strategy.[5] Further, core competencies are resources and capabilities that serve as a source of competitive advantage for a firm over its rivals.[6]

Figure 5.5 TOWS Matrix

	Internal Factors	
	Strengths (S) 1. Brand image and good reputation 2. Good service and warranty 3. Established dealer network, good dealer relations 4. Extensive R&D capabilities 5. Automated efficient plant 6. Manufactures most RV parts	**Weaknesses (W)** 1. One-product vulnerability 2. Concentration at high end 3. Heavy investment in tool-making raises cost of model changes 4. Single plant location 5. Unprepared for transition from family to corporate management
External Factors		
Opportunities (O) 1. Demand for smaller RVs 2. New international markets 3. Demand for low-cost modular housing (FHA subsidy for mortgage loans)	**SO Strategies** *Strategies that use strengths to take advantage of opportunities* 1. Produce smaller, more efficient RVs 2. Expand into foreign markets 3. Diversify into modular housing	**WO Strategies** *Strategies that take advantage of opportunities by overcoming or mitigating weaknesses* 1. Develop and produce smaller RVs 2. Build different plants in different parts of the country and abroad
Threats (T) 1. Gas shortage, higher gas prices 2. Slowing demand for RVs 3. Trading up creates secondary market 4. Increased competition from GM, Ford, International Harvester, VW, Toyota 5. Impending safety regulations	**ST Strategies** *Strategies that use strengths to avoid or mitigate threats* 1. Diversify into farm equipment, railroad cars 2. Consider diesel engines for motor homes 3. Make RVs safer in anticipation of safety regulations	**WT Strategies** *Strategies that minimize weaknesses and avoid or mitigate threats* 1. Sell the company

Source: Craig S. Fleisher and Babette E. Bensoussan, *Strategic and Competitive Analysis: Methods and Techniques for Analyzing Business Competition*, 1st ed. (Upper Saddle River, NJ: Pearson/Prentice Hall, 2002), 100. Fleisher and Bensoussan cite as their source for the technique, H. Weihrich, "The TOWS Matrix—A Tool for Situational Analysis," *Long Range Planning* 15, no. 2 (1982): 54–66. © 2002. Reprinted by permission of Pearson Education, Inc., Upper Saddle River, NJ.

- *Competitive advantage*—a significant edge over competitors, often measured in developmental lead time, such as an 18-month lead over the nearest competitor in software, but otherwise something an organization can do (e.g., integrate systems efficiently) that competitors can't, or that an organization has (e.g., patents, a core competence) that competitors lack.

- *Sustainable competitive advantage*—the ability to *maintain or increase* the edge that an organization has over its competitors over time. Given that a competitive advantage erodes over time, sustaining it takes focused effort and considerable resources. It involves "raising the bar" every time—as soon as a competitor thinks it has caught up, the company in question must have developed something new which maintains the original lead. As Kevin P. Coyne writes, "The most important condition for sustainability is that existing and potential competitors either cannot or will not take the actions required to close the gap."

The relationship between the first three terms (and others) is shown in Figure 5.6.

A list of typical capabilities includes:

- Effective execution of managerial tasks

- Effective organizational structure

- Design and production skills yielding reliable products

- Product and design quality

- Technological capability

- Integrating different technologies to produce a desired system or product for the customer

- Rapid transformation of technology into new products and processes

- Effective use of logistics-management techniques

Figure 5.6 Derivation of Competitive Advantage and Strategic Competitiveness

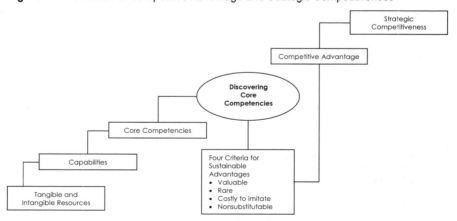

Source: Adapted from Michael A. Hitt, R. Duane Ireland, and Robert E. Hoskisson, *Strategic Management: Competitiveness and Globalization*, 6th ed. (Mason, OH: Thomson South-Western, 2005), 75. © 2005. Reprinted with permission of South-Western, a division of Thomson Learning: www.thomsonrights.com. Fax 800 730-2215.

- Effective promotion of brand-name products
- Strong brand (well known, high value)
- Strong customer service
- Innovative merchandising
- Effective HR policies to motivate, empower, and retain employees
- Excellent training[8]

The four criteria that distinguish capabilities from core competencies are related to competitive advantage and firm performance as shown in Table 5.1. *Valuable capabilities* are those that create value for a firm by exploiting opportunities or neutralizing threats in its external environment. *Rare capabilities* are those possessed by almost no current or potential competitor. *Costly-to-imitate capabilities* are those that other firms cannot develop easily, quickly, or inexpensively. And *nonsubstitutable capabilities* are those that do not have strategic equivalents.

While these criteria appear straightforward, applying them is difficult. Take any of the capabilities in the list above, for example, or others that your firm may have, and try to apply these criteria. It may take some research to evaluate them. For firms without a core competence, or with capabilities that meet two or fewer criteria, the strategic-planning imperative is clear: Work on developing a core competence that meets all the criteria and that produces a sustainable competitive advantage. On the downside,

Table 5.1 Testing for Core Competence: Outcomes from Combinations of Criteria

Criteria for Sustainable Competitive Advantage (A capability that meets all criteria is a core competence.)				Outcomes	
Is the capability valuable?	Is the capability rare?	Is the capability costly to imitate?	Is the capability nonsubstitutable?	Competitive Consequences	Performance Implications
No	No	No	No	Competitive disadvantage	Below-average returns
Yes	No	No	Yes/No	Competitive parity	Average returns
Yes	Yes	No	Yes/No	Temporary competitive advantage	Average to above-average returns
Yes	Yes	Yes	Yes	Sustainable competitive advantage	Above-average Returns

Source: Michael A. Hitt, R. Duane Ireland, and Robert E. Hoskisson, *Strategic Management: Competitiveness and Globalization*, 6th ed. (Mason, OH: Thomson South-Western, 2005), 88. © 2005. Reprinted with permission of South-Western, a division of Thomson Learning: www.thomsonrights.com. Fax 800 730-2215.

Figure 5.7 Example Using the General Electric Matrix

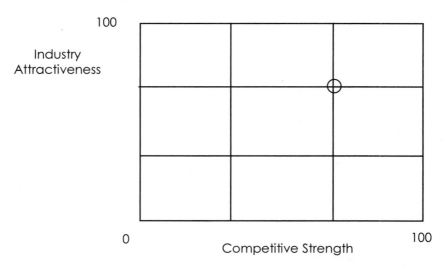

a core competence can be outdated by environmental change, replaced by substitution, or eroded through imitation and competitive action.

Other Analytical Tools

Competitive Strength

How competitive is your company? To find out, do an analysis very similar to the one done to assess industry attractiveness (see Table 4.1) except with different factors. Here, the factors should reflect what it takes to be competitive in an industry—similar to critical success factors. When you have finished, you will have a resultant competitive strength index at the bottom. The higher the percentage figure, the more competitive your company can be considered to be in the industry, assuming realistic ratings. (This technique is also highly subjective.)

Both indices are used to plot your company on the General Electric. Matrix (industry attractiveness against competitive strength). A hypothetical company is plotted on one in Figure 5.7. Notice that the grid is divided into nine cells. If the company ends up in any of the three cells in the top-right corner of the grid, conventional wisdom would suggest a strategy "to grow, invest, and build." If it ends up in any of the three cells in the bottom-left comer of the grid, conventional wisdom would mean pursuing a strategy to "harvest or exit" from the industry. (What else can a weak uncompetitive company do in an unattractive industry?) The remaining three cells are more difficult to assess, and strategies should be developed for these on a case-by-case basis. The value of plotting the company on this grid is to get an early "take" on the strategy the company should follow, as assessed by these two complex variables.

Is the current strategy working?   First of all, what is the company's current strategy? It is remarkable how many companies are hard pressed to answer that question—the answer invariably takes the form of several guesses, and different people asked will give different answers. However, once you can articulate it, answers to only two questions will tell you whether it has been working: (1) Has the company made progress towards achieving, or has it achieved, its vision and strategic intent? (2) Have its stated objectives been attained?

Consider the questions shown in Figure 5.8. If you find that objectives have not been met, resist jumping to the conclusion that the strategy has not been working. The strategy could be appropriate in the circumstances, but the execution of it may be poor; or the company may have underestimated how quickly it could be achieved. However, if you deem that the execution was good, then it is probable that the strategy was not working and should be changed. Also, if you judge that the company has been making satisfactory progress towards achieving its vision and strategic intent but not achieving its objectives, it could be that the objectives were set too high or were otherwise unreasonable. Thus, such a review ought to be done carefully, because what you conclude could set the stage for what strategic alternatives you come up with later in the process.

Figure 5.8 Questions to Challenge the Current Strategy

Questions about scope

- What assumptions about market trends, competitor behavior, new entrants, changes in technology, and customer needs have you made? If those assumptions are wrong, how would the strategy be affected?

- Are there trends that could force you to change the way you do business now?

- If you had to triple your growth, what new business would you enter?

- What is the definition of the market you are in, and what is the logic behind that definition?

- What new uses for your products and technologies have you explored?

Questions about choices

- What strategic choices are you making, and what are you rejecting? What is the rationale? Are there circumstances or situations that would cause you to choose differently?

- Are you pursuing growth aggressively enough? Are you compromising growth by failing to provide adequate resources?

- Can you reverse a basic assumption held in the industry? How, and what would be the benefit?

- How are your plans the same as or different from those of your competitors? How will you ensure that you have a different value proposition?

- What actions have your competitors taken in the last three years to upset global market dynamics? What are the most dangerous things they could do in the next three years?

- What have you done to affect global dynamics over that period, and what are the most effective things you could do in the next three years?

Questions about process

- How many customers did you interview? How many noncustomers?

- How did you involve different markets from around the world?

- What approaches did you use to develop creative or breakthrough strategies?

- Have you committed sufficient resources to your strategic initiatives? Are they linked to your financial and HR plans?

Source: Sarah Kaplan and Eric D. Beinhocker, "The Real Value of Strategic Planning," *MIT Sloan Management Review* 44, no. 2 (Winter 2003): 73.

SPACE Analysis

SPACE stands for Strategic Position and ACtion Evaluation and is used to determine or confirm the appropriate strategic posture of a firm.[9] It is a two-dimensional diagram incorporating four dimensions shown in Figure 5.9. Each dimension is a composite of several factors that are evaluated separately (see Table 5.2). Two of the factors—financial strength and competitive advantage—are major determinants of a company's strategic position. The other two factors—industry strength and environmental stability—characterize the industry and context in which the company competes.

The factors comprising each dimension are given in Table 5.3. Each factor is evaluated on a scale of 1–6 (6 being best). A template for the SPACE chart is shown in Figure 5.9. When the resulting averages are plotted on the SPACE diagram, the averages for competitive advantage and environmental stability *must* be negative. For example, if the average for competitive advantage is 2.4, then what is plotted is [average – 6] or *minus 3.6* on the SPACE chart.

Table 5.4 gives an example for computing one of the dimensions—competitive advantage. Note the appropriate explanations given to each factor that help in rating it.

The following results lead to one of the four strategic positions of Figure 5.9:

- *High on all dimensions*—aggressive posture

- *High on competitive advantage and industry strength, low on financial strength and environmental stability*—competitive posture

Figure 5.9 SPACE Chart

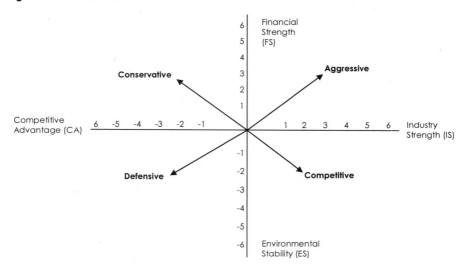

Source: Derived from Alan J. Rowe, Richard O. Mason, Karl E. Dickel, Richard B. Mann, and Robert J. Mockler, *Strategic Management: A Methodological Approach,* 4th ed. (Boston: Addison-Wesley, 1994), 255–265. Copyright © 1994 by Alan J. Rowe.

Table 5.2 Breakdown of the Four Dimensions in a SPACE Chart

Competitive Advantage	Financial Strength	Industry Strength	Environmental Stability
Market share	Return on investment	Growth potential	Technological changes
Product quality	Leverage	Profit potential	Rate of inflation
Product lifecycle	Liquidity	Financial stability	Demand variability
Product replacement cycle	Capital required vs. capital available	Technological know-how	Price range of competing products
Customer loyalty	Cash flow	Resource utilization	Barriers to entry
Competition's capacity utilization	Ease of exit from market	Capital intensity	Competitive pressure/ rivalry
Technological know-how	Risk involved in business	Ease of entry into market	Price elasticity of demand
Vertical integration	Inventory turnover	Productivity; capacity utilization	Pressure from substitutes
Speed of new product introductions	Economies of scale and experience	Manufacturers' bargaining power	

Source: Derived from Alan J. Rowe, Richard O. Mason, Karl E. Dickel, Richard B. Mann, and Robert J. Mockler, *Strategic Management: A Methodological Approach,* 4th ed. (Boston: Addison-Wesley, 1994), 255–265. Copyright © 1994 by Alan J. Rowe.

- *High on financial strength and environmental stability, low on competitive advantage and industry strength*—conservative posture

- *Low on all dimensions*—defensive posture

With all four dimensions plotted, the result in each case is a polygon anchored on each of the dimension axes. Adding the plotted values on the vertical and horizontal axes separately yields the coordinates of a point, and in each case the point ends up being in a particular quadrant. This tool is included in the SAM^tw CD-ROM.

Value Analysis

The term *value disciplines* was developed by Michael Treacy and Fred Wiersema to describe different ways companies create value for customers.[10] They describe three general disciplines that have been successfully used by many companies: product leadership, operational excellence, and customer intimacy. A fourth discipline, not included in Treacy and Wiersema's model, is value-based management. Most successful companies excel in at least one of these disciplines and have, by so doing, strengthened their strategic focus. By fully developing one of these value disciplines, a company can separate itself from its competitors; by fully developing *two* of these value disciplines, an even wider separation can be achieved. The tool, included in SAM^tw, involves a subjective evaluation of the company on the

Table 5.3 Evaluating Competitive Advantage for SPACE

Market share	Small	0	1	2	3	4	5	**6**	Large
Product quality	Inferior	0	1	2	3	4	5	**6**	Superior
Product lifecycle	Late	0	1	2	**3**	4	5	6	Early
Product replacement cycle	Variable	0	1	2	3	**4**	5	6	Fixed
Customer loyalty	Low	0	1	2	3	4	**5**	6	High
Competition's capacity utilization	Low	0	1	**2**	3	4	5	6	High
Technological know-how	Low	0	1	2	3	4	**5**	6	High
Vertical integration	Low	0	1	2	**3**	4	5	6	High
Speed of new product introductions	Slow	0	1	2	3	**4**	5	6	Fast
	Total = 38, Average = 4.2 **Score for SPACE = 4.2 − 6 = −1.8**								

Source: Derived from Alan J. Rowe, Richard O. Mason, Karl E. Dickel, Richard B. Mann, and Robert J. Mockler, *Strategic Management: A Methodological Approach,* 4th ed. (Boston: Addison-Wesley, 1994), 255–265. Copyright © 1994 by Alan J. Rowe.

many factors that comprise the value disciplines listed in Table 5.4. (Further definitions and explanations of these factors are given in SAM[tw].) The idea is to identify those areas in which a company is weak and recognize ways that they may be strengthened as part of any ensuing plan.

Corporate culture   Much has been written about what corporate culture is. A good definition from this literature is the one by Kilmann, Saxton, and Serpa, which states that culture "is defined as the set of key values, beliefs, understandings, and norms shared by members of an organization."[11]

Table 5.4 Value-Discipline Factors

Operational Excellence	Product Leadership	Customer Intimacy	Value-Based Management
Information systems	R&D capability (innovation)	Customer service	Management skills
Production efficiency	Product development	Customer satisfaction	Making managers into owners
Reengineering—simplification	Marketing and sales	Customer loyalty	Managerial performance
Reengineering—automation	Distribution	Employee capability	
Reengineering—integration	Brand equity management	Employee satisfaction	
Reengineering—leadership	Value chain integration	Employee loyalty	
		Employee productivity	

The ability of a culture to enhance or impede the implementation of a particular strategy has also received much comment in, for example, Edgar H. Schein's *Organizational Culture and Leadership*. Because of this last characteristic, it is incumbent on top managers to have a thorough understanding of the company's culture and to evaluate the extent to which the culture can become a strategic enabler or hindrance.

The following examples illustrate some of the most common strategic changes that companies undergo that require the corporate culture also to change:

- High-growth companies transitioning to maturity and slower growth, where the primary emphasis shifts from market share and sales commissions to cost-cutting and cost-savings.

- Sleepy and complacent companies with flat sales suddenly waking up and becoming more innovative, productive, and competitive.

- Companies with declining or flat profits that now turn to lowering costs in all phases of their operations and developing a low-cost mentality.

- Companies deciding finally to do something about quality and, through training, begin infusing every aspect of their operations with higher expectations and teamwork to produce tangibly higher quality.

- Companies trying to develop a core competence to attain a sustainable competitive advantage

- Companies in the midst of a turnaround, where losses have been finally stemmed and operations stabilized, and the germ of a new strategy has just begun to take hold and be implemented

Notice that the extent to which an alternative fits with the corporate culture (or the extent to which a company's culture might be expected to change for each alternative) is used in Chapter 6 as a key criterion when analyzing which of several strategic alternative "bundles" to adopt.

Management and leadership capabilities The final aspect of a company analysis is an assessment of its management and leadership capability. While it was covered cursorily in this chapter under strengths and weaknesses, the following questions will help you make a more insightful and penetrating assessment:

- Do members of the top management team have the right kinds of experience and qualifications?

- How long have they worked together as a team?

- How frequently and openly do they communicate with one another and with others in the organization below them? In what regard are they held by their peers and those who report to them? Do they command respect?

- How open are they to new ideas and new ways of doing things?

- How do they react when things aren't going well? For example, do they blame others and look around for scapegoats? Do they panic?

- What ethical standards do they espouse? Do they model the organization's values?

- Do they put a high priority on developing the people they supervise?

- Are they critical and demanding, that is, do they have high standards, ambition?

- Do they go out of their way to help their people achieve high expectations? Are they good motivators?

- Are they strong leaders, that is, are they visionary, and can they mobilize people and teams to implement their vision?

- Are they good role models? Do they lead by example?

- Are they empathetic and compassionate?

Summary

Corporate executives are often hampered from understanding their own company for two reasons: they view the company from the perspective of a particular functional area, and they are often so close to things, being part of the company's management, that their perspective becomes clouded. That is why doing specific analyses about the company itself and doing it in a shared way makes a lot of sense. An internal situation analysis, then, includes:

- An analysis of the company's recent financial performance and its current financial condition.

- Its strengths and weaknesses, opportunities, and threats.

- Its capabilities and an analysis to determine whether any of them are core competences, and whether it has a competitive advantage over its competitors.

- Its competitive strength.

- Stating its strategy (many executives guess at this) and determining whether it is working or needs to be changed.

- Characterizing its corporate culture.

- Assessing its management team and leadership capabilities.

This chapter also introduces and explains a number of analytic techniques useful in doing an internal situation analysis: financial analysis (most of which is done automatically in the companion CD-ROM upon entering the most recent 3–5 years' of financial statements) *and* drawing a realistic conclusion from the numbers, classifying threats, TOWS matrix, determining which capabilities are core competences, competitive strength, the General Electric Matrix, SPACE analysis, and value analysis. Again, the purpose of doing these analyses is to obtain a deeper understanding of the company's situation, its resources and capabilities, and how it is changing over time.

Notes

1. Identifying weaknesses could be thought of as looking for problems to solve. The best kind of problem-solving, though, is when the problem-as-stated is eradicated altogether. See Russell L. Ackoff, *Creating the Corporate Future* (New York: John Wiley, 1981), 171. There he discusses resolving a problem (satisfying), solving it (selecting an optimal solution), and *dissolving* it (removing it entirely). See also Gerald Nadler and Shozo Hibino, *Breakthrough Thinking: The Seven Principles of Creative Problem Solving* (New York: Prima Publishing/St. Martin's Press, 1994), where a focus on the right purpose often eliminates the problem as originally stated.

2. Derek F. Abell, *Managing with Dual Strategies* (New York: Free Press, 1993), 49. This concept was originally introduced in Abell's *Defining the Business.*

3. Dan Kopp and Lois Shufeldt, "Reader's Digest Association," *Business Case Journal,* 1994.

4. R.M. Grant, *Contemporary Strategic Analysis*, 2nd ed. (Oxford: Blackwell, 1995), 119–120.

5. Adapted from Michael A. Hitt, R. Duane Ireland, and Robert E. Hoskisson, *Strategic Management: Competitiveness and Globalization*, 6th ed. (Mason, OH: Thomson South-Western, 2005), 82–84.

6. A. A. Lado, N. G. Boyd, and P. Wright, "A Competency-Based Model," R. M. Grant, "Resource-Based Theory"; and M. A. Hitt and R. D. Ireland, "Relationships Among Corporate-Level Distinctive Competencies, Diversification Strategy, Corporate Structure, and Performance," *Journal of Management Studies* 23, no. 4 (1986): 401–416.

7. Kevin P. Coyne, "Sustainable Competitive Advantage—What It Is, What It Isn't," *Business Horizons* 29, no. 1 (January/February 1986): 58.

8. Adapted from Michael A. Hitt, R. Duane Ireland, and Robert E. Hoskisson, *Strategic Management: Competitiveness and Globalization*, 6th ed. (Mason, OH: Thomson South-Western, 2005), 83.

9. All the information about SPACE, including Figures 5.9, 5.10 and Tables 5.4, 5.5, are derived from Alan J. Rowe, Richard O. Mason, Karl E. Dickel, Richard B. Mann, and Robert J. Mockler, *Strategic Management: A Methodological Approach,* 4th ed. (Boston: Addison-Wesley, 1994), 255–265.

10. Michael Treacy and Fred Wiersema, *The Discipline of Market Leaders: Choose Your Customers, Narrow Your Focus, Dominate Your Market* (Reading, MA: Addison Wesley, 1995).

11. Ralph H. Kilmann, Mary J. Saxton, and Roy Serpa, "Issues in Understanding and Changing Culture," *California Management Review* 28 (Winter 1986): 87–94.

12. See especially parts II and III in Edgar H. Schein, *Organizational Culture and Leadership,* 2nd ed. (San Francisco: Jossey-Bass, 1997).

6

Creating Strategic Alternatives— Then Choosing One

The purpose of an effective strategy development process is not to avoid but to confront uncertainty: to pose the really tough questions that you do not have the answers to—the issues and opportunities that can make or break the business.[1]

—Dennis Rheault

Chapter 3 surveyed several methods of strategic analysis; however, these methods omit the critically important step of developing strategic issues and strategic alternatives before deciding on a course of action for the company. Those that generate alternatives derive them from the common SWOT analysis. In other words, the alternatives stem from a detailed consideration of both the past and the current situation. Paradoxically, any strategy the firm might choose is played out in the future. Any decision the firm makes now has its consequences in the future. So would it not seem natural that the choice of a strategy depends in part on future trends and on what the future environment is likely to be?

One reason this is not done is that very little is known about forecasting trends and imagining future scenarios. Yet even if not done "scientifically" or rigorously, attempting to do the right thing will yield far better results than doing the kind of routine strategic analysis that many companies do. The critical differences are (1) the injection of creativity and imagination into the process; (2) a decidedly future orientation; and (3) working backwards from some future vision or ideal state to arrive at meaningful alternative strategies for achieving it. Everything discussed in Chapter 2 is future-oriented and captures these differences.

The next step is to make a list of the company's key strategic issues, which essentially summarize the most critical elements of the entire situation analysis.

Identifying Key Strategic Issues

Identifying the key strategic issues is an act of synthesis. That is, taking what you know about the organization and its changing environment and distilling the critical questions and issues the organization must address in its strategic plan. These critical or key strategic issues derive from both external and internal sources. The former includes the company's industry, competitors, customers, suppliers, and other environmental forces—in one or more countries—and what it is about them that constitutes a critical issue for the company. The internal sources include key organizational, resource, culture, technology, or strategic decisions that the company must address. Together, these strategic issues form the basis for generating the strategic alternatives. (Too often, alternatives are generated from only a subset of these categories such as opportunities, which means leaving out a lot of information that is probably known and should be considered.)

There are two kinds of strategic issues, the first "external" and the second "internal":

1. *A trend*—for example, likely increases in the interest rate or price of a critical raw material, the frequency and severity of terrorist acts, an impending event such as legislation about to be enacted, or a large competitor about to enter the competitive arena that will have positive or negative strategic consequences for the firm.

2. *A strategic decision or choice*—one that will have a dramatic impact on the firm and the way it does business such as whether to merge or acquire another firm, go international, vertically integrate, go public, form strategic alliances, change its vision and core character, and so on.

Even after identifying a strategic issue, determining whether it is a strategic issue is still difficult. It is useful to think of a strategic issue as something that keeps the CEO up at night, something that is constantly on his or her mind (in the shower, driving to work, even during a boring meeting), something that his or her subconscious—and conscious—mind constantly wrestles with. So, when reviewing a list of strategic issues, use this imagery as a way of pruning those from the list that do not merit such obsessive attention. Besides, it is easier to do when looking at a particular strategic issue in relation to others in the list—is it as important or less important? Ultimately, the final decision is subjective; what one person might consider critical another might cross off the list. More to the point, a CEO or top manager should really check his or her gut instincts when creating the list of strategic issues: What are the *real* issues, problems, or dilemmas facing the firm?

If there ever was a time for soul-searching, this is it. For the exercise to be meaningful, the issues must be real. (Look again at what Dennis Rheault says at the start of this chapter.) This is not a time to "play back what the CEO wants to hear," or "what the consultant wants to hear." Unless these issues are real and phrased in plain English in a person's own words, the resulting strategic alternatives that are designed will be "suboptimal"—that is, not the best ones that could be devised and thus not in the company's best interests. Engaging in strategic thinking—such as having strategic conversations (see Chapter 2) with colleagues or outside experts—will help to unearth the real issues that the company must confront.

The viewpoint of most strategic analyses is assumed to be that of the CEO or leader of the organization and may include the top management team. However, when examined from the viewpoint of a board of directors, other variables could be added to the list of strategic issues, such as whether to go public, and even whether it is time to replace the CEO.

There is one final check on whether you are dealing with the proper set of strategic issues. Because they constitute the critical questions and issues a company should address, they should all be taken into account explicitly when forming strategic alternatives. But consider the case where the alternatives fail to take into account one of the strategic issues. It could mean that either (1) the strategic alternatives have not been properly formulated and should be further modified to take it into account; or (2) the issue in question is not as important as was initially assumed, and thus could be deleted.

Technically, a firm could have any number of strategic issues at a given point in time. Yet the larger the number of issues proposed, the higher the chances are that some of them are not as critical as others, or could be consolidated with others. Long lists of over 12 items should be pruned down to about eight to ten items, eliminating those that are not so critical or combining some of them (these numbers are not rules, but only guidelines). If you cannot reduce the list now, you will have another chance to do so when the strategic alternatives have been created and you find that they have still not taken into account every issue you had on the list.

Strategic issues are typically expressed in one of two forms, for example:

- Whether the company should acquire XYZ Corporation.

- Should the company acquire XYZ Corporation?

The second is phrased as a question and is a form that is recommended for the following good reason. If you know the answer to the question—for example, "Yes"—then the issue is not a strategic issue. It is something the company is going to do anyway no matter which strategic alternative is chosen. Other examples include:

- Should the company continue to produce with quality? (Not a strategic issue, because the answer is "Yes.")

- Should it try to lower costs? ("Yes.")

But wait. Perhaps the issue is not "whether to lower costs" but rather "How?" So the strategic issue could more accurately be phrased as, "How should the company lower its costs?" For this strategic issue, the answer is uncertain, and so it appears to be a bona fide strategic issue. So also with "*How* can the company pay down its debt?" rather than "Should it pay down its debt?" ("Yes.")

Thus, one criterion for a strategic issue is that the answer to the issue is uncertain. The way in which that uncertainty is resolved is through the design of strategic alternatives or "bundles" and choosing a preferred one. (See Bundles.)

> **Bundles**
>
> In one example of choosing a bundle this question could be posed: "Should the company broaden its product line?" One alternative bundle could say "Yes" and another "No." When later deciding which alternative is preferred—each of course contains more items than the answer to that issue—the one that is chosen automatically "resolves" the uncertainty inherent in the issue.

Creating Strategic Alternative Bundles

Obstacles to Creating Strategic Alternatives

For some companies, the decision-making about their future may involve tweaking their present strategy slightly by adding a distribution channel or starting to advertise on television. In other words, there is no change to the strategy itself, but some change in its implementation. Companies do this because they have a strong feeling at the time that it is the right thing to do.

For other companies, the strategy itself may remain unaltered, but the objectives may change, for example, from 10%/yr to 15%/yr growth in revenues and profits. People mistakenly believe this represents a change in strategy. However, if the same strategy is in place, that is, how the company competes has not changed, there is no change. Again, they do this because they have a strong feeling at the time that it is the right thing to do.

Still other companies may in fact change their strategy. They could go from a concentration (product- or market-development) strategy to a growth-through-acquisition strategy, from a growth to a retrenchment or turnaround strategy, or from going it alone to forming a number of strategic alliances. These changes could be the result of opportunities opening up, of threats that need to be defended against, of competitive realignments, or other environmental changes such as an economic downturn or impending new legislation. And again, they do this because they have a strong feeling at the time that it is the right thing to do.

What many companies do, it would appear, involves simpleminded extrapolations of past accomplishments (i.e., no change in strategy) or the first change that occurs to them that appears to solve the perceived problem. Sometimes it works, or works only for a short time, but more often it does not. As naive as this sounds, how else can we account for so many poor decisions made by various companies over the years? Note that even the best decision made at a given time can lead to a poor result because of unforeseen events and actions. Poor results are also notoriously the inevitable byproduct of poor execution, even with an otherwise sound strategy in place.

In each of these cases, is the strategy the company chose the best one it could have adopted in the circumstances? The only way to tell, really, is to have analyzed the subset of all plausible alternative strategies and chosen one for very good, defensible reasons. If this is done, then any challenge or question about what else might have been done can be preempted because one can argue convincingly why the chosen strategy is superior or, at least, preferable to any other that might be proposed. And if you are that confident about it at the time you make the decision, the chances are that you will be confident it will work as you implement it, and your motivation to see it succeed will also contribute to its success. Contrast this with how enthusiastically you might implement a strategy in which you have relatively little confidence.

Why don't companies do this all the time? Many do—and though this book is directed at managers of companies that do not and to graduate students who want to learn how to craft defensible strategies, the reasons are still illustrative:

1. *It takes a lot of effort and much time (We're in a hurry and competitors won't wait.)*—If you want to do something well, then you will put in whatever time and effort it takes to do it well, so the excuse of being "in a hurry" is just a convenient excuse. (Rather than do a superficial job because they were in a hurry, several client companies have worked around the clock and did a good job.) True, circumstances sometimes demand a quicker decision, but even in this situation, making a decision without considering alternatives is foolhardy. Besides, to make any decision at all, one needs at least two alternatives.

2. *It doesn't guarantee the "right" answer (So why bother?)*—No one can guarantee the correctness of a decision whose consequences play out in the future. But by considering the right kinds of trends and impacts, including the relevant variables, assessing the fit with the company's capabilities and resources, and considering plausible strategic alternatives, the chances of making the "right" decision for the company are substantially enhanced. Only when three, five, or even ten years have passed can you look back in hindsight and know whether a strategic decision was good or not. Otherwise, one has to make the decision while not knowing how things will actually turn out. All one can do in the circumstances is one's best. But companies do not give themselves a chance to make the best decision they can; they short-change themselves.

3. *People are more comfortable thinking about and analyzing the past than the future*—People seem to find nothing wrong about examining past data and then reaching a decision that plays out in the future. In these days of rapidly increasing change—even discontinuous change—past data are often irrelevant. What we need to examine are trends about everything that is changing and likely future moves of competitors. How are industries changing? What will merging industries become? How will technology affect our lives, what we buy, how we use products, how we think, how we do business? People are less comfortable in the future because they are typically unable to predict or forecast it, unable to extrapolate, and unused to ambiguity and uncertainty. The joke is that they would rather be certainly wrong than not sure whether they were right (and with no chance of finding out). The thought that they might even influence the outcome of future events even escapes them—they regard the future as

something beyond their control. (In fact, some things are and some are not.)

4. *People don't take the responsibility seriously enough*—It is not that CEOs do not take the responsibility of managing their companies seriously, but rather, they do not use the time they devote to strategic planning to ask themselves really tough questions and put their companies on a strong course, even a very different one. They do not take strategic planning seriously enough. It is so much easier to keep doing what the company has been doing, to blame a competitor or a piece of new legislation the company did not see coming, a downturn in the economy, or a rise in supplier prices. True, the unexpected often happens. But in hindsight, many "unexpected' occurrences could have been anticipated and taken into account had strategic planning been properly done.

5. *People don't know how*—and would rather avoid it to save face and do what they think is strategic planning as they have always done it. This may be a valid reason, but not after reading this book. While there is no foolproof way of coming up with a good strategy—experts have failed to do so in the past, and for good reason—the process relies to a very large extent on strategic thinking, the results you achieve depend in large part on your strategic-thinking ability and on your experience with and commitment to the approach. Even after you have decided on a strategy, only you can make it succeed; following the approach in this book will not automatically guarantee future success. It will be *your* ideas, creativity, arguments, and skill at implementation that will bring you the results you desire. So, although it is more convenient to hide behind ignorance and stay in one's comfort zone, it may not be the best way to chart the future of the company.

6. *A lack of top-management commitment*—In many companies, staff planners and even some line managers that value the process of strategic planning find only lip service paid to it because of disinterest or a lack of commitment on the part of top management. Reasons could include a tradition or culture of risk averseness, as well as entrenched and threatened interest groups raising additional obstacles to the process. Finally, top-management's reluctance to embrace the process may stem from simple ignorance about what strategic planning really is and is supposed to do (covered above).[2]

7. *Short-term focus*—Companies for many reasons put a far greater emphasis on short-term financial results than on longer-term strategic performance. While short-term financial performance is always important, it should never come at the expense of longer-term performance. CEOs threatened with losing their jobs or the value of their stock holdings (see Greedy CEOs), boards of directors worried about the company's stock price, or the company just trying to survive are all examples where short-run considerations dominate. In this environment,

Greedy CEOs

During 2002, the world witnessed several of the most egregious examples of corporate CEO and top-management greed stemming from actions taken to cover up worsening financial performance and giving stockholders the impression that their companies were continuing to perform well and to maintain stock price. The most notorious examples concerned Enron, WorldCom, Tyco, Adelphia, and Global Crossing.

the company's long-term future and potential is often sacrificed, for example, when expenditures for R&D, new-product development, advertising, and training programs are slashed to show profits for the immediate quarters and year. Clearly, such decisions are suboptimal and not made in the long-term best interests of the company. Such decisions also adversely affect any strategic alternatives the company may consider and the strategic direction the company pursues.

What Is a Strategic Alternative?

An ordinary alternative is one of several means by which a goal is attained or a problem solved. A *strategic alternative* is one of several ways by which a firm might compete in a marketplace, achieve its vision or, if no vision has been articulated, decide where it might go and what it might achieve. Notice two things about the definition: (1) The designation "strategic" is necessary because alternatives are fashioned in a competitive environment, where actions and retaliations of competitors must be taken into account; and (2) the alternatives are created at the level of the whole firm and not any one of its functions or units (see Department-Specific Strategic Planning?). In addition, they provide choices about marketplace strategy or about configuring the organization, address issues of central importance to the organization, have uncertain outcomes, and require resources to develop before action can be taken.[3]

Alternatives are of three general types. "Obvious" alternatives arise from current strategies or simple extrapolations of what the organization is currently doing. "Creative" alternatives take different conceptual approaches than existing strategies do and break away, to some extent, from the assumptions and beliefs underlying current strategies. "Unthinkable"

Department-Specific Strategic Planning?

Is it possible to do strategic planning and develop alternatives at a subunit level? The answer is "yes." Although some care must be taken when doing so, especially in making sure that its vision, strategy, and objectives are aligned with the overall organization. See Appendix C, which describes strategic planning for a university academic department.

alternatives reflect a radical departure from the organization's historic mindset.[4] They are unthinkable because no one before has bothered to break the rules of what is appropriate for how an organization does business. Typically, such alternatives have little chance of being accepted by management unless arguments for their adoption are persuasive and made by someone who commands respect in the organization. Unthinkable alternatives illuminate the current situation in a radically different light and inspire other managers to propose creative solutions. However, this typology is typically not used as a framework to generate alternatives.

How Are Strategic Alternatives Created?

Usually a small group or team of managers brainstorm ideas that later become alternatives. Some follow a specific process, some do not. Marjorie Lyles suggests a process that begins with framing a problem, identifying an initial list of alternatives, extending the list if resources and time permit, then narrowing the list through a process of evaluation and consolidation.[5] However, who is to say that the resulting list contains good rather than mediocre or unimaginative alternatives? Clearly, a worthwhile strategy cannot come from poorly conceived alternatives. Lyles further defines what makes a list of alternatives useful:

- The variety of alternatives.

- Differences among them compared to the present situation.

- The costs and difficulties of implementation (if they are all too easy to implement, the organization is not stretching itself or being ambitious enough).

- The degree to which they challenge existing goals, aspirations, long-held assumptions, and beliefs.[6]

Edward de Bono makes the distinction between choosing from alternatives that already exist, such as ties in a closet or menu choices at a restaurant, and alternatives that do not exist and need to be found.[7] In the latter case, one cannot suggest just any alternative and have that alternative make sense. It has to be related to a reference point. For example: What alternatives are there to achieving this purpose? Or carrying out *this* function?

To help in coming up with alternatives, De Bono suggests thinking of groups, resemblances, similarities, or concepts—for example, as an alternative to an orange, do you search for other citrus fruit, domestic fruit, refreshing beverages, or colors? His technique of lateral thinking is directly concerned with changing concepts and perceptions, especially when used to come up with alternatives in solving problems.[8] It is a systematic way of generating new ideas and new concepts. Besides leading to a defensible strategy, coming up with suitable strategic alternatives is a heaven-sent opportunity to explore whether the organization should be heading in another direction or doing business a different way (i.e., do strategic thinking). Of course, companies that have been operating in a certain way for years—and doing fairly well—are not inclined to change their way of doing business for all the usual reasons. However, one reason often overlooked is that it is almost impossible to even think about doing business in a different way or heading in a different direction when you are an intrinsic part of the organization and have become used to doing what you do. It is an ideal, if somewhat counterintuitive, time to explore other options. Many companies fall into the mindset of "If it ain't broke, don't fix it." They are difficult to persuade otherwise. They address the issue only when their strategy falters, or when competitors overtake them, or some other threat looms (and by then, of course, it can be too late). Opportunities go by the board because they are seldom sought or considered. (Yet another reason why a company—or someone in the company—should be doing strategic thinking all the time.) In cases like this, the organization needs both an outside facilitator and specific exercises to stimulate creativity. (See Comparative Lit.)

James Bandrowski offers one of the most powerful techniques for using creative imagination to find alternatives or, more accurately, breakthroughs.[8] He suggests visualizing the ideal solution and then "filling in the feasibility" afterwards, that is, figuring out how to achieve that ideal solution (see Figure 6.1). The advantages include coming up with something radical, *leapfrogging* the competition instead of just catching up, getting ready for tomorrow's markets, and injecting new life into a possibly complacent and (mentally) tired organization.

Rather than just blindly searching for ideal solutions, Bandrowski offers the following different suggestions for making a creative leap, all of which will improve your ability to think strategically and supplement the ideas you learned in Chapter 2:

- *Year 2010*—Pick a date in the future like the year 2010. Call it "Challenge 2010" like 3M does. Unlock your imagination and visualize what your industry, products, services, markets, and so on will be like then. Bandrowski says, "The future will be invented by those who see it today."

- *Ideal Company*—What would the ideal company look like? Who is the best competitor in the industry? What do you most covet in this competitor? What company would you most like to acquire and why? Bandrowski quotes Lee Iacocca's description of an ideal automobile company: "It would combine German engineering,

---

Comparative Lit

Several helpful books have already been cited so far. The following titles should also make the list:

- James L. Adams, *Conceptual Blockbusting: A Guide to Better Ideas*, 4th ed. (New York: Perseus, 2001).

- Tony Proctor, *The Essence of Management Creativity* (Upper Saddle River, NJ: Prentice Hall, 1995).

- Charles "Chic" Thompson, *What a Great Idea! Key Steps Creative People Take* (New York: Harper Perennial, 1992).

Japanese production efficiency, and American marketing."

- *Ideal Industry*—Reconceptualize your entire industry. How could it become more profitable? How could technology revitalize it? Would it make sense to merge with another industry? How could you tilt the playing field in your favor?

- *Sweeping Solution*—Start with a blank canvas and try to find a total solution, rather than trying to improve various components such as production, marketing, and distribution. Is there a completely different way of doing business that is better (akin to reengineering, but for the whole company rather than a business process)?

- *Perfect Product*—What ideal products could be provided to either existing or new customers, assuming no fiscal or technical constraints? Customers should be included in this fantasy exploration; in fact, how might customers be persuaded to help co-create value? One place to start might be to list all the shortcomings of existing products.

- *Perfect Package*—How could packaging most benefit the product? Could it make the product easier to use, last longer, more convenient, more transportable, and the like? Could it be combined with the product or even eliminated?

- *Ideal Service*—Ask what customer needs are directly or even indirectly related to the product the customer buys. Any time you can make your product easier to use for your customer, or save your customer money, or increase your customer's sales, it may provide an opportunity to improve your service to that customer. (Or, again, get the customer to cocreate value with you.)

- *Ideal Information*—What information must you have to win? What *don't* you know that is hampering your efforts or causing you to be uncompetitive? Include information also about trends and the future. Rank the list in terms of importance to the company, not in terms of what is possible or what costs the least; and then brainstorm how to secure the information the company needs most. What emerges may well be a computer-based system that becomes a competitive advantage and that locks the customer in and increases the customer's switching costs.

- *Ideal System*—Focus on new ways of increasing throughput, reducing costs, reducing cycle time, or bringing new products to market faster. This is an area in which business-process reengineering traditionally takes place. But what do you do for an encore *after* your reengineering has taken place?

- *Comic Relief*—At least for a short period of time during a creativity session, request that "all participants come up with wild ideas—ones that are as outrageous and/or as funny as possible. No logical solutions are permitted. Humor activates the creative imagination."[9]

Figure 6.1   The Creative Leap

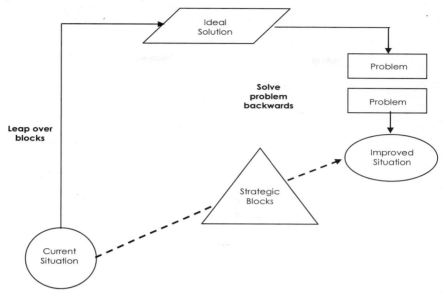

Long before Bandrowski published his book on infusing strategic planning with creativity, Gerry Nadler had been developing his ideas on a more effective way of thinking and solving problems. His Breakthrough Thinking® consists of seven principles:

- *Uniqueness*—Avoid using a solution that has worked elsewhere, or assuming that this situation is "like" any other.

- *Purposes*—Try to expand as far as possible the purposes you are trying to achieve. The expanded array of purposes lets you choose the biggest possible purpose that you think makes sense for your organization or area of concern. This ensures you are working on the "right" problem or trying to achieve the "right" purpose.

- *Solution-After-Next*—Develop many options of ideal solutions to achieve the focus of your selected purpose. Consider how you will solve the problem next time, perhaps three years from now, when you may have to work on it again.

- *Systems*—Everything is a system. To implement the *solution-after-next*, all system interrelationships must be taken into account and planned for.

- *Limited Information Collection*—What would you do with all the information if you had it? Collect only information that is essential to the *solution,* not the problem.

- *People Design*—Using the principles above, give all who might be affected by the changes or their implementation a chance to participate in the planning and selecting of the solution.

- *Betterment Timeline*—Even while designing today's solution, schedule the next change. Install solutions that contain the seeds of future change based on the bigger purposes and solution-after-next ideas. Fix it *before* it breaks.[10]

Using these principles has been shown to have the following outcomes:

- The generation of a significantly higher number of recommended major and innovative solutions.

- A significantly larger proportion of recommendations that are actually implemented.

- Significantly lower costs and time involved in developing and arriving at usable and beneficial results.

- A powerful builder of effective teams.

Notice that the *solution-after-next* principle is virtually identical to what Bandrowski calls the "Creative Leap." The only difference is that Breakthrough Thinking engages in this liberating and powerful act of creativity when focused on the chosen level of purpose from the previous step in the process. This is the built-in reference point that de Bono says is needed when creating alternatives.

Henry Mintzberg was the first strategy scholar to sound an alarm for both academics and practitioners. For years they had promoted strategic planning as an essential part of running a company, but they did not have the slightest idea how strategies were formulated.[11] He maintained, correctly, that "strategy-making is an immensely complex process, which involves the most sophisticated, subtle, and, at times, subconscious elements of human thinking."[12] He believes that strategies can develop inadvertently, without the conscious intention of senior management, through a process of learning. He illustrates this with a story of a salesperson who convinces a different kind of customer to try a product. Other salespersons follow up with their customers and, next thing management knows, its products have penetrated a new market. We try things, and those experiments that work converge gradually into viable patterns that become strategies. This is the very essence of strategy-making as a learning process. Mintzberg believes that deliberate strategies decided from a formal strategic-planning process are not necessarily good, and emergent strategies that grow from informal experiments and learning are not necessarily bad. All viable strategies have both emergent and deliberate qualities, and all must combine some degree of flexible learning with some degree of cerebral control.[13]

This book, proposes a logical process of doing strategic analysis, one that includes the important steps of creating strategic alternatives and choosing from among them a preferred one. To use the process requires strategic thinking—with all the openness, creativity, discipline, research, and experience implied in Chapter 2 and this chapter—and an overriding commitment to do what's best for the company.

Creating Strategic Alternatives

The process proposed here starts with the list of key strategic issues discussed in the previous section. Because these strategic issues represent the most pressing and important problems and strategic decisions facing the organization, any subsequent plan or strategy that is developed should address all of them. So, starting with that list, we create two to four alternatives that must meet certain criteria. Identifying more than four is extremely difficult. Most organizations manage to come up with three. You must be wondering, "Surely one can come up with many more alternatives than four?" Read on, these are not "ordinary" alternatives.

Because of the large number of possible strategies available, students (this technique was refined in graduate courses and later tested on client companies) have always found it extremely difficult to create good strategic alternatives other than the obvious safe ones. Consider the spectrum of strategies shown in Figure 6.2, which are organization-wide "master" or "grand" strategies, and do not include functional or operational strategies, classified as 'programs' in this book. An organization could choose a particular combination of strategies to adopt but, in order to show that it is the best choice at the time, it would have to compare it to all other combinations of strategies, a Herculean and impractical task. It took several years to make the conceptual leap and ask: "What if there were only a *small* number, say two to four choices, available? And what if they constituted 'either/or' choices such as choosing A *or* B *or* C, rather than saying that A + B together was better than A alone, or A was better than B + C + X? And what if the alternative proposed was one that the organization would be proud to implement because it would be both feasible and lead to success? Wouldn't this define a good set of alternatives?"

As the technique took shape, it seemed to make more and more sense. But making it practical proved to be more elusive. At least there were now three conditions (plus a fourth that is discussed at the end of this section). Good alternatives have to:

- *Be mutually exclusive*—that is, doing any one would preclude doing the others.

- *Be plausible*—that is, doable or feasible.

- *Be worthwhile*—that is, implementing it would lead to success.

- *Address all the strategic issues*— to be discussed later.

What also became clear was that these alternatives did not consist solely of strategies, but rather *"bundles"* that comprise strategy, strategic intent, core competence, programs, financing method, geographic scope, and any other parameter that would help define and clarify a future course of action to an observer. The bundles would be derived in large part from the key strategic issues which, in turn, were derived from a comprehensive situation analysis of the external and internal environments. (This sequence of dependencies gives the method a logic that is easy to grasp and learn.)

Figure 6.2   Spectrum of Possible "Master" Strategies

Stay in the same business:
- Concentration (product development, including technological innovation)
- Concentration (market development, including globalization)
- Vertical integration (forwards or backwards)
- Acquisition (horizontal integration) or merger
- Forming strategic alliances (including outsourcing, licensing, joint ventures, etc.)
- Retrenchment
- Turnaround or bankruptcy (Chapters 11 and 13 of U.S. Code Title 11)
- Harvest
- Be acquired (signifies a change of ownership, but company remains a going concern)
- Differentiation
- Low-cost leadership
- Focus or niche player

Exit the business:
- Liquidation or bankruptcy (see Chapter 7 of U.S. Code Title 11)

Enter another industry:
- Diversification through acquisition (related or unrelated)
- Internal diversification

As we shall see later, these bundles are one step away from being business models. That is why creating more than a few is extraordinarily difficult—companies are hard pressed to come up with *one* alternative business model, let alone up to four.

Consider the following case illustration.[14] Carmike Cinemas in 1986 was the fifth largest movie theater chain in the United States and the largest in the Southeast region. (The year of the case in no way diminishes its value as an illustration.) Revenues and *net income after tax* (NIAT) were growing at an average 15.3%/yr and 50.2%/yr respectively between 1982–1985. In 1986, with not enough good movies to show, revenues and NIAT dropped 11.6% and 44.4% respectively. Its debt/equity ratio in 1986 was 1.66, down from 6.66 in 1983 when it acquired another movie theater chain principally through debt. The company is well managed and growing aggressively through acquiring failed theater chains throughout the Southeast, staying mainly in small towns where often it is the only theater. Like other chains at that time, it was rapidly multiplexing, that is, converting single-screen theaters into multiscreen theaters.

Some strategic issues arising from a situation analysis include the following initial list. Should Carmike:

- Stay regional or expand nationally? How fast and where should it grow? ("Should Carmike grow" is *not* a strategic issue—answer "Yes." Its recent history suggests strong growth and the CEO's style and characteristics lean towards aggressive growth.)

- Increase its debt or go public to secure additional capital?

- Invest in screen/projection/sound technology?
- Upgrade the quality and amenities of its theaters?
- Experiment with serving hot food and coffees in its theaters?
- Sell memorabilia associated with the movies it shows?
- Show foreign, classic, cult, or other types of movies?
- Get into domestic or foreign distribution?
- Stay in small towns or expand into urban areas and cities?

If in doubt as to whether or not to include something as a strategic issue, go ahead and include it. Err on the side of having too many strategic issues. Later in the process, you will come to realize which of them are real issues and which are not important enough, so you can then delete them. With experience, you will be able to gauge which strategic issues are meaningful and find yourself adding very few that are later deleted. The process is iterative.

After much trial and error (adding, moving, erasing, changing items in each bundle until the three conditions are met), you can arrive at a set of strategic alternatives. Remember that *at least two* alternatives are required; otherwise there can be no decision. One alternative is a no-brainer that also has no way of telling whether it is the best strategy to pursue in a given situation. (Among the very few instances where a single strategy (i.e., no choices) makes sense are startups and turnarounds.) Creating two is not difficult—the strategy the company is currently pursuing and a different or potentially better alternative—three takes substantially more effort and thought, and four is extremely difficult. The reason is that these are not just strategic alternatives, but rather different business models with alternative visions. Table 6.1 presents three alternative strategy "bundles" for Carmike Cinemas as an illustration. Giving each bundle a label helps distinguish it from the others and underscores how they are mutually exclusive.

The first check is for mutual exclusivity—doing any one means not being able to do the others. To be sure, components of one alternative might be common with another one, but the question refers to the whole alternative and not just particular components. The check shows the three bundles to be mutually exclusive. However, if the check revealed that the bundles were not mutually exclusive, for example, you might think it possible to combine #1 with some aspects of #3, and if there were general agreement as to that point, then the bundles would have to be reconfigured. In other words, the process of creating them was not yet finished. Only when the resulting bundles meet all the criteria *and* do not change any more is this part of the process complete.

Are the bundles plausible? How do you know that they are "good" alternatives and not just mediocre ones? Are there any others that should be considered? If you were a manager of the organization in question, you would be in a better position to judge whether the course of action suggested by a particular bundle is doable. In addition, organizations that include lower-level managers, who implement the strategy in forming alternative bundles and choosing a preferred one, do a much better job with the bundles because feasibility is a principal criterion.

Table 6.1 Alternative Strategy Bundles for Carmike Cinemas (1986)

1. Go National	2. Stay Regional	3. Go International
Target #4 ranking near-term and #1 ranking nationally eventually	Maintain #5 ranking nationally but continue to dominate the Southeast region	Maintain #1 ranking regionally and become a major player internationally
Grow very rapidly, say 27%/yr in revenues	Grow moderately, say 15%/yr in revenues	Grow moderately, say 18%/yr in revenues
Increase D/E ratio	Lower D/E ratio	Maintain D/E ratio
Strive for market share	Strive for profitability	Strive for international recognition
Look for acquisitions in small towns first in the Northeast, then Midwest, then Southwest and West	Look for acquisitions in small towns primarily in Florida but also in other Southeast and Southern states	Look for acquisitions in United Kingdom and Australia, Canada, European countries (in large cities), and also in the Southeast United States (small towns)
Do not go public unless a very large acquisition is contemplated	Experiment with serving hot foods and coffee, and selling movie memorabilia in selected theaters	Go public to finance international acquisitions
	Upgrade facilities and technology of the worst 1/5 of all theaters	

Are the bundles worthwhile? Would implementing each one lead to success? While "success" means different things to different people and companies, we will assume for the moment that it means becoming a stronger competitor and realizing a strategic intent. (It could mean the "purpose" that the chosen strategy fulfills in the definition of "strategic planning" in Chapter 1.) Furthermore, we are not concerned with the objectives that the organization needs achieved and defines as "success." Some firms set objectives first and then find a strategy. The process described here does it the other way around for reasons that will become clear later.

The answers to the questions posed in the previous two paragraphs will always be uncertain because the outcomes occur in the future; though this is less the case the more experience you have. The best approach is to be constantly critical of what you come up with except when brainstorming, and go with what appears to be the most convincing argument when including or analyzing anything.

When analyzing a company with which you are unfamiliar, such as MBA students do in a strategy course when analyzing a case, you need to juxtapose in your mind each bundle with your situation analysis and determine whether the bundle is something that the company would implement, is capable of implementing, and would benefit from if implemented. This is why the key people who would be involved in implementing the strategy have to be part of this process: They will have a better feel for whether a particular bundle is feasible, and what it might take to implement it. Remember that we are not yet at the point of arguing which is the best bundle, but simply whether each bundle meets the criteria of plausibility and success. If they are mutually exclusive, plausible, and worthwhile, then they are decent alternatives, by definition. If not, then the process of tweaking them should continue. Keep in mind Marjorie Lyles's criteria, mentioned earlier, that the alternatives should have a high degree of variety, be as different as possible from the status quo, "stretch" the organization, and challenge existing goals, aspirations, long-held assumptions, and beliefs.

So often, particularly in cases when an analyst comes up with one strong strategic bundle, coming up with a second or even third one is very difficult. The strong alternative has preoccupied the person who has chosen it prematurely and any other alternative gets added as an afterthought and, in the case of a student, because the instructor has said that at least two alternatives are needed. Be careful that you do not "decide" what to do before even coming up with alternatives—the mistake is easily spotted, and the result lacks rigor and persuasion. Many companies are guilty of doing this when they decide on the strategy that they will pursue without contemplating or contrasting it with other alternatives. Without generating and considering good alternatives, the company has no way of knowing whether the strategy it will pursue is the best it could pursue in the circumstances.

Let's examine for a moment some strategic alternatives that were suggested but later discarded:

- *Vertical integration*—Nothing in the case information suggests that vertically integrating backwards would benefit the company. Movie production and distribution are very different businesses and demand a level of investment and risk that is beyond the capability of the company to bear. Because it is already the "retail" arm of the movie industry, it cannot vertically integrate forwards.

- *Strategic alliances*—Unfortunately, the case contains no competitive information. This is like a company having competitors that are privately held and about which no information is available; only managers experienced in the industry and who can obtain information by "picking up the phone" can get around this obstacle. However, two avenues of thought should be pursued: (1) Which of all considered courses of action might benefit more from, or be done better with, a strategic alliance? (2) What kind of strategic alliance might benefit the company? (Both considerations are an important part of strategic thinking—see Chapter 2.)

- *Being acquired*—Again, the case suggests precisely the opposite. Carmike is run confidently and entrepreneurially by CEO Mike Patrick, and he believes that Carmike not only is a strong competitor, but smarter than most of the others. First, there is no need to be taken over, unless one argues that it would provide a source of equity capital, and Patrick seems to have *no desire* to be acquired.

- *Diversification*—*Related diversification* means getting into another segment of the entertainment industry. Even though the case gives no information about other segments, that does not mean to say that none of them contains an opportunity! (This sort of thinking comes under the heading of "unthinkable" alternatives mentioned above. However, suggesting a course of action into another segment such as live theater, broadcasting, TV, professional sports, and the like has to be justified and defended, which is hard to do without more information and research. In the real world, if an idea has merit, it can only be supported and defended as a viable alternative with an effort to collect relevant intelligence and data, especially about applicable markets and competitors. This is precisely what one has to do when doing strategic thinking.

As you can see, coming up with two to four alternative bundles may mean coming up with a far greater number, like six or seven, then determining whether they are mutually exclusive, plausible, and worthwhile, and finally deleting those that do not meet the criteria or combining them with others until they do. To summarize, the best set of alternatives, echoing Lyles's list, are those that:

- *Contain significant variety*—that is, show that some creative and daring thinking has been done and are not so close to what the firm is doing now unless one of the bundles embodies the current strategy or the *status quo*. (Despite Lyle's criterion of variety, using a status quo alternative is quite understandable if the company is currently performing very well.)

- *Are feasible*—given the circumstances, resources, and capabilities of the firm.

- *Would all lead to "success"*—for the firm, even though the firm might end up in a very different place in each alternative.

- *Are mutually exclusive.*

- *Challenge the organization's existing goals, aspirations, long-held assumptions, and beliefs*—to improve its performance, competitive position, value proposition, and economic value.

Dave Francis advocates a method called "clustering ideas" to help generate strategic alternatives.[15] The clusters he mentions include grouping ideas on a particular theme, such as competing on the basis of superior service, on the degree of "radicalness," on their likely appeal to stakeholders, or on their likely appeal to the top management team. Here are other categories for clustering that might prove even more useful, that all involving strategic thinking:

- Ways of attaining a competitive advantage (if none exists), or ways of sustaining or increasing a competitive advantage that the firm already possesses.

- Ways of attacking or overtaking a key competitor.

- Ways of exploiting a core competence or core technology.

- Ways of differentiating your product or service.

- Ways of diversifying, including acquisition.

- Opportunities for forming strategic alliances.

Bandrowski suggests a number of "strategic actions" (programs) designed to increase profitability and revenue growth. Profit improvement requires cost reduction, productivity improvement, and attention to price and quality. While divesting some assets will not improve profitability, it will raise capital. Revenue growth, on the other hand, requires accurate targeting of customers, developing new products or broadening the product line, extending or finding new markets, and sometimes acquisitions.

Finally, there are several strategic choices that international or multinational firms should consider, shown on a two-dimensional grid in Figure 6.3. A *multidomestic strategy* is most appropriate when customer demands and needs vary substantially from country to country, forcing a company to modify any combination of product features, packaging, advertising, service-delivery methods, and pricing. With this strategy, no centralized control or integration is possible. A *regional strategy* involves marketing to a trading bloc of several countries, such as NAFTA, the European Union, or South America, giving managers in that region a high degree of autonomy, including the opportunity to achieve economies of scale by leveraging any location advantages that may exist in the region. A *global strategy* is warranted in those few instances where country-specific tastes are nonexistent and a standardized product can be marketed and sold to all countries. Such a strategy requires a high degree of centralization and integration to achieve efficiencies in production, advertising, and distribution. Finally, a *transnational strategy,* best thought of as a cross between a global and multidomestic strategy, is most effective in industries where a high degree of integration and efficiency is as important as the ability to tailor the product to different country markets. An example is a product that can be mass-produced in modules, allowing the firm to put together different combinations for different markets. Firms will produce the product in multiple plants wherever it is cheapest to do so and closest to suppliers and customers, yet give country managers the competitive edge of being able to demand certain models, colors, features that are in demand in a particular country.

Closing the Loop with Strategic Issues

One last check needs to be performed before beginning to analyze the strategic alternatives and argue for a preferred one, and that is to compare the final bundles with the list of strategic issues. Every strategic issue should have been addressed in some way by the components in each bundle. In our example, two strategic issues were not addressed:

- Should it show foreign, classic, cult, or other types of movies?

- Should it get into domestic or foreign distribution?

This means that (1) these issues are not as important as we first thought and can be deleted from the list of strategic issues; or (2) they are important and the bundles need further work to take them into account. Either solution is acceptable—there is no right or wrong answer. What matters is what is realistic and in the organization's best interest. If, for example, the film dis-

Figure 6.3 Mapping International Strategies

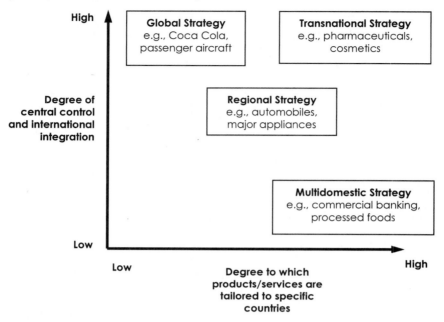

Source: Adapted from Dean B. McFarlin and Paul D. Sweeney, *International Management: Strategic Opportunities and Cultural Challenges*, 2nd ed. (New York: Houghton Mifflin, 2003), 242; P. W Beamish, A. J. Morrison, P. M. Rosenzweig, and A. C. Inken, *International management: Text and cases*, 4th ed. (Burr Ridge, IL: Irwin McGraw-Hill, 2000), 143; and J. D. Daniels and L. H. Radebaugh, *International business: Environments and operations* 9th ed. (Upper Saddle River, NJ: Prentice-Hall, 2001), 529.

tribution business was not considered before, a great deal of research and data collection about that business—domestic and foreign—need to be done before an intelligent analysis and decision can be made. For the moment, let's assume that we are satisfied with the bundles as they are and delete these two issues from the list.

Notice also that the third alternative bundle contained the notion of going international. In fact, going international is the dimension that made Alternative #3 different from the other two. And whether the company should go international was never identified originally as a strategic issue. Clearly, as a bona fide bundle, the issue is important. So it should be added to the list. The final list of strategic issues would seem to be the following:

- Should Carmike stay regional, expand nationally, or expand internationally?

- How fast and where should it grow?

- Should it increase its debt position or go public to secure equity capital?

- Should it invest in screen, projection, and sound technology?

- Should it upgrade the quality and amenities of its theaters?

- Should it experiment with serving hot food and coffees in its theaters?

- Should it sell memorabilia associated with movies it shows?

- Should it stay in small towns or expand into urban areas and cities?

Recommending the Preferred Choice

While generating strategic alternatives is a difficult and creative act, by far the most difficult part of strategic analysis, the odds of choosing a potentially good, let alone best, strategy without them are greatly reduced. Arguing persuasively for the preferred choice is also difficult. In part because, as Michael E. Porter says, "The essence of strategy is choosing what not to do."[16] If the alternatives have been skillfully created and meet the criteria of mutual exclusivity, plausibility, and success, as well as address all the strategic issues, provide variety, stretch the organization, and challenge its long-held beliefs and assumptions, then one is faced with alternatives that are, at first glance, equally good, making the choice very difficult. Picture the president of a division or subsidiary trying to persuade corporate top management why they should go along with his or her choice of strategy. At such meetings, corporate management grills the president mercilessly, trying to expose faulty assumptions or sloppy thinking, and trying to find a hole in the argument for the strategic choice. The only way to be prepared for such scrutiny is by having explored all reasonable alternatives and using defensible arguments for the chosen one. This section provides guidelines for doing this.

Establish Criteria

Choosing among alternatives becomes a little easier when each alternative is compared, one at a time, against a set of criteria and the results used to support the choice. Because such an analysis is often insufficient to decide an issue, the decision may eventually turn on more subjective analysis. What kinds of criteria are appropriate? Depending on the company and its particular situation, the following should be candidates, but do not imply an exhaustive list (see also Other Criteria):

- *Shareholder value*—This criterion is becoming increasingly common, not only for choosing from among alternative strategies, but also from among alternative investments. It requires the firm to have a model for computing shareholder value so that the computation for each alternative uses common values of discount rates and common assumptions about the future environment. In this way, the results become comparable. Students at universities, unless they have been taught how to use such a model, cannot use this criterion because they cannot calculate resulting shareholder value using different strategies. Still, many managers and companies believe that one of the principal purposes of strategic planning is to adopt the strategy that increases shareholder value the most. So managers should know how to compute shareholder value.[19]

- *Revenues*—This criterion is used more often when a firm's revenue growth has been inadequate or flat, or when issues of market share and market positioning are strategically significant.

- *Profitability*—This criterion should be used when a firm is highly leveraged, has insufficient working capital or inadequate or negative cash flow, or even when profits in recent years have been flat or negative. (Leveraged buyouts [LBOs] rely on huge cash flows (profits) during the first year following the LBO, so that the huge debt can be rapidly paid down and owner's equity rapidly rise as a result.) However, as a note of caution, it is relatively easy to "mortgage the future" in favor of present profits—for example, by reducing investment in R&D or new product development—so that, as a criterion, shareholder value may be superior, taking into account as it does a 10-year future stream of earnings.

- *Degree of risk*—Firms vary in their propensity to take risk. They are more inclined to take risks the more that risks have paid off for them in the past and when they have sufficient capital, so that

Other Criteria

Bandrowski suggests similar criteria:

- Financial benefit, including revenue and profit potential.

- Low investment, return on investment, including payback period.

- Strategic fit, that is, with present strategy and leveraging present strengths.

- Feasibility, availability of talent, resources, technology, culture, and the like.

- Low risk, including reaction from competitors.

- Timing, time period to see results.[17]

Richard Rumelt asserts that most tests applied to strategies fall under these broad criteria:

- Consistency, that is, mutually consistent goals and policies

- Consonance, an adaptive response to the changing external environment.

- Creation or maintenance of a competitive advantage.

- Feasibility, which must not overtax available resources or create unsolvable subproblems.[18]

they can *afford to* make mistakes. But it is more than this. A firm's culture can, for example, be risk averse, in which case it will avoid risk even when the risk has odds of success that appear to favor it. Risk can be analyzed and measured; but few have the skills to perform such analyses. Instead, they prefer to make a risky decision according to "gut" instinct, or assess risk by venturing an opinion or two (guessing), or even ignoring any underlying risk. One way in which "risk" can be discussed among a group of people who are not risk analysts is as follows: Because all alternative bundles except "status quo" involve doing something the company has never done before, "risk" can be used as a subjective measure of the likelihood that it can implement the bundle successfully. Some alternatives are sure to score "higher" or "lower" than others when risk is viewed this way.

- *Amount of investment required*—This criterion is one of practicality. If a particular strategic alternative requires an amount of capital the firm does not have or cannot secure, then it shouldn't even be considered a bona fide alternative, because it fails to meet the criterion of feasibility. Of course, it could borrow more money, but it must be careful not to exceed some value of debt-to-equity ratio required by its creditors, or increase its debt to the point where its cash flow cannot service the debt. Obtaining equity capital may be relatively easy for a public company that has been performing well, but not so for a private company. In certain circumstances, the firm could go public and raise some equity capital; in other circumstances, that may not be possible. A firm could find a partner to share some of the risk and put up some of the capital required. But in this case, profits from the strategy must also be shared. Finally, being acquired by the right company could provide the capital needed to finance a strategy, but this step is drastic and should be taken only in the best interests of the company, not just as a means of raising capital.

- *Return on investment (ROI) and breakeven point*—Even when a company can come up with the investment required by a particular alternative, an appropriate criterion might be return on investment (a profitability measure) and how soon the investment can be recouped (breakeven point in months). Clearly an alternative with a much shorter breakeven point is more attractive to a firm with scarce resources, and one with a higher ROI is more attractive to a firm for which ROI is a critical measure of performance.

- *Match with the existing company culture*—All other things being equal, a firm would choose an alternative that suited its existing corporate culture to one that needed a different culture to make the strategy succeed. Just as "form follows function," so also does "culture follow strategy." This means that changing the culture to support the right strategy might be preferable to limiting a company to a strategy that fits the existing culture, or where the existing culture constrains the choice of strategy. Having said that, firms that try to change their strategy assume their culture will also change, then find the strategy almost impossible to implement because the unchanged culture is impeding it. It is well known that changing a corporate culture is very, very difficult and, for large organizations, takes a lot of time. If every alternative considered required the culture to change, the alternative that would require the least change should, perhaps, be chosen.

- *Attainment of a core competence or competitive advantage*—If a firm does not have a core competence or competitive advantage, it should certainly try to attain one, because competing without one results in below-average industry profits and a weak competitive position. Thus, the firm should look for a strategic alternative that would, in time, provide it with a core competence and competitive advantage. If the firm already possesses these attributes, then the alternative that increases the size (e.g., lead time over competitors) or duration of the competitive advantage, both of which are components of sustainability, the most should be preferred.

- *Increasing its bargaining power*—If the industry in which a firm competes has little or no bargaining power with its market (customers) or suppliers, its profitability will be low or sub par and competitive conditions very difficult. Clearly in such a situation, improving its bargaining power and giving it some leverage is highly desirable. One of the most effective ways of doing this is through differentiating. So, would any of the alternatives in question increase the firm's bargaining power with either its customers or suppliers?

- *Timing*—There may be issues of timing to consider among the alternatives in question. Some alternatives are sensitive to when they are implemented, such as accelerating introduction of a new product or entering a particular market. If implementing an alternative now increases its likelihood of success as opposed to doing it later, this may be reason enough to choose it, all other things being equal. Conversely, if doing it now reduces any advantage you otherwise might have, such as investing in a market push just as the economy turns down sharply or when a competitor introduces a better and cheaper product, that may be reason enough to reject the alternative.

- *Clearly defined value proposition*—You will find it easier to articulate a value proposition for some alternatives than for others, and some value propositions are stronger (more persuasive) than others.

- *Passion and Be the Best in the World*—Inspired by Jim Collins's Hedgehog Concept in his book *Good to Great,* a management team that seriously wants to be best in the world at what the company does would select only that alternative bundle about which it feels passionate and believes would allow it to be the best in the world. (On reflection, for companies using this criterion, they would not need any other.)

As was stated earlier, while this list contains useful criteria for most corporate situations, the criteria you ultimately use in your analysis must fit the organization you are analyzing. For example, most of these criteria do not fit the circumstances of a nonprofit organization. The strategic-planning process described in Appendix C, of an academic department at a university, used the following criteria to help it choose from among several alternatives:

- In the best interests of the department's faculty

- Raises the quality of education and programs

- Enhances reputation with employers

- Increases the department's finances

- Makes the department more competitive externally

Other criteria not mentioned so far include:

- Maintaining or increasing a technological lead

- Developing a global presence

The list is really endless. It depends on your company and what success means to it. Try also not to use similar criteria such as profitability and return on investment, or revenue growth and market share.

Apply the Criteria

Except in the case of using the above-stated criterion about "being the best in the world" in your quest for the best strategy, you should choose *several* of these criteria to evaluate the bundles. Which you choose is entirely up to you and your management team. In fact, you might "play" with several combinations of criteria just to learn of the bundles' sensitivity to various combinations of criteria, and to arm yourself against questions that might be asked of you when you present your analysis to others. In addition, and this applies more to practitioners than students, you should supplement this analysis with detailed forecasts and analyses. For example, to assess which bundle might yield the most revenues were each one implemented, you should conduct a more detailed sales forecast for each bundle over the planning horizon (three or five years). Similarly, profitability and shareholder-value analyses should be conducted, rather than using "guesses." Even though such projections are still estimates and based on assumptions, they require more reflection and thought, and so should be more valuable.

Notice also that many of these criteria are alternative purposes to doing strategic planning in the first place. (Look again at the definition of strategic planning in Chapter 1.) The purposes that are important to an organization will also be the purposes it chooses as criteria to select a preferred bundle.

To evaluate the bundles against multiple criteria, it is useful to have some method or scoring system that enables the results of using each criterion to be consolidated. Table 6.2 illustrates the method.

The first (subjective) issue is to choose a subset of these criteria including any other criterion that makes sense for the company but is not on the list. Secondly, you should assign a rating from 0–10 for some criteria

Table 6.2   Criteria Matrix—Assessing Alternative Bundles against Criteria (unweighted method)

Criteria	Alternative A	Alternative B	Alternative C
Shareholder value	9.0	7.0	8.0
Change in culture required	−6.5	−8.0	−7.0
Core competencies/competitive advantage	6.5	7.5	9.0
Investment required	−7.0	−8.5	−9.5
Revenues	8.0	8.0	9.0
Profitability	7.0	7.5	8.5
Totals	**17.0**	**13.5**	**18.0**

and zero to −10 for others (see Table 6.3). Rate the bundles against each criterion independently of any other criterion. When all the ratings are done, see which alternative has the higher or highest total score.

Experience with using this method has shown that some criteria are positively correlated and some negatively correlated. An example of the former is revenues—an alternative that might yield a lot of revenues or high revenue growth is good for the company, but only a little revenue or low revenue growth is bad. The two go in the *same* direction so to speak (lot (high) − good, little (low) − bad), so the criterion "revenues," or "revenue growth" if you prefer, is positively correlated. An example of the latter is "size of investment required"—an alternative requiring a lot of investment is bad for the company, but only a little investment is good. The two go in opposite directions (lot − bad, little − good), so this criterion is negatively correlated. Table 6.3 shows 13 criteria and whether they are positively or negatively correlated:

For positively correlated criteria (identified as P in SAM[tw]), rate the alternatives against them using a scale from 0 to 10, 10 being best. Use subjective estimates; the absolute value of your rating is less important than spacing them according to your belief as to how close or far apart the alternatives are. It is relative ratings that are critical. For negatively correlated criteria (identified as N in SAM[tw]), use a scale of −10 to 0, 0 being best. Thus, an alternative that is not risky at all would get a 0 score, one that is moderately risky a score of −4 to −5, and an extremely risky one a score of −8 to −10.

In Table 6.2, the "quantitative" winner is alternative C. However, the total score of alternative A is so close to that of C that it makes arguing for C being the best alternative more difficult. This is where other considerations might take over. If market share is very important to the company (most revenues), or profitability, or if the company badly needs a core competence or competitive advantage, then choose C. But the table shows that alternative C requires the most investment, and if the firm couldn't raise the needed capital, that could be the one reason to reject it. (Of course, alternative C should not have made it as a bundle if the needed capital couldn't be raised—feasibility is one of the four criteria for creating bundles.) The two advantages that A has over C are the least change in corporate culture and the biggest boost in shareholder value. The diffi-

Table 6.3 Positively and Negatively Correlated Criteria

Positively Correlated (P)	Negatively Correlated (N)
Revenues or revenue growth	Capital investment required
Profits or profit growth	Change in culture required
Contribution to shareholder value	Competitive retaliation
Return on investment	Time to breakeven
Adverse effect on competitors	Overall riskiness
Strength of value proposition	
Gaining or extending a competitive advantage	
Increasing its bargaining power	

culty with A is that the strategy is unlikely to yield a competitive advantage. This illustration is hypothetical and unrelated to the Carmike example presented in Table 6.1.

To avoid the situation where you have to deal with two alternatives that achieve almost equal ratings, revise your selection of criteria and your ratings until you have a clear winner by at least three points. While this has the semblance of "fixing" the result, it is not. Whoever said that your first attempt at using criteria and doing the ratings is suddenly your final result and one you must stick with when doing your final recommendations? You are still in an "analysis" mode, and are free to try different criteria and ratings until you are satisfied you have something you can defend. After all, defending and being comfortable with your choice of strategy is what this whole exercise is about. It is that ultimate defense before your top management, board of directors—or professor, as the case may be, that will keep you from "fixing" the ratings to yield a preordained result. Anyway, a preordained or poorly argued result can be spotted a mile away and will damage your credibility. So while you are doing this analysis, remember to choose only that alternative that you can argue for persuasively, and use the scoring system to help you do that. The *criteria matrix* and the associated process of selecting criteria and rating your bundles against them is simply an opportunity for you to develop arguments you can use to defend or "sell" your preferred choice to others. It is your thinking time. It is a fallacy that using numbers makes the result more "accurate."

You may also do this analysis using a weighted method, as shown in Table 6.4 using the values of Table 6.2 but adding some weights. Each alternative has two columns: The first is the rating, and the second the product of the weight *and* the rating. Sometimes, it makes a difference, but not in this example.

The danger with using such a quantitative, but still subjective, method to choose a strategic alternative is that it invites criticism precisely because your criteria and ratings may not—in fact, will not—match anyone else's. (You will find your results very sensitive to the criteria you choose. Use shared or consensus ratings among a group of managers as one way to get around this problem, and do try out different combinations of criteria.) Its

Table 6.4 Criteria Matrix—Assessing Alternative Bundles Against Criteria (weighted method)

Criteria	Weight	Alternative A		Alternative B		Alternative C	
Shareholder value	20	9.0	180.0	7.0	140.0	8.0	160.0
Company culture*	13	−6.5	−84.5	−8.0	−104.0	−7.0	−91.0
Core competencies/ Competitive advantage	15	6.5	97.5	7.5	112.5	9.0	135.0
Investment required	12	−7.0	−84.0	−8.5	−102.0	−9.5	−114.0
Revenues	25	8.0	200.0	8.0	200.0	9.0	225.0
Profitability	15	7.0	105.0	7.5	112.5	8.5	127.5
Totals	100		414.0		359.0		442.5

principal value, however, is to force you to test your alternatives against different criteria in case other people believe such criteria are important, in which case you will have "done your homework" and will be able to discuss—and perhaps refute—another person's point of view.

The example illustrates that you *will* encounter alternatives with pros and cons that make the final decision difficult. In the event of a stalemate, the chairman of the board or CEO could cast the deciding vote. At least you know that whichever alternative you choose, it will be one that's good for the company—one of the key criteria for creating the alternative in the first place—and will lead to success if implemented well. The only thing you won't know is whether in the circumstances it really was the best one, and no one will know this for certain until several years have passed, giving us the benefit of hindsight.

Summary

This chapter introduced and outlined a method for coming up with the key strategic issues that a company or organization faces, a set of mutually exclusive, plausible, worthwhile, and varied "bundles" or strategic alternatives (akin to business models), and a useful technique for evaluating them against criteria and choosing a preferred bundle. In the process, it discusses the following related topics:

- Why companies and managers often do not take the time and trouble to find out whether the strategy they want to adopt is really the best one under the circumstances.

- How creativity and strategic thinking can improve both the strategic issues and alternative bundles that are developed.

- What makes for good—as opposed to mediocre—alternative bundles.

- Ways of challenging your thinking to come up with the best bundles possible (strategic thinking in action).

- Useful criteria with which to evaluate the alternative bundles.

- Not to rely solely on the numerical scoring system for evaluating the alternative bundles, but to use the analysis to think through the choices ("do the homework") and sharpen one's arguments for choosing the best one.

Notes

1. Dennis Rheault, "Freshening Up Strategic Planning: More than Fill-in-the-Blanks," *Journal of Business Strategy* 24, no. 6 (2003): 33.

2. See Thomas Marx, "Removing the Obstacles to Effective Strategic Planning," *Long Range Planning* 24, no. 4 (August 1991): 21–28; and Henry Mintzberg, "The Fall and Rise of Strategic Planning," *Harvard Business Review* 72 (January/February 1994): 107–114.

3. Marjorie A. Lyles, "Identifying and Developing Strategic Alternatives," Chapter 10 in *The Portable MBA in Strategy,* Liam Fahey and Robert M. Randall, eds. (New York: Wiley, 1994), 274.

4. Ibid.

5. Ibid., 279

6. Ibid., 278

7. Edward de Bono, *Serious Creativity: Using the Power of Lateral Thinking to Create New Ideas* (HarperBusiness, 1992), 121–128.

8. James F. Bandrowski, *Corporate Imagination Plus: Five Steps to Translating Innovative Strategies into Action* (New York: Free Press, 1990), 31–39.

9. Ibid., 33–39.

10. Gerald Nadler and Shozo Hibino, *Breakthrough Thinking: the Seven Principles of Creative Problem-Solving* (Roseville, CA: Prima, 1990). See also Gerald Nadler and Shozo Hibino, with John Farrell, *Creative Solution Finding: The Triumph of Full-Spectrum Creativity over Conventional Thinking* (Roseville, CA Prima, 1995), 296–297.

11. Henry Mintzberg, *The Fall and Rise of Strategic Planning* (New York: Free Press, 1994).

12. Henry Mintzberg, "The Fall and Rise of Strategic Planning," *Harvard Business Review* 72 (January/February 1994):111.

13. Ibid., 111.

14. Based on Marilyn L. Taylor, "Carmike Cinemas, Inc.," in *Strategic Management: Text and Cases,* 8th ed., Arthur A. Jr. Thompson, A. J. Strickland III, eds. (New York: Irwin, 1996), 897–916.

15. Dave Francis, *Step-by-Step Competitive Strategy* (London: Routledge, 1994), 131–132.

16. Quoted in Joan Magretta, with Nan Stone, *What Management Is: How It Works and Why It's Everyone's Business* (New York: Free Press, 2002), 71.

17. Bandrowski, 61.

18. Richard Rumelt, "The Evaluation of Business Strategy," Section 1.3 in, *Strategy: Process, Content, Context,* 2nd ed., by Bob de Witt and Rob Meyer (Cincinnati, OH: International Thomson Business Press, 1998), 34.

19. Alfred Rappaport, *Creating Shareholder Value: A Guide for Managers and Investors,* rev. ed. (New York: Free Press, 1997).

7

Proposing Recommendations

The recommendations phase brings the strategic-planning process to a close that ultimately allows for implementing the recommendations—and the strategy. Recommendations include setting objectives, defining strategic intent, identifying key programs to achieve the objectives, and exploring triggers and contingencies if things do not go as planned. Creating or revising mission and vision statements are also part of this final phase if the organization's existing statements are no longer valid or if it desires such statements.

It may seem odd to some that setting objectives comes after choosing a strategy. They may find it more logical to first set objectives and then choose a strategy to achieve them. The truth is, it doesn't matter which is set first. Ideally, they should be set together, that is, iteratively until they fit with each other. But that is hard to do. Deciding on a strategy first makes sense for three reasons:

- It follows naturally from identifying the company's key strategic issues, which in turn follow logically from the situation analysis phase.

- Construing the selection of a strategic alternative bundle as creating a road map or direction for the company, one can then turn one's attention to deciding how far and how fast to go along that road (i.e., objectives).

- Deciding on the strategy first allows many criteria to be used, enriching the assessment and ultimately the choice of strategy.

In addition, there are two problems with setting objectives first:

- Where does the objective—the number—come from? Other than the case where the current strategy is being continued, setting an objective first lacks a context. For example, to meet a 20% revenue growth objective in two years may be possible by expanding internationally, but not by investing more in R&D. Yet the latter may be the better strategy in the long run. Wouldn't it make more sense to ask which of the two were capable of generating more revenues over the next several years? Wasn't the 20% number derived "from thin air"?

- The objective (say, revenue growth) becomes the sole criterion for picking a strategy, that is, having set an objective, a strategy is chosen that will best enable the company to meet the objective. Wouldn't it make more sense to use, say, revenue growth as one of *several* important criteria? Would one be as content to achieve the revenue growth objective with negative net earnings, for example?

In the end, whichever one is done first—the strategy or the objectives—they must both match, that is, be consistent with one another. The strategy determines how the company will compete and where it is going, while the objectives determine the rate of growth and how fast the company can go (what it can achieve) given its resources, capabilities, and aspirations. Great care must be taken to distinguish objectives from strategies. For example, executives often talk of "high growth," "moderate growth," and "low growth" strategies. Clearly, these growth "strategies" are really objectives reflecting a high, medium, or low increase in sales or revenues. Strategies constitute any of the broad actions shown in Figure 6.2 in the previous chapter.

Setting Objectives

While this model advocates setting objectives after deciding on a preferred strategic alternative, the two must be so well matched that an observer would imagine that they were done together. It is impossible to evaluate or judge a strategy without knowing what the objectives are, and likewise impossible to judge whether the objectives make sense without knowing the strategy.

Consider this hypothetical example. A company decides to pursue an accelerated product development strategy and, at the same time, change its fairly conservative culture into an innovative one that also values quality. Is this a good strategy? It is impossible to tell unless you know what the company is trying to achieve, that is, know its objectives. If you were now told that in three years' time the company expected sales to double and profits to increase by 50%, and that it had the resources to carry out this preferred strategy, now one has a basis for either criticizing the strategy or believing that it will work (or even criticizing the objectives). So a strategy without objectives is meaningless. However, there are some companies that choose a different strategy and implicitly decide to "see what we can achieve with it." In a sense this is not to have any objectives, but these kinds of companies are rare.

Consider a second hypothetical example. A company whose sales have been flat and that has been losing money for two years wants to increase sales by 20% next year and at least break even. Are these good objectives? Again, it is impossible to tell unless you know how the company intends to achieve them, which means knowing its strategy and programs. Merely trying to increase sales, typically a market development strategy, may be insufficient. The company's product may be outdated and its cost structure too high. So with the competitive environment the company faces, it will take a well-thought strategy to give an observer confidence that the objectives could and would be achieved. Again, objectives without a strategy are meaningless.

Setting objectives is a three-step process:

1. *Decide on a small number of measures critical to firm performance*—such as revenues, profit (choose which of several make sense for the company), debt structure, and the like. There is no rule as to how many objectives a firm should have. But the more it has, the more difficult it becomes to achieve them and the greater is the likelihood that some objectives will conflict with others, that is, achieving one will result in worse performance on another. About three to four companywide objectives is typical, one of which is revenues, or market share if it can be accurately measured, and some kind of profit measure: EBIT, NIBT, NIAT, EPS, ROI, ROE, ROS, or ROA—NIAT being the most commonly used.[*] The remaining one or two can be anything of critical importance to the company such as sales per square foot for a retailer, operating income per screen for a movie-theater chain, debt–equity ratio for a fairly leveraged company, and the like. Do not include cost-reduction objectives as one of them because any efforts to reduce costs will show up in improved profit; cost-reduction objectives are important only at an operational rather than strategic level. Similarly, other operational or programmatic objectives, such as number of new products produced, percentage of international sales, number of retail outlets served, or increasing production capacity or throughput by X%, while important, should not be part of this set.

2. *Decide on annual values for these critical measures for the next three years*—This is difficult to do well. Theory tells us that objectives, to be effective, should be set at a "challenging" level—set too high, they demotivate because people consider them impossible to achieve, and set too low, they also demotivate because they are too easily achieved. So how to find that perfect level? The following five-step process may help:

   a. Extrapolate from historical data to establish *initial* values for each objective for the next three years. This is easier to do when you have at least five years of historical data available.

   b. Ask yourself what external and internal forces or changes might act to decrease these beginning values over time, such as intensifying competition, scarcity of borrowed funds, a conservative culture, rapidly accelerating technological innovation in the industry with which the firm cannot keep up, and so on. Make a list and, for each item, indicate, even sub-

---

[*] EBIT = Earnings Before Interest & Tax; NIBT = Net Income Before Tax; NIAT = Net Income After Tax; EPS = Earnings Per Share; ROI = Return On Investment; ROE = Return On Equity; ROS = Return On Sales; and ROA = Return On Assets.

jectively, the strength of the negative effect on the objective (H, M, or L).

c. Ask yourself what external and internal forces or changes might act to increase these beginning values over time such as a new strategy, companywide training, a new CEO, a change to a more productive culture, new quality programs, strategic alliances, a new advertising campaign, and so on. Make a list and, for each item, indicate, even subjectively, the strength of the positive effect on the objective (H, M, or L).

d. Compare the two lists and decide, for each objective, whether the initial value deserves to be increased or decreased and by how much, depending on the extent to which the positive effects outweigh the negative effects or vice versa. Create a "first cut" of each objective for each of the next three years.

e. This is the most important step, and often omitted. Get feedback from those who are going to implement the objectives that your "first-cut" objectives are challenging yet achievable in the circumstances. In fact, get these other people involved in steps (b) through (d) too. For some companies, deciding on such strategic objectives cannot be done unless the whole range of operational objectives have been created, thought through, and approved, to make sure that the resources to achieve them are available and that they are feasible to achieve in the timeframe specified. If they have been well designed, achieving operational objectives should result in automatically achieving the strategic objectives.

3. *Check that the objectives match the preferred strategy*—The preferred strategy and the set of objectives must be consistent with each other. For example, if the strategy decided upon is aggressive, the objectives set should also be aggressive. If the strategy is a turnaround, the objectives should reflect this unusual state, showing first stabilization at a lower level followed by growth consistent with the new strategy. If the strategy is designed to maintain market position in a highly competitive, mature market, the objectives should not show high growth, but reflect the status quo to a high degree. If the strategy requires a period of heavy investment before it pays off, the objectives should reflect that reality. Remember, the objectives indicate what the company considers to be successful performance over time given the changing realities of the industry, marketplace, and the company's own strategies, resources, and commitments. Thus, not achieving these objectives (indicators) means less-than-successful performance, while meeting or exceeding them indicates intended or superlative performance in the circumstances.

One final point on the kind of objectives to set here. The above discussion implicitly assumes that these are company or companywide objectives, rather than partial, functional, or operational objectives. Examples of these kinds of objectives (all of which could well show up during implementation of a strategy) include:

- *Partial*

  - International sales to increase by 10%/yr (does not address domestic sales).

  - Sales from new products created during the past three years to total 40% of total sales (does not address sales from existing products).

  - Sales to mass merchandisers must grow by 30%/yr (does not address sales to other retail channels).

- *Functional*

  - Double the number of retail outlets (marketing).

  - Increase throughput by 5%/yr (production).

  - Redesign the product to reduce purchasing costs by 5% (engineering).

- *Operational*

  - Reduce costs by 12%/yr (cost-reduction programs are important in most companies, but the higher-order objective of net profit takes this into account).

  - Improve quality by reducing the costs of quality by 30% (insofar as improvement in quality is measured this way, it is taken into account by the higher-order objective of net profit; however, it could also be measured by a customer-satisfaction index or a ranking by J. D. Power and Associates).

  - Improve the sales "hit rate" to 6% at year-end from 2% at year-end (this would be one of marketing's operational objectives). (See Hit Rate.)

So take care to set *companywide* objectives in sales or revenues, net profits (or other profit objective), and one or two other ratios or nonfinancial measures that the company as a whole would commit to achieve.

Identifying Major Programs

For purposes of the strategic plan, only the major programs or operational tasks need be identified. (Later, during operational planning, an essential ac-

---

Hit Rate

Hit rate is defined as the ratio of number of customers who actually purchased something to the number visited over a given period (per month, quarter, or year). Hit rate can also refer to the number of proposals that win contracts to the total number written over a given period: per month, quarter, or year.

tivity before anything can be implemented, the programs and objectives are "fleshed out" for and by every operating unit and department in the company.) The programs can and should include successful and needed programs that the company is currently implementing. In addition, the company may have to initiate new programs called for by the strategy. Programs implemented the very next year are often called *tactics*.

Every strategy implies a set of programs, as shown in general form in Table 7.1.

Other common programs include hiring a new CEO or Vice President, seeking a strategic alliance with an external organization (an international distributor that knows the market in a particular country, an offshore manufacturer that can produce the required quality at a lower cost, a university laboratory to lower R&D costs, or a small company that has a new technology), automating a production process, networking or upgrading the company's computers, installing an integrated accounting system, embarking on a planned-change program, or improving product quality. Remember that key programs are already included in the chosen strategic-alternative bundle.

Bundles should also contain the method by which the bundle, if implemented, would be financed. This topic merits some discussion. An organization typically generates funds from three sources:

- *Operations and other internal sources*—such as net income after taxes, depreciation, sales to dispose of excess inventories, factoring accounts receivable (i.e., selling them at a discount to a factoring firm for ready cash), or selling assets no longer needed.

- *Assuming additional debt consistent with the financial structure of the organization*—such as getting extended lines of credit from banks or certain suppliers or leasing rather than buying equipment or facilities.

- *Adding new long-term debt or equity funding that would change the financial structure of the firm*—such as issuing new stock or taking on additional long-term debt.

Funds available to the business are usually of two kinds: (1) "baseline" funds that are needed to support the firm's current business and ongoing operations, that is, pay current operating expenses, maintain adequate working capital, and maintain current plant and equipment, and (2) "strategic" funds that could be invested in new strategic initiatives, that is, purchase assets such as facilities, equipment, and inventory, increase working capital, increase R&D or marketing/ promotion expenses, or acquire another company.[1] For example, increasing market share usually requires strategic funds, while maintaining market share needs only baseline funds. Firms are in serious trouble when they do not even have the level of baseline funds they need to maintain current operations.

Contingency Planning

To counteract Murphy's Law ("If anything can go wrong, it will,"), it is a good idea to contemplate what could go wrong in the future (a trigger) and what the company would do differently were that to happen   (a contingency).

Table 7.1 Program Components of Common Strategies

Product Development	Market Expansion	Acquisition	Turnaround	Diversification	Differentiation
R&D programs	Market research	Define criteria	Control cash	Choose industry	Marketing. research
Engineering	Hire sales force	Search lists	See creditors	Set criteria	Develop concept
Prototypes	Train salesmen	Analyze candidates	See customers	Acquire company	Invest capital
Design Engineering.	Ad campaign	Due diligence	Divest assets	Invest capital	Ad campaign
Testing	Distribution channels	Negotiate deal	Reduce staff	Negotiate objectives	PR campaign
Quality program		Get financing	Form new strategy		Redesign product
		Consolidate			Raise price

We therefore talk about *trigger-contingency pairs,* typically one or two that pertain to next year—the short term—and one or two that may occur three years from now—the long term. The planning horizon, however, can be different. For example, a company like Boeing views the next several years as "short-term," about 10–15 years as "medium term," and 20–30 years as long term." Companies in the fashion business view two weeks as "short term" and a season (4–6 months) as "long term." For most companies, however, the long term of five years has now shrunk to three years because of the rapid pace of change, especially in high-technology industries.

Triggers

Triggers should be specific and quantitative; otherwise the company will not know when to invoke the contingency plan. It is no use saying, for example, "If profits decline," or "When things get tough." Decline how much? Get how tough? Even when trying to address phenomena that cannot be measured—such as a competitor infiltrating your territory or, for the movie theater paradigm discussed in the last chapter, "worse" movies being made in a certain year—try to gauge their effect on your sales. For example, if they were to cause your sales to decline, would you do something differently if your sales fell below target projections by 5%, 10%, or 15%? In this way, you will monitor something you constantly measure, and so can bring into play the contingency plan at just the right moment.

Triggers also come from assumptions you make about the future that are "soft," that is, about which you lack confidence. For example, if you are engaged in strategic planning and your company is sensitive to interest rates, you may not know what is going to happen to interest rates next year. You may have tried to obtain information from various economic forecasts on this variable but, sadly, all of them differ in their predictions. So here is something you can do. Assume that interest rates are not going up next year (if this makes sense) and base your planning on that. However, because the assumption is "soft," create a trigger that admits the possibility that interest rates could go up: "If interest rates go up by more than six percentage points, then . . ." (substitute any number you like in place of the six).

Triggers can also emerge from the timing of various imminent occurrences. For example, if new federal legislation is being created to nationalize healthcare, you may be unsure if this would take place next year or two to three years from now. So create your plans with your best assumption in mind—for example, no healthcare legislation will be enacted during the period of the planning horizon. However, because the assumption may be "soft," create a trigger, too, that says, "If healthcare legislation were enacted within the next two years, then . . ." Notice that this trigger is quantitative. You can tell exactly when it happens, and can therefore invoke the contingency plan. Similarly, you may want to do something differently if two competitors merge, or if quota restrictions into some foreign country are imposed or lifted.

For companies focused on increasing sales or market share, it is tempting and understandable to create triggers having to do with not meeting revenue objectives. Once is perfectly fine, but to have such a trigger every year gives the impression of obsessive focus in one area. Management is about directing and coordinating many aspects of a company to work together seamlessly to create value, and indeed things could go wrong in many areas, not just in failing to make a revenue objective. So make a list of all the possible things that could go wrong or where your assumptions are soft, and choose the most likely of them as your triggers. Try to choose a different trigger for the short term from what you choose in the long term.

Contingencies

Contingencies are *precursors* to contingency plans. They are a response to a particular trigger, what you think a company should do differently if that trigger occurred. Later, when the strategic plan is operational, the contingency should be translated into a contingency plan complete with who is responsible for it, its budget and schedule, and who must keep it relevant as conditions change.

Good contingencies should meet three conditions:

- *Do not renege on the adopted preferred strategy*—For example, suppose you chose a market-expansion strategic bundle, but have reason to believe it would be difficult to implement and pull off. If sales were to drop more than 10% from target projections at any time, do not put, as a contingency, "Cancel the market-expansion strategy and implement a differentiation strategy." Once you do that, you are in effect saying that the strategic bundle you chose was not a good choice, and you will instantly lose credibility. Besides, companies cannot—and should not—go through life changing their strategies at the first sign of difficulty. Strategies typically take anywhere from two to five years to implement, and you must give the chosen strategy a chance to succeed by not changing it until you are absolutely certain it is not working. So for any new or modified strategy you are implementing that does not seem to be working, suspect first your execution of the strategy, *but not the strategy itself.* That way your contingency should focus on operational changes you could make to enable the strategy to succeed, not changing the strategy itself. Examples are:

  · Change the ad campaign, or change advertising agencies.

  · Replace the VP Marketing (or any other VP).

  · Give the salespeople additional or more technical training.

  · Do additional and specific market research.

  · Increase the rate of new product development.

  · Broaden your distribution channels.

  · Increase links to your customers and increase their switching costs.

- *Do not put down something that the company is already doing*—Think about it. What the company has been doing up to the time the trigger is invoked is what got the company into trouble in the first place. If sales are not meeting expectations, do not put as a contingency, "Continue advertising" or "Do more R&D." The company is already doing those things and, clearly, they have not helped. So think of something it can do differently, that is, an adjustment to its operations or execution, one that can be implemented quickly.

- *Make the contingency a solution to the problem implied in the trigger*—If inadequate profits are the problem, the contingency should be directed towards increasing profits, not sales. If market share is the problem, do not suggest lowering costs as the contingency, even if it is something different; the two are unrelated.

Because contingencies are in fact back-up plans, they have to be spelled out in great detail, and those responsible for developing them and carrying them out must know who they are and what they must do. Those details are added during the operational phase prior to implementation, and are intentionally outside the scope of this book. Companies that go this extra mile will reap rewards in three ways:

- They will be better prepared for specific uncertainties than companies that have no triggers and contingencies, especially if they work to adjust the contingencies over time as conditions change to make them current and workable.

- They will become more adept at anticipating what might go wrong and come up with better triggers and contingencies over time.

- They will appreciate the need to be alert to key changes in the environment and their company and, over time, create a more flexible company culture

Summary

Once the strategic direction of the firm or organization has been decided, several strategic decisions also need to be made, namely, the strategic intent, a limited set of annual companywide objectives, and the major programs—particularly new programs. The firm or organization must also implement key trigger/contingency pairs in preparation for anything that might go wrong and revise vision and mission statements if necessary.

This chapter covers those topics in detail, and offers addition guidance in three related areas:

- The reasons why strategies and objectives must be synchronized.

- How to set challenging strategic objectives.

- How to identify triggers and develop reasonable contingencies that address them.

Notes

1. Alan J. Rowe (with the collaboration of Richard O. Mason, Karl E. Dickel, and Peter A. Westcott), *Computer Models for Strategic Management* (Reading, PA: Addison-Wesley, 1987), 43–44.

Part Three

DOING STRATEGIC PLANNING

8

Managing the Strategic-Planning Process

In a company, strategic planning is usually carried out by a group of people and to get such a group to coordinate their efforts and work as one, a formal process needs to be established. This chapter presents guidelines for carrying out strategic planning in a company, and builds on the discussion in Chapters 4 through 7, which describe a process for conducting a strategic analysis. However, with the variation in the abilities of different companies to perform strategic planning and implement a formal process, such guidelines are difficult to write. Nevertheless, initial assumptions—right or wrong—were made in formulating them:

- Most small- to medium-sized organizations do not have a good understanding of strategic planning and, therefore, either do not perform it or do something they "think" is strategic planning.

- Companies that do strategic planning and use a formal process could benefit by "benchmarking" their process with the guidelines presented here.

- Many companies do strategic planning without reflecting (i.e., without the benefit of any strategic thinking) on whether it is done well or provides the organization with value.

Setting up the Process

Deciding to Do Strategic Planning

Even though an individual manager believes in and can perform strategic planning, the rest of the company and the other top managers need to participate. Ultimately the decision to do strategic planning comes from the CEO, the owner, or a similar executive body. He or she must believe that it is worthwhile and will benefit the company—hopefully from experiencing successful strategic planning in the past or having learned strategic planning as part of an MBA program, continuing education, or working with a consultant with expertise in strategic planning. A perception of *need* is important for the leader, too. He or she must see their company at a crossroads, where it would benefit from strategic planning. After all, as the saying goes, "necessity is the mother of invention." If the company is to either do strategic planning for the first time or change the way it has been doing it in the past, the top person or persons in the organization must be 100% behind it. Persuasion, nevertheless, is often part of achieving this 100%:

- Give the CEO a short quiz to take to determine how strategic the organization is. (See Strategy Quizzes.)

- Give the CEO some of your favorite articles to read on strategic planning.

- Explain the benefits of strategic planning to the CEO, that he or she can:

  - Understand the many changes occurring both outside and inside the organization that affect it, including how the industry, competition, and markets are changing. Often the preexisting understanding of these is imperfect.

  - Thoroughly assess the company's recent financial performance and competitive strength, and whether it has a core competence or competitive advantage. A leader may well have his or her opinion, but would not know what the planning group might think or conclude.

  - Identify the key strategic issues the company faces, as well as all its viable and desirable strategic alternatives, many of which would not be known without carrying out the process and doing strategic thinking.

  - Choose the strategy that most benefits the company—the best in the circumstances—and which the company is excited to pursue. Again, good planning demands that those who implement the plan participate in formulating it, and this is impossible without going through the process.

  - Have operational plans that achieve the objectives and strategic intent. This forms the foundation for developing accountability and the company budget, something that may not be tied to a viable and preferred strategy.

  - Achieve the ultimate purposes for the company—increasing its shareholder value, helping it deliver more value to its customers, and improving its competitiveness and reputation. In other words, can the company currently measure performance on these important indicators?

Most importantly, explain to the CEO (or owner, whatever the title of the organizational head is) that the process of strategic planning educates and enlightens all the key managers in the company about what is changing in the world, resulting in a shared perspective of those changes, the options the company has in the circumstances, and ultimately what the company should do and why. With such a shared understanding—and one

Strategy Quizzes

One such quiz can be found at **www.futurebydesign.biz**.

FUTURE BY DESIGN

Create your future by design, not by default   Home | Contact Us

Strategy Quiz
What Would You Do?   **How Strategic Is Your Organization?**
Strategic Resources
Services Offered
Benefits of Engaging Us
Our Experience
Examples of Previous
Engagements
About Dr. Abraham

How Healthy Is Your Business?
Answer the following questions either with a YES or NO by clicking on the
checkboxes next to it. Your answers will be calculated based on the number of
NOs you answered.

1. Are you realizing the full potential of your company and people? ☐ Yes ☐ No

2. Do you have a five-year vision for the company? ☐ Yes ☐ No

3. If you do, do you believe the organization can achieve it? ☐ Yes ☐ No

4. Are you pleased with your company's profitability over the last three years? ☐ Yes ☐ No

5. Do you believe the value of your company is increasing over time? ☐ Yes ☐ No

6. Are your company's sales (revenues) growing fast enough? ☐ Yes ☐ No

7. Do you have enough money (including ability to borrow) to get the job done? ☐ Yes ☐ No

8. Do you have a significant advantage over your competitors? ☐ Yes ☐ No

9. Are your products (or services) competitive? ☐ Yes ☐ No

10. Do you know what your costs are? ☐ Yes ☐ No

11. Are you getting new products to market quickly enough? ☐ Yes ☐ No

12. Does your company do strategic planning every year? ☐ Yes ☐ No

13. Can you state what your current strategy is and why it will work? ☐ Yes ☐ No

14. Do you have at least three opportunities you are deciding whether to pursue? ☐ Yes ☐ No

15. Do you know what your company's principal problems are? ☐ Yes ☐ No

16. If so, do you know what to do about them? ☐ Yes ☐ No

17. Do you have a set of annual measurable objectives you are trying to achieve? ☐ Yes ☐ No

18. Are you getting the most out of your people? ☐ Yes ☐ No

19. Do your employees know where the company is going and how it will get there? ☐ Yes ☐ No

20. Is your company culture collaborative, innovative, and trusting? ☐ Yes ☐ No

[Click here for your score] [0]

View Result Here

Credits   Copyright © 2003 Future by Design

they helped create—their willingness and enthusiasm to make the plan operational and implement it is very high. (The last and not always obvious suggestion, of course, is to have him or her read this book.)

If a CEO is still reticent about strategic planning—because of little or no experience in strategic planning, discomfort with change, or a lack of requisite knowledge—suggest that he or she talk to other CEOs or consultants who have such experience. Point out that an experienced consultant would manage the process and teach it to everyone in the organization, especially if strategic planning is being considered for the first time.

Whose Responsibility Is It?

In small companies that perform strategic planning, the CEO or owner typically drives the process. Sometimes, he or she might use a consultant—or an executive within the organization—to conduct the process and help the group decide on the strategies. Most small companies and new ventures, however, do not do strategic planning. The most common reason is that there is only one strategy possible and the company's energies are focused on executing it. Examples are restaurants, retail outlets, or small service businesses. Such companies address strategic planning when faced with several choices or intense competition and, for the first time, are put in a position of not knowing what to do.

In midsize to large companies, the job of controlling the process is typically delegated, even though the responsibility for it never is. Ideally, the director of strategic planning, if there is one, manages the process, otherwise whoever in the opinion of the CEO can do a good job or has some experience with strategic planning (e.g., the CFO, VP Marketing, or another functional VP). If no one wants the assignment or feels they cannot do it, someone from outside is often brought in to do it. If manufacturing, R&D, and distribution can be outsourced, so can facilitating the strategic-planning process. However, only planning and conducting the process and achieving its purposes should be subcontracted to a trusted consultant. The actual decisions must be made by the CEO and managers. They alone are accountable for acting on those decisions and achieving the company's objectives.

The person in charge should make sure all those involved understand what they have to do and give them time to do it. Additionally, he or she should:

- Create standard reporting formats that everyone understands and that facilitate comparisons with later years.

- Create a schedule for the process and then stick to it, except if a company crisis intervenes.

- Remember that these planning tasks are superimposed on people's regular jobs and are likely to produce negative attitudes and reactions. Only if those involved see the activity as crucial for the company—and taken seriously by everyone—will they be motivated to do a good job.

Choosing the Process

As Chapter 3 showed, many models of strategic planning exist. In fact, there are as many models as there are companies and consultants. In the absence of a good process—because the company does not have one or is dissatisfied with the one it has—choose one that meets the following criteria:

- Key company managers must understand it, particularly the person in charge of the process (what it is, what is involved, who should be involved, why it is needed, how to realize the benefit from using it).

- The process must be perceived as appropriate and feasible for the company—in terms of sophistication, complexity, and culture.

- The company must be prepared to commit to the process and its outcomes, that is, to agree to take it seriously and implement those strategies and decisions that result from the process.

The person in charge should explore several different approaches, or invite several consultants—hopefully those who have been recommended by others in one's network—who specialize in this area to discuss their approaches. The process outlined in this book provides a benchmark and the resources to ask good questions when discussing the approaches of others (e.g., consultants).

Hire a consultant to help with doing strategic planning the first time. Ceding this control (and worry) frees managers and executives to participate in the process. Furthermore, a consultant can control the quality of the discussion and strategic ideas that are proposed, as well as ensure that real data and analyses are used as much as possible instead of opinions and pontificating—typically, consultants are more subtle in getting the message across. Finally, a consultant, as facilitator, can make sure that all voices are heard clearly, not just the one or two people who dominate discussions, and that people are not just saying what they think the CEO wants to hear, which is a major problem in many companies. Ideally, a consultant should be trusted and one with whom the CEO is comfortable, who can do a good job of guiding participants in the strategic-planning process that is the best fit for the company. Pay the going rate—getting a "cheap" consultant may result in a process that is flawed and decisions that are very conservative and provide little benefit to the company. Table 8.1 summarizes the benefits of using an expert outside facilitator as opposed to in-house strategic planning.

A Suggested Strategic-Planning Process

The following process would work with firms of almost any size. While there are similarities with the topics and discussion presented in earlier chapters, this process is designed to perform strategic planning in a company. Nevertheless, it is generic and can be tailored to fit your particular company. The process shown in Figure 8.1 has at least ten steps, and could have more to the extent that some of them are broken down into two or more steps.

Perhaps the most crucial element in strategic planning is to involve the right people—particularly those who will be called upon to implement the plan. Different kinds of people going through the same process of strategic planning make completely different decisions and achieve completely different results. So consider carefully who is involved in the process. Do not confine the group to just the top management, but include managers two or three levels down. If this yields a number that becomes unwieldy for simple meetings, you may have to either intentionally limit the number that participate or cascade the meetings from one level to the next to accommodate everyone. What is crucial is to obtain as many different perspectives in the planning process as possible as well as the involvement of people who implement the strategies. The need for a professional facilitator becomes more pronounced the larger the group of people that are involved in the process.

Make decisions you mean to implement   The biggest waste of time and money—and it happens frequently—is to bear the cost of top

Table 8.1 Using an Outside Expert Facilitator versus "In House"

Having an Expert Facilitator	Doing It Alone
Leaves executives free to participate in the process.	One or more executives must manage the process, hence cannot participate fully.
Facilitator applies his or her expertise and experience to guide the process.	Company will miss an outside perspective and the experience of having guided many companies in strategic planning.
Facilitator has experience in designing a suitable process and in meeting process objectives.	Inexperienced facilitators or the absence of a facilitator may result in a process that is poorly controlled and whose objectives are not realized.
Quality of participation rises—all get to participate, even those who do not normally speak up. The facilitator will set ground rules that encourage open communication and honest dialog.	The same people will voice the same old arguments; the same people who like hearing themselves speak will speak. People will offer opinions to support their view, against which no one can argue
Facilitator can recognize "group think" and take steps to eliminate it, as well as instances where people are not being candid, but only saying what the CEO wants to hear.	The group may develop "group think" and not listen to a lone dissenter. Some participants will not speak up or say what needs to be said in front of top management, and whatever top management or the CEO wants is what will transpire.
Presence of paid facilitator ensures that follow-up takes place.	Without any pressure to follow through, people are tempted to go back to their old ways of doing things (and often do).
Imparts a sense of confidence to the participants that the process is going well and that appropriate decisions are being made based on the best information available.	No one will know how good the process or the decisions were, or if things were done correctly. Whatever mistakes were made in previous years will be made again. Companies will fall into the trap of believing their own stories; the status quo will prevail.
Cost of the consultant—not really a cost but an investment when one considers: (a) the training implicit in the facilitation, and (b) the quality of the strategic decisions.	Cost savings that otherwise would have been spent on a consultant, but possibly at the expense of poorer decisions made.

managers meeting at a retreat making important decisions, sometimes with an expensive facilitator, and then no one follows up. The result is back to business as usual. One can only conjecture some possible reasons for why this happens. Perhaps "going through the motions" of strategic planning soothes some executives' consciences. Perhaps they believe that "doing the planning" is all there is to it, a belief that no one has bothered to correct for them. Perhaps it is the golf game at the resort where the retreat is held that has their real interest. However, it is a waste of time just to go through the motions. So do not do it unless it is for real.

The key strategic decisions to be made or at least revisited include the following:

- A vision for the company to aspire to.

- The best strategic bundle it can come up with in the circumstances, even if that happens to be what the company is currently doing.

- Overall companywide objectives.

- Major programs and resource allocations that are to be implemented.

Following through will be much more likely if the participants see these as being the best decisions that could be made, that they are feasible yet challenging to achieve, that some urgency attaches to getting them implemented, and that would result in a stronger and more competitive company. Focusing on a small set of objectives increases the chances of them being attained, considerably lessening the likelihood of conflicting objectives with a larger number, and would help focus the company.

Below, the description of each step in the process shown in Figure 8.1 includes some pointers for making the whole process successful.

1. *Situation Analysis (a)*—Table 8.2 suggests key categories of data that need to be collected in this initial research step. Any time data are collected, try to obtain a copy of the source document or at least a complete citation of the source. Get the most recent data possible. If you are fortunate enough to obtain forecasts, again be sure to record the source, because it has a huge bearing on the credibility of the forecast itself. Finally, appoint key people in the company to act as "gatekeepers" for particular categories of data, and tell everyone in the organization who they are. Everyone can then send items of information or leads about a particular category to these gatekeepers throughout the year. (If you do this throughout the year, this first step is not needed; if not, then allow sufficient time to collect and analyze the data and

Figure 8.1   A Company Strategic-Planning Process

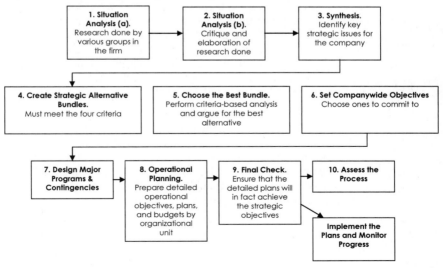

prepare useful summaries.) Every month, these gatekeepers should summarize and make sense of the data collected to-date (e.g., write a summary that is sent to everyone on the planning team and encourage ongoing dialogs).

Do substantial preparation for each step. Research and data collection must be based on fact or analysis, not on opinion. Where you cannot obtain data, for example, on competitors that are privately held, make assumptions and move on. Consider paying for critical data such as economic forecasts or competitive intelligence, and consider it an investment. Also consider adding an economist or competitive-intelligence professional to your permanent staff if it turns out to be cost-effective.

2. *Situation Analysis (b)*—Each gatekeeper should make a brief, 30-minute summary presentation of what is going on in his or her particular category—the categories shown in Table 8.2 are suggested categories; the list should be tailored to the needs of the company in question. Such presentations should be based on the data collected and analyzed during the previous 12 months (or portion thereof if the activity was begun less than 12 months ago), and should include numbers, trends, graphs, and sources wherever possible. The gatekeeper should interpret all the data and conclude with the most significant and relevant facts and trends that will affect the company. This is one way of educating the planning team about changes and implications arising in that particular category, and enough time should be allowed for questions in order for complex issues or trends to be understood (or challenged). (This process should appeal to companies that value structure; an alternative is a series of strategic conversations, as discussed in Chapter 2.)

The presentations should be made into handouts for all participants and sent to the planning team in advance if possible. About 1–2 hours should be enough time.

However, if every category in Table 8.2 were actually assigned, this step would consist of 12 sessions, each lasting 1–2 hours and it would take planning to accomplish. Two categories could be done per session—or a weekend (1.5–2 days) could be taken to do all 12. And it might be possible to squeeze everything into one day if some categories are "light" and consume little time, or if fewer categories were chosen in the first place.

3. *Synthesis*—This step allows the participants to list all critical uncertainties (i.e., the key strategic issues) that could have a positive or negative impact on the company. "Critical," means those issues that must be addressed in the ensuing strategic plan. Take care in this step to get everyone's suggestions first before combining or eliminating any issue.

4. *Create the Strategic Alternative Bundles*—This is a creative activity well suited to an extremely diverse group of people—from different functional areas and levels of the company, with very

different business and industrial backgrounds, men as well as women, and young and seasoned veterans alike.

Starting from the list of strategic alternatives and working

Table 8.2   Categories of Data to Research

Category	Items
Industry	How the industry is changing and why, total industry sales and growth, market shares of top 10–20 firms, details about the segments related to the one in which the company competes (create an "industry map"), an assessment of how attractive the industry is, and so on.
Competitors	Details about the firm's top-10 competitors (especially strategies and strategic intents), core competencies and competitive advantages of each competitor, comparison among the competitors and the company along critical success factors, knowledge of all competitive products and, if possible, about their technologies and next-generation products, financial data on each competitor.
Markets	Size and growth rate of the company's target markets, customers' current and future needs, what value and service the company currently provides customers (from their point of view), perception of brand reputation, how distribution channels are changing, and how price-sensitive the customers are.
Economic Environment	Current and near-term interest rates, inflation rates, unemployment rates, exchange rates with major countries the company does business with, and other key economic indicators.
Technological Environment	The current and forecast state of key technologies underlying the product(s) the industry produces without regard to which firm uses a particular technology, and an assessment of potential technologies that could be relevant to the industry and company, and investments in R&D of key competitors.
Political/ Regulatory Environment	Identification of potential legislation or regulations that could adversely affect the company, background of key legislators involved and who or what is influencing them, and history of bills in Congress (or State Assembly) that relate to potential new legislation.
Social/ Demographic Environment	Any trend with the general populace that might affect what the company is doing, and forecasts and trends of the demographic group(s) the company targets (if applicable).
Company (Marketing/ New Product Development)	Assessment of marketing strategies—sales, distribution, advertising and promotion, exports, brand image, customer service, new product development, and comparison between marketing budget and actual expenditures (could include comparison with competitors' marketing budgets).
Company (Production)	Assessment of production and operations—purchasing efficiency, inventory control, quality, cost-reduction initiatives, distribution, and comparison between production budget and actual expenditures, also trends in gross profit margin.
Company (Engineering/ R&D)	Assessment of progress with current projects, rationale for proceeding with the chosen slate of projects, payoff of recent R&D projects, assessment of pipeline (future) projects, and comparison between engineering/R&D budget and actual expenditures.
Company (Finance)	Assessment of financial performance over the past five years, current financial condition, trends in the financial markets, and the fluctuations in the company's current cost of capital and credit rating.
Company (Core Competence)	An analysis of whether the company has a core competence and, if so, the competitive advantage it gives to the company.

in small groups, each group should come up with its version of alternative bundles and check to see that they meet all four criteria. Formal group meeting time could be devoted to creating the bundles, or this could be assigned to be done before the group as a whole gets together, using group time more efficiently only to present the alternatives and discuss and critique them. The idea is to synthesize the efforts of the various subgroups into a final grouping of three or four really good bundles that meet the criteria. (In planning this step, be warned that it always takes longer than you think to do well.)

One idea to force an intelligent critique of the alternatives is to "murder-board" them. Assign a subgroup to tackle each alternative bundle, and instruct them to come up with all the reasons they possibly can as to why that alternative would *not* work. It is amazing how this "extra" step adds a humiliating dose of reality to the process, can result in important modifications to the bundle in question, and can even cause one bundle that was going to be considered by the group to be discarded.

5. *Choose the Best Bundle*—Select a subset of 5–6 relevant criteria. (It may take considerable discussion to reach consensus on such a list.) Evaluate the bundles on each criterion. The entire group of participants should be convinced that whichever bundle is finally selected really is the best one the company could choose in the circumstances, and they should all be clear as to why it is the best one. As the process proceeds, people will try to argue for a particular bundle before it is time to do so; someone should capture those arguments as they might prove very useful in the end. They should be clear that this is how the company will compete over the next 3–5 years.

6. *Set Companywide Objectives*—As discussed earlier, this is a three-step process. Depending on the preferred key indicator, such as revenues, NIAT, market share, and D/E ratio, the company needs to simply answer the question: "How far do we want to go this next year, and each of the two succeeding years as well, towards implementing the chosen strategic bundle"? It will depend on the firm's current resources and those it could additionally access, as well as the nature of the chosen strategies. In addition, it will depend on whether the competitive environment is becoming more difficult or any other threats are looming. So take a good look at how the company has been doing in the recent past and set the objectives at a challengingly high level while still being achievable. Most importantly, those who must be accountable for achieving these objectives should agree to the level at which they are set, and that level should be challenging.

Of course, the model assumes a participative way of setting objectives; some CEOs still reserve the right to do this on their own. However, a wise CEO knows that when managers charged with implementing a strategy set their own objectives, they are more likely to achieve them.

7. *Design Major Programs and Contingencies*—Some of these major programs are included in the chosen bundle, while others may need to be added. It is this list of programs that will guide the creation of the operational plans. "Contingencies" here refer to the trigger/contingency pairs that were discussed earlier in Chapter 7.

8. *Prepare Detailed Operational Objectives and Plans*—The bad news is that this is one of the more complex steps in the process. The good news is that there are many ways to create operational plans. Given the companywide objectives and major programs that were already identified, the functional (e.g., marketing, production, finance) and other heads (e.g., materials lab, purchasing) take these as mandates to their respective units and get them to generate detailed operational plans that would contribute to achieving the objectives and chosen bundle (business model). At a minimum, these plans should include:

   · A timeline of specific tasks the unit will undertake during the year.

   · A proposed budget to accomplish them by task and month.

   · Who will be participating in these activities and, in particular, the person who will be responsible for each activity.

   · Whether additional staff (what kind?) and/or resources (what kind and level) will be required to complete the proposed tasks.

9. *Perform a Final Check*—Once these plans have been drafted, they should be reviewed by top management and/or the Director of Strategic Planning to check their feasibility, make sure that the totals of all the requested budgets do not exceed available funds—if they do, a process of negotiation ensues with affected managers to trim certain budgets to stay within available funds—and that completing all the planned activities in fact will achieve the overall objectives for the company. In fact, this mixture of top-down and bottom-up planning may have to endure one or more iterations before the operational plans and budgets are finally approved as shown in Figure 8.2. For this reason, be sure to allow enough time to complete this process properly and break it down into components as shown in Figure 8.2.

10. *Assess the Process*—Those who participated in the strategic-planning process should be asked to complete a detailed questionnaire about how well the process went and the quality of the decisions made. (See appendix D for a list of suggested questions for such a survey.) The person responsible for the process should analyze the responses and present the results—with constructively critical commentary—at a meeting of those that participated, giving each participant a personal copy. Unless such a review takes place, there is little chance that the company will improve the way it does strategic planning from one year to the next. Any mistakes that are made are likely to be repeated unless

Figure 8.2   One Way to Do Operational Planning

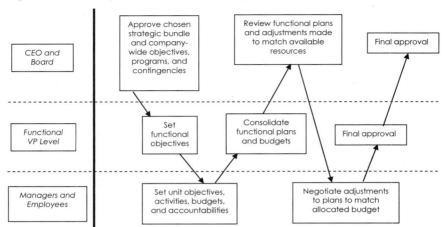

those involved are made aware of them. For example, if the quality and quantity of data collected was not sufficiently high, steps can and should be taken the next time around to collect better data, being very clear as to what "better" means.

Finally, everything should be timed so that by the time the fiscal year starts, all the strategic decisions, operational plans, and budgets have been completed. Final approval of the plans and budgets should be completed within a couple of weeks before the start of the company's fiscal year. Each unit should therefore be armed with monthly (or even weekly) objectives, activity schedules, and budgets. These, in fact, constitute the simplest kind of control system that the company and its units use to monitor progress as the activities are carried out. Monthly meetings at the VP level with unit heads and at the CEO level with the functional VPs should be held to review progress against plans and discuss deviations, problems, and corrective actions.

Summary

Transposing the steps in the strategic-planning model to a process for the whole company must be carefully orchestrated and planned, particularly if the company or organization is doing strategic planning for the first time. It goes without saying that undertaking to do strategic planning must come from the CEO or top executive (or sometimes the board of directors), otherwise it will be a fruitless exercise and a waste of everyone's time. Several considerations should guide how this is done:

- Whether expertise exists in-house to plan and facilitate the process or whether a consultant should be engaged to do it.

- How many and what kind and level of people should participate in the process.

- What process (model) should be adopted, and ensuring that those participating understand the process and their roles in it.

- What are the purposes of the strategic-planning process (specific strategic decisions that need to be made), and ensuring that those involved in the process commit to implementing those decisions (i.e., "following through").

- Ensuring that operational plans mesh with the strategic direction and objectives, and that the firm has the resources to support the budget.

The chapter covers all these points, and also discusses the research and data collection that needs to underpin analyses about the changing environment and the firm itself. This is not research for its own sake, but rather a means to educate the strategic-planning team and develop a shared understanding as to what has changed in the last year and to correct any misunderstandings people may have about key issues. This enlightenment and "unfreezing" and "refreezing" of one's mental model is, according to experts like Peter Schwartz, the principal reason for doing strategic planning. Only when such understanding is shared and reached can strategic decisions properly be made. It is serious business. And it is enormously valuable if conducted in the right spirit—with ruthless candor, equality of voice, skepticism, openness, and a desire to do what is best for the firm.

9

Operational Planning
and Implementation

After the multistage strategic-planning process is complete, the various strategic decisions have been made, and after going through still more stages of operational planning and budgeting until all plans and budgets have been approved, one could heave a sigh of relief. However, the relief would be short-lived as any seasoned manager will tell you: The real work begins with implementation.

The simplest implementation scenario occurs when a company has a clear strategic direction, challenging objectives, well-thought plans to achieve those objectives, and can over the next 2–3 years implement those plans in a straightforward manner and achieve its objectives. But this rarely happens.

Implementing a strategy or strategies in the real world is unlike swimming from one end of a calm pond to the other on a sunny day. It is more like crossing from one bank of a raging river to the other, encountering hidden eddies, fog, driving rain, lightning, and riptides along the way. While not impossible to reach the other bank—the goal, the task often becomes difficult and one of overcoming obstacles and making constant adjustments without losing focus or sight of the goal. Implementation is like that. Even the most brilliant strategy is worthless if it cannot be implemented. It is for this reason that managers implementing a strategy must participate in coming up with strategic alternatives, choosing a preferred strategy, and creating operational or implementation plans.

Without going into the topic in great detail, as every firm or organization is different, this short chapter touches on five aspects of implementation that might help make it more successful.

Have faith in the strategy you chose Most strategies take 3–4 years to play out before anyone can tell whether or not they are successful. Along the way, things may not go as planned. Remember when you made your arguments for this strategy as the best strategy? Those arguments were based on assumptions, estimates and, yes, sometimes guesswork. Those assumptions and estimates could well be wrong. The market you thought was full of potential really was not. The competitors you thought had not changed at all have been developing dynamite products based on new technology. The economy you thought would come out of its recession is still mired in it. Perhaps you recognized some of these risks when you developed contingencies if certain triggers were reached. In any case, the last thing you should do is abandon the strategy at the first or second sign of things not going according to plan.

Find a way to make it work   Make adjustments. Be creative. Unleash the creative power of your people to come up with ideas and tactics that would improve performance with no increase in expenditures or get the company back on track if circumstances force it to veer off. Again, implementation is about making operational changes and adjustments while still being focused on the strategy and on achieving the objectives that were set. In this respect, when the strategy is in fact achieved and the objectives for the first three years have been fully met or even exceeded, the true heroes are not those that came up with the strategy originally—they will tell you otherwise—but those in the trenches, including the operational managers and supervisors, who made it work.

If, after exhausting all possible operational changes and adjustments, the company's performance is still way below expectations—that is, the likelihood of achieving objectives remains small—then managers have to decide whether: (1) the objectives that were set were unrealistic and should be revised downwards; or (2) the strategy is in fact not working and needs to be changed. This should trigger another round of strategic planning during which other strategic alternatives are considered and the best one is chosen. Those rare organizations that can do strategic planning "on the fly" are truly fortunate. They save a lot of time as they blur the distinction between "planning" and "implementation," doing both seamlessly—often without a formal meeting but through intense conversations with many people, slowly coming to a consensus, and acting on that consensus immediately.

Keep an eye open for emergent strategies   Because everything is changing during implementation, making the task of realizing the chosen strategy quite difficult, it is easy to remain so focused on that task that you miss emerging opportunities as they arise. Change brings both threats and opportunities. If implementing the chosen strategy becomes difficult and performance begins to fall below expected results, a variant of trying to get back on track is to explore whether slight changes to the strategy, such as selling to a slightly different market, have any effect. If the result of any such small experiment is successful, the experiment's scope can be expanded. This is precisely what Henry Mintzberg describes as an emergent strategy, one that is "discovered" in the field or in the lab, tried out, and found successful. It certainly was not argued for at a strategic-planning meeting. Managers should be constantly weighing whether to pursue the intended strategy or, at some point, shift slightly to take into account a successful emergent strategy.

Trust your managers and your people   During implementation, it is easy to set up control systems that actually give lower-level managers and workers very little leeway, making them accountable not only for achieving set objectives, but also for achieving them in predetermined ways. If this is so in your organization, it may be because those people need such close monitoring or because very little trust exists (probably the latter). Another approach is to agree on the objectives that lower-level managers are to achieve, but be less insistent on how they should be achieved. With the additional leeway and freedom, managers are more motivated to be creative, act on their own initiative, act more like a leader, look for emergent strategies, and take advantage of opportunity shifts as they occur. But such additional freedom cannot come without trust. With trust, those managers will know when to consult with their bosses should they find themselves straying too far from the strategic direction that was set.

Be wary of playing catch-up   Much of the implementation of any strategy involves becoming as efficient, quality conscious, and reengineered as your competitors. While the resulting gains could mean the difference between profit and loss, they do little in terms of positioning yourself to out-compete your rivals or differentiate yourself from them. The resources and effort expended serve simply to "catch up" to your competitors, during which time most of them have widened the gap in other ways. It is a depressing race to run. It makes more sense to embark on a course that, in time, will have your competitors trying to catch up to you! By all means strive to accomplish what you must by not exceeding your budget—your profitability depends on it—but do not get caught in a catch-up game.

Don't get into an "implementation rut"—stay agile and flexible It is easy to surmise, when reading a book such as this one, that once a preferred strategy has been chosen and implemented, one simply goes on to choose the next one and implements that. However, the world is not so simple. The truth is that even the annual strategic-planning exercise is a convenient artifact, having little relationship to events going on in the real world. The truth is that strategic-planning meetings and decisions should be taken at all sorts of odd times dictated by current events, competitor moves, and opportunities that suddenly open up—in fast-moving industries, this is more often true than not. Organizations that wish to be successful have to be prepared to "think on their feet," to make sudden changes when called for so long as they are in the best interests of the organization, and to adapt their systems to constantly changing realities. Don't get me wrong. I am not advocating changing strategic direction every month! But I am saying that whenever there is good reason to *change,* the organization should be prepared to quickly adjust its objectives, tactics, and control systems to take advantage of the changing realities and still end up being successful. Yes, this is immensely hard to do, but not impossible if trust is high, communication is open, and the best interests of the organization are paramount.

Summary

It has been said that implementation is "95% of the battle." Whatever the real percentage is, no strategy is worth anything unless it can be implemented. What makes implementation difficult is both the considerable time it takes to do, often 2–5 years and, during this period, the fact that everything is changing, sometimes with alarming speed.

This short chapter offers five "tips" to bear in mind while implementing any strategy:

- Have faith in the strategy you chose and give it time to be successful—do not change it at the first "hiccup."

- Be alert for emergent strategies, that is, if you find that deviating from the current strategy for whatever reason produces good results, consider doing more of it.

- Trust your managers and your people, giving them the freedom to decide how to achieve operational objectives instead of prescribing the method.

- Try not to play the "catch-up" game. It is like being on a treadmill where you expend a lot of effort and resources and get nowhere.

- Find ways to be agile and flexible, especially in situations where change occurs faster than you expected. Your organization must develop the capability of thinking and acting "on its feet."

A good way of keeping abreast of changes as implementation moves forward is to discuss what they might be every week formally or informally. Frequent strategic conversations can be productive, even in a corridor, cafeteria, or break room. Give yourself more time and opportunity to deal with them without losing sight of your strategic objectives or purposes.

Appendix A

Some Definitions of Strategy

The 66 definitions of strategy in this appendix are assigned a number to make it easy to refer to them in the text. They have the following general sources:

- Twenty-two are from strategic-management textbooks arranged in chronological order (1–22).

- Thirty-three are from trade books and journal articles on strategy and strategic planning arranged in chronological order (23–55).

- Nine are from individual strategists from author's correspondence (56–65).

- Two are from dictionaries (65–66).

Strategic Management Textbooks

1. Business strategy is the determination of how a company will compete in a given business and position itself among its competitors.—Kenneth Andrews, *The Concept of Corporate Strategy,* 2nd ed. (Homewood, IL: Irwin, 1980), 18.

2. Corporate strategy is the pattern of decisions in a company that determines and reveals its objectives, purposes, or goals, produces the principal policies and plans for achieving those goals, and defines the range of business the company is to pursue, the kind of economic and human organization it is or intends to be, and the nature of the economic and noneconomic contribution it intends to make to its shareholders, employees, customers, and communities.—Kenneth Andrews, *The Concept of Corporate Strategy,* 2nd ed. (Homewood, IL: Irwin, 1980), 18–19.

3. A strategy is the pattern or plan that integrates an organization's major goals, policies, and action sequences into a cohesive whole. A well-formulated strategy helps to marshal and allocate an organization's resources into a unique and viable posture based on its relative internal competencies and shortcomings, anticipated changes in the environ-

ment, and contingent moves by intelligent opponents.—James Brian Quinn, Henry Mintzberg, and Robert M. James, *The Strategy Process: Concepts, Contexts, and Cases,* 2nd ed. (Englewood Cliffs, NJ: Prentice Hall, 1988), 3.

4. Business strategy [is] a set of objectives and integrated set of actions aimed at securing a sustainable competitive advantage.—Frederick W. Gluck, Stephen P. Kaufman, and A. Steven Welleck, "Strategic Management for Competitive Advantage," Chapter 19 in Richard G. Hamermesh, ed., *Strategic Management* (New York: Wiley, 1983), 303.

5. A grand strategy is a firm's integrated approach to achieving a vision while responding to a constantly shifting external environment.—Alan J. Rowe, Richard O. Mason, Karl E. Dickel, Richard B. Mann, and Robert J. Mockler, *Strategic Management: A Methodological Approach,* 4th ed. (Reading, MA: Addison-Wesley, 1994), 82.

6. Strategy refers to the ideas, plans, and actions used to help firms and people compete successfully in their endeavors. Strategy is designed to help firms achieve competitive advantage.—Robert A. Pitts and David Lei, *Strategic Management: Building and Sustaining Competitive Advantage* (St. Paul, MN: West, 1996), 6.

7. Strategy is a pattern in a stream of decisions.—L. J. Bourgeois III, *Strategic Management: From Concept to Implementation* (Fort Worth, TX: Dryden, 1996), 95.

8. In the simplest terms possible, strategy refers to either the plans made, or the actions taken, in an effort to help an organization fulfill its intended purposes.—Alex Miller and Gregory G. Dess, *Strategic Management,* 2nd ed. (New York: McGraw-Hill, 1996), 5.

9. Strategy is the determination and evaluation of alternatives available to an organization in achieving its objectives and mission, and the selection of the alternative to be pursued.—L. L. Byars, *Strategic Management: Formulation and Implementation, Concepts & Cases,* 3rd ed. Harper Collins, 1992), 13.

10. Strategy is the broad program for defining and achieving an organization's objectives; [it is also] the pattern of the organization's responses to its environment over time.—J. A. F. Stoner and R. E. Freeman, *Management,* 4th ed. (Englewood Cliffs, NJ: Prentice Hall, 1989), 193.

11. Strategy is about the firm's positioning vis-à-vis its rivals. [It is also] about the efficient conversion of resources into customer value.— Jeremy G. Davis and Timothy M. Devinney, *The Essence of Corporate Strategy: Theory for Modern Decision Making* (Sydney: Allen & Unwin, 1998), 41.

12. Strategy is the "game plan" management has for positioning the company in its chosen market arena, competing successfully, pleasing customers, and achieving good business performance.—Arthur A. Thompson Jr., and A. J. Strickland III, *Strategic Management: Concepts and Cases,* 10th ed. (New York: Irwin McGraw-Hill, 1998), 2.

13. Strategy is a commitment to undertake one set of actions rather than another.—Sharon M. Oster, *Modern Competitive Analysis,* 3rd ed. (New York: Oxford University Press, 1999), 2.

14. Strategy is a set of concrete plans to help the organization accomplish its goal of outperforming the market.—Adapted from Sharon M. Oster, *Modern Competitive Analysis,* 3rd ed. (New York: Oxford University Press, 1999), 2.

15. Strategy can be defined as the determination of the basic long-term goals and objectives of an enterprise, and the adoption of courses of action and the allocation of resources necessary for carrying out those goals.—Alfred D. Chandler Jr., as cited in Pankaj Ghemawat, *Strategy and the Business Landscape* (Reading, MA: Addison-Wesley, 1999), 1.

16. A strategy statement must have components of goals, scope, competitive advantage, and logic otherwise it is not a statement of strategy.—Adapted from Garth Saloner, Andrea Shepard, & Joel Podolny, *Strategic Management* (New York: Wiley, 2001), 19–38.

17. Strategy is not the means for achieving a limited objective, but rather encompasses an overall approach to running a business.—Adapted from Garth Saloner, Andrea Shepard, & Joel Podolny, *Strategic Management* (New York: Wiley, 2001), 4.

18. A grand strategy is the general course of action through which an enterprise seeks to accomplish its corporate objectives . . . and ensure the long-term prosperity of the organization.—Adapted from A. J. Almaney, *Strategic Analysis: An Approach to Building Distinctive Competencies* (Salem, WI: Sheffield, 2001), 19.

19. A strategy is an integrated and coordinated set of actions designed to exploit core competencies and gain a competitive advantage.—Michael A. Hitt, R. Duane Ireland, and Robert E. Hoskisson, *Strategic Management: Competitiveness and Globalization, Concepts & Cases,* 6th ed. (Mason, OH: Thomson South-Western, 2005), 7.

20. A business-level strategy is an integrated and coordinated set of actions designed to provide value to customers and gain a competitive advantage by exploiting core competencies in specific, individual product markets.—Michael A. Hitt, R. Duane Ireland, and Robert E. Hoskisson, *Strategic Management: Competitiveness and Globalization, Concepts & Cases,* 6th ed. (Mason, OH: Thomson South-Western, 2005), 105.

21. Strategy is a series of goal-directed decisions and actions that match an organization's skills and resources with the opportunities and threats in its environment.—Mary Coulter, *Strategic Management in Action,* 2nd ed. (Upper Saddle River, NJ: Prentice Hall, 2002), 7.

22. A strategy is an organizational plan of action that is intended to move an organization toward the achievement of its shorter-term goals and, ultimately, toward achievement of its fundamental purposes.—Jeffrey S. Harrison and Caron H. St. John, *Foundations in Strategic Management,* 2nd ed. (Cincinnati, OH: South-Western, 2002), 6.

Trade Books and Journal Articles

23. Strategy is the framework which guides the choices that determine the nature and direction of an organization.—Benjamin Tregoe and John Zimmerman, *Top Management Strategy* (New York: Simon & Schuster, 1980), 17. *Note*: Tregoe and Zimmerman advocate basing the firm's strategy on one and only one "driving force," and list nine possible driving forces: products offered, market needs, technology, production capability, method of sale, method of distribution, natural resources, size/growth, and return/profit.

24. What business strategy is all about is, in a word, competitive advantage. . . . The sole purpose of strategic planning is to enable a company to gain, as efficiently as possible, a sustainable edge over its competitors. Corporate strategy thus implies an attempt to alter a company's strength relative to that of its competitors in the most efficient way.—Kenichi Ohmae, *The Mind of the Strategist* (New York: Penguin, 1983), 36.

25. Strategy is defined as the way in which a corporation endeavors to differentiate itself positively from its competitors, using its relative corporate strengths to better satisfy customer needs.—Kenichi Ohmae, *The Mind of the Strategist: Business Planning for Competitive Advantage* (New York: Penguin, 1982), 92.

26. Strategy is the search for a favorable competitive position in an industry, the fundamental arena in which competition occurs. Competitive strategy aims to establish a profitable and sustainable position against the forces that determine industry competition.—Michael E. Porter, *Competitive Advantage: Creating and Sustaining Superior Performance* (New York: Free Press, 1985), 1.

27. The Five Ps of Strategy—strategy is a plan (intended), a pattern (realized), a position (a strong presence in a particular market), a perspective (doing things a unique way), and a ploy (a specific maneuver intended to outwit a competitor).—Adapted from Henry Mintzberg, Bruce Ahlstrand, and Joseph Lampel, *Strategy Safari: A Guided Tour through the Wilds of Strategic Management* (New York: Free Press, 1998), 9–18; and Henry Mintzberg, "The Strategy Concept 1: The Five Ps for Strategy," *California Management Review* 30, no. 1 (June 1987): 11–24.

28. Strategy is the long-term pattern of actions aimed at altering a firm's competitive position.—N. T. Taylor and L. H. Rosansky, *What Managers Do*, 3rd ed. (New York: AMACOM, 1988), 18.

29. A set of decisions and behavior (what managers and organizations do); a pattern of resource allocation.—Robert Allio, *The Practical Strategist: Business and Corporate Strategy for the 1990s* (New York: Harper & Row, 1988), 8.

30. The goal of strategy is to beat the competition. . . . [But] before you test yourself against the competition, strategy takes shape in the determination to create value for customers.—Kenichi Ohmae, "Getting Back to Strategy," *Harvard Business Review* 66, no 6. (1988): 149–156.

31. Strategy is a deliberate search for a plan of action that will develop a business's competitive advantage and compound it.—Bruce D. Henderson, "The Origin of Strategy," *Harvard Business Review* 67, no. 6 (November–December 1989): 139–143.

32. We define vision or strategy as the framework which guides those choices that determine the nature and direction of an organization.— Benjamin B. Tregoe, John W. Zimmerman, Ronald A. Smith, and Peter M. Tobia, *Vision in Action: Putting a Winning Strategy to Work* (New York: Simon & Schuster, 1989), 33.

33. The purpose of strategy is to gain and maintain long-term competitive advantages.—Spyros G. Makridakis, *Forecasting, Planning, and Strategy for the 21st Century* (New York: Free Press, 1990), 176.

34. The overall strategy statement should pull together into one seamless picture your high-priority options for both what you are going to do with your existing business and how you will attack new businesses.— James Bandrowski, *Corporate Imagination Plus* (New York: Free Press, 1990), 75.

35. Strategy is...an underlying logic beneath the flow of decisions which create the future.—Dave Francis, *Step-by-Step Competitive Strategy,* (Cincinnati, OH: International Thomson Business Press, 1994), 18.

36. Strategies are the means, the ways, the hows, the devilishly detailed methods by which organizations accomplish their objectives.—C. Davis Fogg, *Team-Based Strategic Planning: A Complete Guide to Structuring, Facilitating, and Implementing the Process* (New York: AMACOM, 1994), 12.

37. Strategy is as much about competing for tomorrow's industry structure as it is about competing within today's industry structure.—Gary Hamel and C. K. Prahalad, *Competing for the Future: Breakthrough Strategies for Seizing Control of Your Industry and Creating the Markets of Tomorrow* (Boston: Harvard Business School, 1994), 42.

38. Strategy [is] a general policy for achieving a number of specified objectives.—Tim Hindle (chief contributor), *Field Guide to Strategy: A Glossary of Essential Tools and Concepts for Today's Manager* (Boston: Harvard Business School Press, 1994), 202.

39. Strategy is a dynamic learning process that encompasses deliberate (planned) strategies that are then tested for strategic fit with customers and markets, and may include strategies that evolve from past experience as well as strategic foresight based on discovering unanticipated markets and unarticulated customer needs. Adapted from Stephen J. Wall and Shannon Rye Wall, *The New Strategists: Creating Leaders at All Levels* (New York: Free Press, 1995), 18.

40. Strategy states how you will achieve competitive advantage by providing target customers a good deal at a profit over time, while still generating cash for future needs.—Eileen Shapiro, *Fad Surfing in the Boardroom* (Reading, MA: Addison Wesley, 1995), 31. *Note:* Thanks to Sam Felton for this one.

41. Strategies are specific plans to achieve the objectives one sets after creating the vision. Objectives are the ends, strategies are the means. . . . Strategies are plans that identify and convert opportunities on the one hand and respond to changes on the other.—Kerry Napuk, *The Strategy-Led Business: Step-by-Step Planning for Small- and Medium-Sized Companies* (New York: McGraw-Hill, 1996), 65.

42. Whereas operational effectiveness can help a company catch up to or do things better than competitors, strategy focuses on doing things *differently*. . . Strategy means deliberately choosing a different set of activities to deliver a unique mix of value.—Michael E. Porter, "What Is Strategy?" *Harvard Business Review* 74, no. 6 (November–December 1996): 61–78.

43. Strategies [are] the primary bases upon which an organization allocates resources to differentiate itself from competitors, create customer value, and achieve exemplary performance in order to realize its vision.—Robert H. Miles, *Leading Corporate Transformation: A Blueprint for Business Renewal* (San Francisco: Jossey-Bass, 1997), 36.

44. A company's business design has four elements: customer selection (target), value capture (protect profit margins), strategic control (differentiation), and scope. Good strategy involves creating the right business design and reinventing it (every 3–5 years) so that it continues to keep the company successful.—Adapted from Adrian Slywotsky and David Morrison, *The Profit Zone: How Strategic Business Design Will Lead You to Tomorrow's Profits* (New York: Times Business, 1997), 10–13.

45. Strategy at its heart is about positioning for future competitive advantage. That is its essence. Any strategic thinking must reflect this essence. It is the purpose that drives strategy.—Stuart Wells, *Choosing the Future: The Power of Strategic Thinking* (Boston: Butterworth-Heinemann, 1998), 52.

46. Strategy describes a clear set of organizational intentions that together present a coherent set of decisions about what businesses the organization is to be in and how to run those businesses. . . Sustainable competitive advantage is in the end what a successful strategy is all about.—David A. Nadler, *Champions of Change: How CEOs and Their Companies Are Mastering the Skills of Radical Change* (San Francisco: Jossey-Bass, 1998), 153, 156.

47. Strategy in any business (or nonbusiness) context is meaningless without reference to customers and competitors. The dominant aim of strategy . . . is to deliver superior value to customers compared with current (and potential) rivals.—Liam Fahey, *Outwitting, Outmaneuvering, and Outperforming Competitors* (New York: Wiley, 1999), vii.

48. Strategy is defining a unique market position and occupying it. . . The essence of strategy is selecting one position that a company can claim as its own. (A strategic position is the sum of the company's answers to three questions: (1) Who should the company target as customers? (2) What products or services should the company offer? (3) How can the company do this efficiently?)—Constantinos C. Markides, "A Dy-

namic View of Strategy," *Sloan Management Review* 40, no. 3 (spring 1999): 56.

49. Strategy at its heart [is] identifying discontinuities, determining their impact on markets of today and tomorrow, and developing new business models. [Success depends on] both strategic thinking and flawless execution.—C. K. Prahalad and Jan P. Oosterveld, "Transforming Internal Governance: The Challenge for Multinationals," *Sloan Management Review* 40, no. 3 (spring 1999): 39.

50. Strategy is about positioning an organization for sustainable competitive advantage. It involves making choices about which industries to participate in, what products and services to offer, and how to allocate corporate resources to achieve such a sustainable advantage. Its primary goal is to create value for shareholders and other stakeholders by providing customer value. (Value, unless constantly maintained, nourished, and improved, erodes with time.) Strategic thinking focuses on taking *different* approaches to delivering customer value [and] on choosing *different* sets of activities that cannot easily be imitated and thereby provide a basis for sustainable competitive advantage.— Cornelis A. de Kluyver, *Strategic Thinking: An Executive Perspective* (Upper Saddle River: Prentice-Hall, 2000), 3–5.

51. Within the Value Dynamics context, corporate strategy concerns the effective design and execution of a business model to create and realize value.—Richard E. S. Boulton, Barry D. Libert, and Steve M. Samek, *Cracking the Value Code: How Successful Businesses Are Creating Wealth in the New Economy* (New York: Harper Business, 2000), 248.

52. Strategy is a handful of decisions that drive or shape most of a company's subsequent actions, are not easily changed once made, and have the greatest impact on whether a company meets its strategic objectives. . . . This handful of decisions consists of selecting the company's strategic posture, identifying the source or sources of competitive advantage, developing the business concept, and constructing tailored value-delivery systems.—Kevin P. Coyne and Somu Subramaniam, "Bringing Discipline to Strategy," *The McKinsey Quarterly*, no. 3 (2000): 61–70.

53. Strategy is the art of deploying resources toward market opportunities in a way that distinguishes a business from its competitors.—Robert Allio, *The Seven Faces of Leadership* (Philadelphia: Xlibris, 2002), 96.

54. Strategy [is the] driving force that shapes the future nature and direction of the business; it defines the means that will be employed to achieve the corporate vision.—Ian Wilson, *The Subtle Art of Strategy* (Westport, CT: Praeger Publishers, 2003), 154.

55. Strategy describes how an organization intends to create sustained value for its shareholders.—Robert S. Kaplan and David P. Norton, *Strategy Maps: Converting Intangible Assets into Tangible Outcomes* (Boston: Harvard Business School Press, 2004), 29.

Individual Strategists

56. Strategy is an experiment in making smarter choices through a process of exploring, selecting, testing, evaluating, prioritizing, investing, motivating, implementing, monitoring, and adapting.—Robert M. Randall, January 22, 2002.

57. Strategy is positioning for competitive advantage and sustaining it.— David Crain, adapted from Markides, January 22, 2002.

58. Strategy is a clear compelling description of your competitive distinction and how your organization will deploy it to win in your industry.—James F. Bandrowski, January 29, 2002.

59. Strategy is about uniqueness and competitive differentiation for achieving leverageable advantage in the marketplace. Most definitions of strategy equate it with planning, which in my opinion is wrong. While planning is needed to execute any project, you need strategy only when you have competitors and a need for competitive differentiators. Strategy is also about uniqueness, especially when you want to position yourself and identify yourself uniquely in a competitive environment. [Finally,] because competitive advantage is not sustainable in today's world, you need to focus on the art of leveraging an advantage.— Deependra Moitra, March 13, 2002.

60. Strategy spells out how you plan to be the market leader in served markets of your choice while earning more than the cost of capital employed to do so.—Sam Felton, based partly on his extensive experience with PIMS (Profit Impact of Market Strategies), August 29, 2002.

61. Strategy is about creating and optimizing value deliverance to customers, shareholders, and employees. Definitions of strategy ignore the employee dimension, even though we call our economy a knowledge-driven economy, human-capital-intensive economy, etc. If human capital is the raw material for today's business, how can we afford not to integrate employees into the definition of strategy?—Deependra Moitra, September 5, 2002.

62. Strategy is a pattern of resource allocation to achieve (or maintain) a competitive advantage.—Robert Allio, May 1, 2002.

63. Strategy is how a company continuously increases value to customers in order to create ever-increasing value for all stakeholders.—James F. Bandrowski, October 29, 2002.

64. Strategy is trying to understand where you sit in today's world. Not where you wish you were and where you hoped you'd be, but where you are. And [it is trying to understand] where you want to be . . . [it is] assessing with everything in your head the competitive changes that you can capitalize on or ward off to go from here to there. It's assessing the realistic chances of getting from here to there.—Jack Welch's "definition-in-use," from an informal presentation he made to a management class at Crotonville (GE's "school") as quoted by Ian Wilson, August 29, 2002.

Dictionary Definitions

65. Strategy is a plan, method, or series of maneuvers ("stratagems") for obtaining a specific goal.—*Oxford English Dictionary*.

66. Strategy. 1. (a) The science of planning and directing large-scale military operations, specifically (as distinguished from tactics) of maneuvering forces into the most advantageous position prior to actual engagement with the enemy, (b) a plan or action based on this. 2. (a) Skill in managing or planning, especially by using stratagem, (b) a stratagem or artful means to some end. ("Stratagem" is defined as "a trick, scheme, or plan for deceiving an enemy in war," as well as "any trick or scheme for achieving some purpose.")—*Webster's New World Dictionary*.

Appendix B

Guidelines for Using the SAM^{tw} CD-ROM

The companion CD-ROM to this book, entitled SAM^{tw} (Strategic Analysis Model—that works), has been designed as a standalone. In other words, SAM^{tw} can be used without constant reference to this book. It is self-contained. However, anyone who has first read this book to understand the concepts, and who wants to apply them, will be in a better position to use SAM^{tw} with more success. That is why SAM^{tw} is bundled with the book and not sold separately. So read the book, especially Chapters 4–7, before trying to use SAM^{tw} to do a strategic analysis of a company or as a prelude to strategic planning.

SAM^{tw} follows the same model as that described in the book, so there will be a welcome familiarity with how it is laid out. You should have no difficulty navigating its various sections. In addition, the following design features add to its convenience and ease of use:

- An introductory Microsoft PowerPoint slideshow (included on the CD-ROM) that provides a valuable tutorial to all parts of the software. First-time users should spend 15–20 minutes and "take the tour."

- Context-sensitive comment boxes that define terms and reinforce instructions, making the information available when and where it is needed.

- An online version of the glossary that comes with this book that defines the terms used in this book.

SAM^{tw} is an interactive workbook. It is a place to think, organize your ideas, describe your perceptions, and even make mistakes. Ideally, you should communicate to other people the results of your work either through a written report or slide presentation—and one of the outstanding features of SAM^{tw} is the neat and organized look of its printouts when you print out the steps of your strategic analysis. You can even assemble the SAM^{tw} printouts into a report that looks quite professional.

SAM^{tw} as a Tool for Strategic Inquiry

Once you become used to the various analysis steps, you will have "internalized" the kinds of information needed to do a thorough strategic analysis. You will be in a position to ask the hard questions at a strategic presentation, a strategic-planning retreat, or any similar venue when no one is asking them. Initially, however, as you go through each step and try to answer the questions posed to you in your role as analyst, you could find yourself unable to answer all of them. Either you do not know or cannot get the information. It could be that the information may even be unnecessary. In this case, use the blanks in the worksheet as questions that you might ask the president or CEO of the company to determine if that information is critical.

Some of the tools in SAM^{tw} require data and others subjective estimates. The accuracy or credibility of such estimates runs from low to high as one goes down the following list:

- Completed by an individual not familiar with the company or its industry.

- Completed by a group of people unfamiliar with the company or its industry.

- Completed by an individual very familiar with the company and its industry.

- Completed by a group of people very familiar with the company and its industry.

Yet even for someone unfamiliar with the company or its industry, the act of attempting to use some of the analytical tools has value far beyond getting answers that are reasonable and credible. Trying to make estimates and thinking through the analytical methods are a learning process, and that process prepares one to discuss his or her perceptions and results even with people who are very experienced in that industry. This is difficult to appreciate for anyone new to strategic analysis, for the line between "pure guessing" and making subjective estimates as part of a learning process is a fine one.

Using SAM^{tw} on Your Computer

As soon as you place the CD-ROM in the computer, just wait a few moments—the SAM^{tw} Launch Pad will automatically open. All modules contained on the CD-ROM can be accessed from the SAM^{tw} Launch Pad.

If for some reason the Launch Pad does not open automatically, simply click **start** , **Run...** , **Browse...** , and locate the CD-ROM. Double-click the file **autorun.exe,** and then click **OK** . (All files on the CD-ROM are accessible using Windows Explorer without the Launch Pad.)

The *Strategic Analysis* and *Financial Analysis* workbooks must be copied to a user's hard drive in order to save data for a particular company. After launching any of the Microsoft Excel modules (**Strategy.xls, Financial_3.xls, Financial_4.xls** or **Financial_5.xls**), simply select from the menu bar **File** and click **Save As...** and enter a filename that is meaningful to you. Make sure to "Enable Macros" when opening the Excel workbooks.

The following tips will help you get the most out of the *Strategic Analysis* and *Financial Analysis* workbooks:

- Look for the small red triangles at the top-right corners of certain cells. These denote comment boxes. By moving your cursor to that cell, the comment box will pop up. The comment boxes offer explanations, definitions, and instructions that will help you complete the worksheets. When your knowledge has increased and you no longer need them, you will learn not to run your cursor over those cells and not be bothered by them.

- With the financial analysis workbooks, choose only *one* of them: the one that matches the number of years of available company data. Do not change the formatting of the income statement or balance sheet by adding or deleting rows. The row heading you do not need can be deleted, *but not the whole row*. If you do not have enough rows for the data you have, then combine some of the rows together, *but do not add rows*.

- You can customize the worksheets. To make changes to non-input fields or to customize a tool, you must first unprotect the worksheet Click ☰ Tools , Protection , and then 🔒 Unprotect Sheet... . Unless you have advanced Excel skills, you would be better served *not* make changes to the model because of the many embedded macros and automated controls.

- To print any part of the analysis, use either the button at the top of the sheet or on the workbook's "Start" sheet, which is its table of contents for the model. *Do not use the menu options in Excel to print.* The Excel worksheets on the SAM^{tw} CD-ROM contain special print macros attached to the button controls that have specific formatting instructions to enhance SAM^{tw} printouts. While you are preparing drafts of your output, you may want to print in grayscale or in draft mode. To do so, change the default printer options using your printer's Properties dialog box. (Because printers differ, it is beyond the scope of this book to provide procedures. Consult your printer's manual.)

There are two Acrobat .PDF files on the CD-ROM. If you do not have Acrobat Reader installed on your computer, you should download it from the Adobe website. Navigate your web browser to **www.adobe.com** and click the Get Adobe Reader button on the left side of the page.

Minimum Requirements for Using SAM^{tw}

System Requirements

Windows 98 or higher, a Pentium 3 or Pentium 4 personal computer with 10MB of free disk space.

Table B.1 Contents of the SAM^tw CD-ROM

Description	File Name	File Type
SAM^tw Launch Pad	Launch.pdf	Acrobat .PDF File
Introduction to SAM^tw	Introduction.ppt	PowerPoint Slide Show
SAM^tw Strategy Workbook	Strategy.xls	Excel File
SAM^tw Financial Analysis Workbooks	Financial_3.xls Financial_4.xls Financial_5.xls	Excel Files – choose based upon number of years of available financial data
SAM^tw Glossary	Glossary.pdf	Acrobat .PDF File

Software Requirements

Microsoft Excel (2000 or higher), Microsoft PowerPoint (2000 or higher) or PowerPoint Viewer (free to download from **www.microsoft.com/downloads/**), and Acrobat Reader 5.1 or higher.

Feedback

SAM^tw is a work in progress. With feedback from more and more users, we find many ways to improve its process, worksheets, and ease of use. The goal is to improve the quality of strategic thinking and analysis being done in companies—and also to help MBA students learn to do a sound strategic analysis. Comments from SAM^tw users are always welcome as well as questions about its use—and to report something that is not working right. You can e-mail feedback directly to the author at **scabraham@csupomona.edu**.

Appendix C

The Strategic-Planning Process of Cal Poly Pomona's Computer Information Systems (CIS) Department

Dr. Steven Curl, Chair

Mission Statement

The Mission Statement of the CIS Department is to provide quality education opportunities to a diverse and multicultural student body in computer information systems at the undergraduate and graduate levels, with particular emphasis on undergraduate preparation, and to provide support courses for other departments of the College to enhance their understanding of the increasingly critical role of information systems and information technology in organizations.

About the Organization

The Computer Information Systems (CIS) Department provides undergraduate and graduate courses and degree programs for individuals seeking careers in business computing and information technology. CIS faculty members' outstanding academic credentials and years of industry experience in computer information systems enable them to better prepare students for entry-level, specialized, consulting, and entrepreneurial opportunities.

Background

More than 35 years ago, Cal Poly Pomona was one of the first universities in the country to develop a university level program in business information systems. Since then, Cal Poly Pomona's Computer Information Systems (CIS) Department has maintained a national reputation for the quality of its academic programs and the level of technical preparation of its graduates. During this entire period, the CIS department, along with the industry, has faced incredibly rapid rates of change in both the technology and the organizational environment in which that technology is used. This has necessitated on-going and rapid change in the skill-sets required of graduates and in the tools and techniques needed to prepare them.

As a leading edge provider of business information systems education, Cal Poly Pomona must anticipate the technologies and skill sets that will be required by employers and graduates, and then respond across the whole range of its operations, including providing faculty development to teach new technologies, instructional and materials development, and curriculum design and reform. In the past, the CIS department has responded to its continuously changing environment with various homegrown planning processes. Approximately every four years, often coinciding with leadership changes, the CIS department would initiate a major self-appraisal and planning effort. The intervening years would fill up with the ongoing activities of a university (e.g., annual incremental changes to curriculum, faculty hiring, etc.), most of which were only loosely guided by the department's previous planning efforts. This "ad hoc" planning process served the department adequately, but not well, until recently.

Today, as the rate of change of technology has continued to increase, the competitive environment is far different; the competition for critical resources (funds, faculty, quality students, etc.) is far more intense and more sophisticated. The processes used by the department in the past to maintain its status and reputation were no longer working, and the faculty as a whole were concerned that they were in danger of losing their cutting-edge reputation and competitive standing. The department knew it needed to change, but wanted to do so in a thoughtful, comprehensive and consistent way. This, then, was the environment in which the CIS department's strategic-planning process took place during the Fall 2003 and Winter 2004 quarters.

1. The Strategy-Formulation Process

Impetus for doing real strategic planning this time around grew from the faculty members' growing dissatisfaction of trying to do more and more with fewer resources, which meant that very little of what it was doing was done well. Clearly, the time had come to make some hard choices. But how?

This led to the CIS department's decision to undertake strategic planning for the first time. The process was carried out in eleven stages (arrived at in retrospect) as shown in Table C.1. Below the table, each stage that was carried out is described, the information that was used, and how the process progressed to successive stages. In the end, the department succeeded in setting a strategic direction for itself together with a detailed implementation plan that everyone is excited to implement.

Stage 1 Preplanning

The chair of the department created a Development Plan Committee (DPC), consisting of two professors (one senior and one new faculty) and himself. Based on its previous planning experience, this committee outlined the objectives the plan should achieve and that the conditions under which the planning should proceed (i.e., every body should participate in the process, and the process should proceed in an environment of freedom to participate regardless of rank). An important decision was to engage an experienced facilitator to help the department through the planning process.

Table C.1 CIS Department Strategic-Planning Process, 2002–2003

Stage	Responsibility	Output
1. Preplanning	Development Plan Committee	Objectives Meeting outline Tentative activities Desired outputs
2. Meeting Logistics	Development Plan Committee	Date, coordinator, venue Select expert facilitator
3. Adoption of Model and Design of Retreat	Development Plan Committee and facilitator	Meeting conditions Retreat agenda
4. The One-Day Retreat	CIS faculty and facilitator	Strategic Issues Potential activities Strategic alternatives ("bundles")
5. Bundle Composition	Subcommittee	Retreat report
6. Bundle Grading (1)	CIS faculty and facilitator	Evaluation criteria and voting
7. Scenarios Definition	Member of the Development Plan Committee	Four scenarios
8. Bundle Grading (2)	CIS faculty and facilitator	Selecting a preferred bundle (was not achieved this round)
9. Scenarios' Champions	Faculty members	Scenario analysis and scenario presentations
10. Bundle grading (3)	CIS faculty and facilitator	Selecting a preferred bundle
11. Development Plan	CIS faculty	Tasks/responsibilities/dates

Stage 2 Meeting Logistics

The DPC set the date and venue for the first faculty meeting and selected the expert facilitator.

Stage 3 Adoption of Model and Design of Retreat

Based on the experience of the facilitator, the DPC and the facilitator together agreed to base their process on the strategic-planning model used by the facilitator in both his courses at the university and with his clients (and described in this book). The model consisted essentially of becoming aware of changes in the external environment, candidly evaluating the strengths and weaknesses of the organization, identifying strategic issues, creating strategic alternatives (bundles), selecting a preferred bundle using relevant criteria, and, finally, creating an implementation plan. The DPC and the facilitator together agreed on the ground rules that would apply to all strategic-planning meetings (like free expression), and designed the retreat agenda.

Stage 4 The Retreat

CIS faculty and the facilitator held a one-day retreat at the home of one of the DPC members (offsite). The intent of the retreat was to go through the entire strategic-planning model and end with a preferred strategic alternative. However, the rich nature of the information discussed and the difficulty the faculty experienced going through a decision process that affected their very jobs practically ensured that the process would not be completed. The following narrative summarizes what was done during the retreat and how it ended.

After introducing the facilitator, setting the ground rules, and outlining the agenda for the day, the group of 22 people was divided into smaller groups, each of which tackled the following topics:

- *The industry*—What is changing in higher education and, in particular, in computer information systems education?

- *Competitors*—Which particular schools are the best in the country at CIS education and why? How does this department compare with them?

- *Market*—Here, the department is serving two markets simultaneously: *students* that take their courses, especially majors in their department, and *employers* that hire CIS graduates. What is changing in the needs and qualifications of students and in what employers are looking for in graduates?

- *Environmental variables*—How is the economy changing and how will it affect the department? How are demographics changing and will that affect enrollment? What is changing in the State of California budget and how will that impact the university and ultimately the department?

- *Strengths and weakness of the CIS Department*—A candid listing of its strengths and weaknesses.

Faculty members were extraordinarily well informed about trends in both industry and education regarding computer information systems, information technology, and related fields such as telecommunications and security issues. Being on the cutting edge and aware of trends is part of their job description. Unlike other organizations that need to collect such data when doing strategic planning, the faculty simply relied on its extensive experience, research (including their own survey research, that is, industry, alumni, and student surveys to support a graduate program proposal in telecommunications and computer networking), attendance at many national and international conferences, and conversations with industry contacts throughout the year to analyze and list the major issues under each topic. (Recall that all faculty members have held positions in industry and commerce before coming to teach at Cal Poly Pomona.) While students—one of its major customer groups—were not involved in the strategic-planning meetings, they were included in the process via offline discussions and consultations with student leaders.

The small topic groups reported back to everyone a summary of their findings, both to share the information and receive critical feedback from everyone. Then, based on that shared information, the facilitator elicited a listing of strategic issues from everyone (see Figure C.1). These were to form the foundation of the strategic alternatives that were subsequently created with suggestions from everyone.

The retreat ended with the identification of preliminary bundles. A *bundle* is a set of activities oriented to support a strategic direction for the department. By the time we finished identifying the potential bundles, we had run out of time.

Stage 5 Bundle Composition

Two professors and one member of the DPC worked on developing the five bundles that were identified during the faculty retreat. They took the notes from the afternoon brainstorming session and began to flesh out the bundles. The five bundles were:

1. Align closer with industry needs.

2. Stress graduate education.

3. Focus on advanced and specialized courses.

4. Innovate in terms of delivery of content.

5. Improve the quality of undergraduate students.

Note that each bundle includes the Department continuing to do what it has to do as part of the College of Business Administration, and what it must do in the future regardless of the bundle chosen; the differences lie in what the Department chooses to do on top of that.

Figure C.1   Strategic Issues for the CIS Department

- Will external online programs impact enrollment?
- For how long will we have to endure State budget cuts?
- For how long will the IT slump continue?
- How quickly will competitors match our offerings and quality?

Should the CIS Department . . .
- . . . offer more online teaching?
- . . . review and reorganize existing specialization tracks with the department's curricula?
- . . . give more priority to graduate education than we are giving now?
- . . . develop a substantially expanded outreach program to high schools and community colleges, reentry, etc.?
- . . . put more time/effort into recruiting more higher-quality students?
- . . . set up a new Advisory Board?
- . . . require laptops for all the students?
- . . . spend time and effort to supplement State funds with private?
- . . . increase security offerings throughout the curriculum?
- . . . get involved with noncomputer-software education (appliances)?
- . . . offer more courses that require team projects?
- . . . offer more certificate programs and workshops?
- . . . host academic conferences?
- . . . offer more B2B vs. B2C projects?
- . . . improve the specialized MBA in Information Management program?
- . . . include Enterprise Resource Planning in the curriculum?

Stage 6 Rating the Bundles (1)

In order to evaluate the bundles, the DPC selected five evaluation criteria. With these criteria and now four bundles (Bundle 3 was eliminated because it overlapped with two other bundles), a Criteria Matrix was developed (see Table C.2). The purpose of the Criteria Matrix is to rate each bundle against each criterion and arrive at a "best" bundle. The first time the department faculty discussed and tried to evaluate the bundles, three of them tied for the lead—the faculty was clearly uncomfortable with choosing only one bundle, and still clung to their habit of trying to do everything.

Stage 7 Scenarios Definition

In order to break the deadlock, the faculty decided to develop a scenario for each bundle. Each scenario would represent the future state of the department if the corresponding bundle were selected. Figure C.2 presents summaries of the four scenarios that were developed.

Stage 8 Rating the Bundles (2)

The CIS faculty again tried to evaluate the bundles using the Criteria Matrix. This time, while not identical in their final scores, the three leading bundles were still too close to decide the strategic direction for the department. At this stage, Bundle 3 (innovate in terms of delivery of content) was eliminated because of its relatively low score in the evaluation.

Stage 9 Scenarios' Champions

How to break the deadlock? Someone had the idea for each bundle to have a champion who would forcefully argue the merits of that bundle in an effort to sway people's opinions and break the tie. Accordingly, three faculty members volunteered to prepare a case and arguments for each bundle.

Table C.2 Criteria Matrix

Criteria	Bundle 1 Align with Industry	Bundle 2 Stronger Graduate Program	Bundle 3 Innovative Delivery	Bundle 4 Improve Students & Outreach
1. In the best interest of the Department's faculty				
2. Raises quality of education and programs.				
3. Enhances reputation with employers.				
4. Increases the Department's finances.				
5. Makes the Department more competitive externally.				

Figure C.2   The Four Scenarios (alternative futures five years out)

Bundle 1   Align Closer with Industry Needs

After closely working with an Industry Advisory Board for five years, the CIS Department has reached a unique alignment with industry in Southern California. All CIS students participate in an eight-month internship in which they are responsible for developing a project under the supervision of one CIS faculty member and one manager from a specific organization. Monitoring and supervising industry projects allows faculty to update the CIS curriculum constantly. The quality of the program is considered outstanding in Southern California and is facilitated by constant industry feedback, exemplifies the university's "learning by doing" teaching philosophy, and technology orientation. Next year, the CIS Department will open the new Information Technology Center (ITC). Supported by industry, the ITC will manage University-Industry projects oriented to develop, test, and implement information-technology solutions for small and medium-size organizations.

Figure C.2   The Four Scenarios (alternative futures five years out) (cont.)

Bundle 2 Stress Graduate Education

The CIS Department offers three academic programs: two graduate programs (Information Audit and Information Assurance, and Telecommunications and Networking), and one undergraduate program in Computer Information Systems. The CIS undergraduate program is recognized for its quality, technology-orientation, and relationship with the graduate programs that together are considered leading programs in the field. Two hundred graduate students and 800 undergraduates work with 25 faculty members, including two visiting professors. Each faculty member publishes four articles per year and supervises three Master's degree theses per year in addition to his or her teaching responsibilities. Next year, the Department will start the publication of Information Technology Quarterly (ITQ), a journal oriented to publishing creative research focused on ways to translate IT into business success.

Each professor would act as the bundle's champion. In this stage, the three professors prepared arguments in support of his or her bundle.

Stage 10 Rating the Bundles (3)

Over several department meetings, the CIS faculty repeated the evaluation process using the Criteria Matrix with the three remaining bundles. They heard presentations by the proponents of each of the three bundles. After extended discussions, the rankings were tabulated again and, this time, clearly discriminated among the bundles. Bundle 2 (Stress Graduate Education) was the clear choice of the faculty. They understood, and were excited about, finally having chosen their strategic future. They left that meeting with a sense of relief and incredible excitement. The process—and the investment they had made in it—had produced a result that they were persuaded to adopt and they felt good about their decision.

Figure C.2   The Four Scenarios (alternative futures five years out) (cont.)

Bundle 3 Innovate in the Delivery of Content

After five years of working on pedagogical innovation with information technology, the CIS Department has achieved international recognition. Two years
ago, three faculty members published the highly debated article "Distance
Learning, Distant Impact." In this article the authors demonstrated the critical
conditions for "distant" and "presencial" learning. Faculty members at the CIS
Department have reinvented teaching. Some teachers focus on course requirements, while others focus on designing and testing course content and
new courses. Students only come into contact with some of the faculty. These
professors are experts in the management of student learning through learning
by objectives. Onsite and remote learners walk through the different activities,
labs, and writing assignments that have proven to be the most effective means
to learn a given topic (e.g., B2B), information assessment, software engineering). The CIS faculty has been awarded four new major grants to continue to
study the role of information technology in education and learning assessment.

Figure C.2   The Four Scenarios (alternative futures five years out) (cont.)

Bundle 4 Improve Quality of Undergraduate Students

Over the past five years, the CIS Department has been very successful in at-
tracting the best students in the IS field. Operating a program that serves more
than 1,100 students, the Department manages three promotion programs: one
with high schools, one with community colleges, and one with other national
and international universities. The base of the Department's promotion effort is
the quality of its alumni and the recognition of our graduates' quality by industry. Corporations regard highly our students' writing, critical-thinking, and problem-solving abilities. Service learning and other "active" teaching strategies
contribute to the Department's success. Last year, for example, the CIS Department won the "Education for a New Society" award for the way its undergraduate program teaches and promotes ethical behavior. Next year, the CIS
Department will expand its international program to enroll more students from
Chile, Brazil, and Costa Rica in Latin America; Poland and Slovenia in Eastern
Europe; and South Korea and China in Asia.

Stage 11 Development Plan

Now that the strategic direction for the department was set, the DPC, together with the facilitator, began planning the meeting that would develop
the implementation plan. Tasks were created that were essential to implement Bundle 2, and were each initially assigned to a professor or group of
professors. The next step would be, at a subsequent department meeting, to
agree on the initial assignments, and the due dates for, and likely resources
needed to accomplish, the tasks.

Planning Horizon

The planning horizon chosen was five years in recognition of the fact that
implementing any plan would take at least that long given the slow bureau-
cratic processes of the university. For example, it takes two years just to get

a new course approved by the College of Business Administration and the Academic Senate.

Implementation

Progress in implementation over the next few years will be measured informally every academic quarter and in detail in a strategic-planning meeting every year. Measurements will essentially consist of progress in completing the complex tasks within the time stated. In the future, surveys will be necessary to gauge "soft" issues such as reputation and external perception.

Summary

The following aspects of the process were considered to be particularly innovative:

- Forming a steering committee (the DPC) to plan and be responsible for the process (and not delegate that to the external facilitator) and to communicate that process with the rest of the department and prepare them for each stage of the process.

- The (small-) size and democratic composition of the DPC to include the department chair, a senior faculty member, and a new faculty member.

- Elevating key aspects of the strategic-planning process to be paramount:

  · Involving the entire department (including part-time faculty).

  · Pursuing only that strategic direction that the whole department could get behind.

  · Allowing free expression (a junior faculty member's opinion would have the same weight as the chair) and respect for all at all meetings.

- Creating strategic alternatives and selecting the best one based on specific criteria.

- Using scenarios as an aid to arguing for each alternative.

Postscript

The CIS department is well on its way to achieving its chosen strategic direction, and could not have done this without following a strategic-planning model and process and getting unanimous buy-in from every faculty member to the chosen direction. Clearly, the impact of the strategic-planning process on the organization was enormous. This first effort exceeded its expectations and could well form a model for the other academic departments within the college and the university.

Appendix D

Suggested Survey Questions for Assessing the Strategic-Planning Process

Situation Analysis

1. Were sufficient data collected for various parts of the situation analysis? If not, which particular parts were shortchanged?

2. Was enough time allowed for data collection? (If a system is in place in which such data are collected year-round, omit this question.) Where would more time allowed have been beneficial?

3. Was enough analysis performed on the data? If not, where would more analysis have been beneficial?

4. Were credible sources used for data and forecasts? If not, for which kinds of data were they not credible?

5. For those analyses that used subjective estimates, did you agree for the most part on how those analyses turned out? Where particularly did the subjectivity affect the credibility of the analytic findings? Were the opinions of some people given unfair attention over those of others?

6. Would the use of outside experts have improved any part of the situation analysis (e.g., having an economist talk to the managers about economic trends for the coming year)?

7. Do you believe that the participants in general understood the terms and terminology used in the situation analysis (e.g., core competence)? Were there any terms or concepts that you personally did not understand?

Strategic Analysis

8. Were enough key strategic issues identified? If not, what might you have added?

9. Do you believe they really represented the most critical issues facing the company? If not, why not? Which ones were left out? Was the omission an oversight, or were some people afraid to articulate it?

10. Did the strategic issues reflect the kind of far-out strategic thinking you imagined should have occurred? If not, why not?

11. Could you have suggested any that was not on the list? If so, what is it?

12. In your mind, were the strategic-alternative bundles sufficiently creative and realistic?

13. When creating them, do you think participants were unduly influenced by what the company is currently doing, by its current strategies or by what you know the CEO really wants? If so, how could we correct for this in the future?

14. Do you believe that anyone who could have contributed usefully to the process of creating these alternative bundles was allowed to do so and actually did so? If not, how could this be corrected?

15. Do you think the criteria that were used to evaluate the alternative bundles were reasonable for this company? If not, which others would you like to have seen used?

16. Do you believe that the analysis that was used comparing the alternatives against the criteria produced a believable result? Why or why not?

17. Which of the alternative bundles would you have preferred that the company follow other than the one chosen? Why? Were you able to voice your point of view? If not, why not?

18. During the sessions choosing a preferred strategic bundle, did you feel you had ample opportunity to express your feelings, agreements, or misgivings? If not, why not?

Recommendations

19. Do you think that the objectives that the company decided on for the next year were appropriate and achievable? If not, why not?

20. What about the objectives for three years from now? In your opinion, are they unattainable? Or are they "stretch" objectives (challenging yet attainable)? Are they set without much careful thought (e.g., an extrapolation of last year's)? Or are they set too low? Why do you feel this way? What do you think they should have been?

21. Are you pleased and excited about the direction the company is taking now as a result of the strategic-planning exercise? If not, why not?

Some General Questions

22. Did you think the whole process took too long? Why? Where could it have been shortened?

23. Did the process stick to the original schedule? If not, where did it deviate? Do you think the schedule might have been unrealistic?

24. If the process did not keep to the original schedule, did you notice any adverse effects? If so, what were they?

25. What lessons did you learn about the process this year that might be put to good use next year?

26. Has your own knowledge of strategic planning increased? How do you know? If not, why not?

27. Do you believe that everyone that participated in the process is substantially "on the same page," or did the process conclude with a number of people in significant disagreement? If the latter, what suggestions do you have for airing such disagreements more fully and resolving them?

28. Overall, do you believe the company is better off for having been through this strategic-planning exercise? Why or why not?

Glossary

Acid-test ratio See *Quick ratio*.

Acquisition strategy A legitimate way of growing by acquiring and controlling another company. Typically, a company acquires a competitor to increase its customer base, sales, and market share. But other good reasons include acquiring a company for its technology and know-how, as well as diversifying into an industry about which the company knows very little. The track record of successes in acquisitions over the past 20 years or so is about 20%. Among the principal reasons for acquisitions not succeeding are paying a hefty premium for the company in the first place (almost never recouped), realizing potential "synergies" (seldom realized), and integrating the cultures of the two companies.

Altman Z-score The Altman Z-score is a bankruptcy indicator. The Z-score is used for a manufacturing firm, and the Z_2-score for a non-manufacturing firm. Each score is computed using a regression equation that employs financial ratios, as follows:

X_1 = Net working capital divided by total assets

X_2 = Retained earnings divided by total assets

X_3 = EBIT divided by total assets

X_4 = Market value of equity divided by book value of debt (if this information is unavailable, total equity divided by total debt is an acceptable substitute)

X_{4a} = Net worth divided by total debt

X_5 = Total sales divided by total assets

Z-score = $1.2X_1 + 1.4X_2 + 3.3X_3 + 0.6X_4 + 1.0X_5$

If the Z-score is > 2.99, the company is financially healthy (safe zone); if it is < 1.81, the company is in the bankrupt zone and in serious financial trouble. Between the two zones lies the gray area.

Z_2-score = $6.5X_1 + 3.26X_2 + 6.72X_3 + 1.05X_{4a}$

If the Z_2-score is > 2.59, the company is financially healthy (safe zone); if it is < 1.11, the company is in the bankrupt zone and in serious financial trouble. Between the two zones lies the gray area.

Average collection period Calculated by dividing 365 by accounts receivable turnover (annual credit sales divided by accounts receivable). Indicates the average number of days the firm must wait for payment after making a sale.

Bargaining power In any negotiation, any party that can dictate the terms of the negotiation is said to have bargaining power. In an industry, who has bargaining power—the producers (rivals) or customers? Who needs the other more? Are buyers' switching costs high? Typically, in a commodity industry, where all rivals produce identical products and buyers choose the lowest price, the buyer has bargaining power. When all rivals are differentiated, the industry has bargaining power. A similar logic is used to assess whether the producers (rivals) or the suppliers have bargaining power. Industries that have bargaining power are profitable; those that don't experience subpar profitability.

Barriers to entry High barriers to enter an industry deter potential entrants from becoming competitors. Barriers to entry include capital investment required, the need to set up a distribution system, the time it takes to develop a brand identity (especially if companies compete on the basis of brands) and loyal customers, technological know-how, and manufacturing expertise. A common mistake is to imagine barriers to entry to be very high, whereas certain companies deciding to enter would find the barriers much lower. For example, a company wanting to enter the U.S. motorcycle industry would find the barriers to entry very high, but a foreign motorcycle manufacturer would find the barriers to entry low.

Bundle A strategic alternative that includes elements such as the technology on which the product is based, the product, capabilities, knowledge, integration skills, systems, value-chain management, supply chain, distribution, source of financing, strategy, strategic intent, and much more. Such elements, when integrated into a cohesive "story," form a business model. See also *Strategic alternatives*.

Business model A description of the way in which a firm does what it does to deliver customer value, often expressed as a story. The company's strategy should be considered part of the business model, although some authors disagree.

CEO style To characterize a CEO's style, think of 3–5 adjectives that best describe it, for example, aggressive, democratic, ambitious, knowledgeable, charismatic, personable, conservative, cost-conscious, customer-focused, innovative, autocratic, and the like. Particularly in small companies, the company's culture is a reflection of the CEO's style.

Channel markups The price a manufacturer charges for a product is not the same as the price the eventual customer pays. At each stage of distribution, the price increases reflecting the value added by that stage of the distribution process. So on top of the factory price must be added the markups of the wholesaler, the distributor, and the retailer.

Company objective This is a measurable target for the *whole company* to achieve, for example, total revenues, NIAT, any financial ratio, and the like. If the company has different lines of business or sources of revenues, or subsidiaries or divisions, objectives for these individual lines of business or divisions are not company objectives because they would not take into account the whole company. A company objective could be expressed as either an absolute dollar figure or a percentage increase over the previous year. The keys are that it: (1) is measurable, and (2) must be achieved within a specified timeframe. With financial ratios, it is better to state the value of the ratio itself as the objective.

Competition, basis of The most common bases include: *price*—typical in commodity industries, or where people sacrifice quality or service for a lower price, *quality*—where people will pay more for higher perceived quality, *service*—where customers go because of how well they are treated, *technology*—where advantages accrue through superior technology or patents, and *low-cost leadership*—power through having the lowest costs in the industry.

Competition, intensity of When analyzing how competitors compete within an industry, it is useful to characterize the intensity of that rivalry on a continuum from low to very high. The intensity could be high and getting even higher if, for example, there are many competitors, customers are price-sensitive, demand is falling, customer-switching costs are low, and a lot of technological innovation is taking place, that is, if it is getting more difficult to compete.

Competition, types of The most common types include: *monopoly*—the only competitor in the business (true if first to market, or if granted an exclusive territory), *duopoly*—only two competitors in the industry, *oligopoly*—a small number of independent rivals, *monopolistic competition*—a small number of rivals having strongly differentiated and branded products, *monopsony*—a monopoly on the buyer's side, that is, the whole industry serving one customer, and *pure competition*—a large number of competitors competing largely on price.

Competitive advantage An edge over its competitors that a company possesses. It could take the form of a proprietary product or process, a developmental lead time, or a discipline or level of service that cannot easily be emulated. Companies that have a core competence usually have a sustainable competitive advantage. A competitive advantage can erode over time if the company does not work at sustaining it or if it is too easily imitated.

Competitive strength There is an analytic method, very similar to that used for determining industry attractiveness, for coming up with a measure or index of competitive strength (CS Index). However, the factors used are different, being similar to critical success factors. Think of 5–8 factors that form the basis of the company's competitive strength in its industry, enter them in the table as row headings, assign weights to each one that add up to 100, and rate your company on each factor on a scale of 0–1.0, 1.0 being best. The final column contains the product of the weight for each factor and its rating, and the sum of the products yields the CS Index as a percentage. The CS Index is used to position the company in the GE Matrix (see *General Electric matrix*).

Competitor Anyone that takes sales away from you. Usually, competitors include companies that produce similar products or services targeted at the same market. Even if your company has many competitors, you should be able to name the key or most feared competitors in doing a competitive analysis. Often, such a short list would include the market leader, but just as often it would include competitors very similar to your company in market share, for example, if your company ranked 15th in market share, your key competitors could include companies perhaps ranked 12th to 18th. Competitors also include buyers or customers that might vertically integrate backwards (or make what they used to buy), suppliers that might vertically integrate forwards (or even bypass you in the value chain), substitutes, and potential entrants if the industry's barriers to entry are low. Finally, in an industry with disparate competitors, the ones your company really competes with are strategically similar to you (those in the same strategic group).

Concentrated industry An industry where only a few competitors account for a large percentage of sales. At one end of the continuum is a monopolist that has 100% of industry sales (the maximum concentration), while at the other end are tens of thousands of competitors, not one of which has more than a fractional share of the market (a very fragmented industry). In between are varying degrees of concentration: the big four public auditing firms that account for 96% of the business of auditing public companies in the United States (very concentrated), to the top 15 firms in the industry accounting for 65% of industry sales (moderately concentrated), to the top 20 firms accounting for 40% of industry sales (somewhat concentrated).

Concentration strategy Either product development, market penetration, market development, or any product market combination; the strategy implies that the company will remain in the business it is in.

Contingency A contingency plan is a backup plan. It is invoked only when a trigger point is reached. It must be something the company would do operationally and differently if the trigger occurred. A good contingency must meet three conditions: (1) It cannot change the chosen strategy to one that had been previously rejected; (2) it cannot be something that the company did regularly that gave rise to the trigger in the first place; and (3) it must address the problem inherent in the trigger. When things go wrong implementing a chosen strategy, a good manager would first try to correct or improve implementation of the strategy, that is, the operations or programs. Only when those have been tried and still found wanting should a change in the strategy be considered.

Core Competence A specialized expertise or blend of capabilities around which a company's strategy is built, and which may well form the basis of its competitive advantage. If a company does have a core competence, it usually has only one (more than one is possible, but rare). Many companies do not have a core competence. Also, it could be thought of as a capability that has strategic significance for the company. A core competence is a capability that meets all of the following four criteria: Is it valuable? Is it rare? Is it costly to imitate? Is it nonsubstitutable?

Corporate constraints A constraint is something that, during the planning horizon, cannot be changed and must therefore be planned around. Examples include banks that, at one time, could not have branches or do business in more than one state, and a CEO or company owner mandating that no acquisitions would be made or no debt financing be allowed as long as he or she was CEO or an owner.

Corporate culture The set of key values, beliefs, understandings, and norms shared by members of an organization. Culture refers to how a company goes about its business—the atmosphere that prevails in a company that either enhances or stifles what people try to do. A simple way to characterize a company's culture is to use adjectival descriptors suggested by comparisons such as informal versus formal; aggressive versus laid back; autocratic versus democratic; or participative low-cost versus costs be damned; high quality versus whatever quality; customer is king versus customer does not matter; respect tradition versus do whatever you want; go through channels versus talk to anyone; speak when you are spoken to versus speak when you have got something to say; seniority matters versus knowledge matters, and so on.

Coverage ratio See *Times-interest-earned ratio.*

Criteria matrix A matrix that compares alternative bundles against a number of appropriate criteria, so that one may be chosen as the best one. The criteria may be weighted or not. Typical criteria include revenues generated; profitability; investment required; return on investment; time to recoup the investment (breakeven); effect on company culture; strength of value proposition; bargaining power; riskiness; degree of competitive retaliation provoked; and extent to which it provides or builds on a competitive advantage. This list is by no means complete. Also, because all the criteria may not be relevant in a particular instance, only the most relevant five or six should be used.

The criteria mentioned are of two types—positively and negatively correlated. Positively correlated criteria are scored on a scale of 0–10, 10 being best, while negatively correlated criteria are scored on a scale of 0 to -10, 0 being best. For example, if bundle A generates much more revenues or higher revenue growth than B, it might merit a score of 8 compared to 4 for B. If bundle A is riskier than B, it might merit a score of -8 compared to -4 for B. The scores should reflect the relative strength of each bundle with respect to a particular criterion. In the previous revenue example, the two scores could just as easily have been 9 to 4, 8 to 6, or 7 to 3, depending on the revenue projections of each one compared to how the company might have fared had it continued what it is doing. In the end, the scores for each bundle are added and the one with the largest total is the one that should be chosen (a clear winner by a margin of at least three points is more credible than one with a margin of less than three). Notwithstanding the criteria matrix being a quantitative tool, its real purpose is to help the person or group doing the analysis to articulate persuasive arguments in favor of the chosen bundle.

Positively correlated criteria include revenues, profits, return on investment, strength of value proposition, degree of competitive retaliation provoked, bargaining power, and provision or extension of a competitive advantage. Negatively correlated criteria include investment required, time to recoup the investment, competitive retaliation, effect on company culture, and riskiness.

Critical success factor (CSF) Something a company must do well to succeed in the industry. CSFs attach to an industry and *not* to a company. For example, one could say, "The disk drive industry's CSFs are such and such," but not, "Seagate's CSFs are such and such." Think of these as "rules of the game" for a particular industry. Every industry has its own rules, which a company must "play by" if it wants to succeed in the industry. A brainstorming session could yield as many as 10 such factors; choose the most salient six or so in order to do a CSF analysis. A CSF analysis involves comparing a company's 3–5 key competitors with the company on each CSF.

Current assets These are assets that can be converted into cash within one year (assets whose benefits extend beyond one year are called *fixed assets*). They include cash, marketable securities, accounts receivable, inventory, and payments not due that have already been made such as prepaid taxes.

Current liabilities Financial obligations that the firm must meet within one year. (Those that extend beyond one year are grouped under long-term debt.) They include the current portion of long-term debt, accounts payable, short-term notes and loans, and payment received for products not yet delivered or services not yet rendered.

Current ratio Calculated by dividing current assets by current liabilities. The ratio indicates the extent to which the claims of short-term creditors are covered by assets that could be converted into cash during the period corresponding to the maturity of the liabilities (one year). This ratio should be greater than 1.0. If it is less than 1.0, the company has negative working capital.

Debt-to-assets ratio Calculated by dividing total debt by total assets. Indicates the extent to which borrowed funds have been used to finance the firm's operations. The ratio is typically less than 50%, but could be larger for growth companies or special circumstances. Creditors become anxious if the ratio rises beyond 75%. Ratios above 100% denote negative equity and serious financial problems.

Debt-to-equity ratio Calculated by dividing total debt by total equity, the ratio of borrowed funds to those provided by owners. The ratio is typically less than 1.0, but could be larger for growth companies or special circumstances. Creditors become very anxious if the ratio exceeds 3.0. A negative ratio denotes negative equity and the existence of serious financial problems (the company owes more money than is represented by the entire assets of the organization).

Differentiation strategy One of three generic strategies (see also *Low-cost leadership strategy* and *Focus strategy*) designed to attain a competitive advantage and achieve above-industry-average returns. It entails being unique or different from competitors to the extent that customers will pay more for your product/service (customers must perceive the differentiation). If they do not, then you are in fact not differentiated, even though you may think you are. The strategy involves an initial investment in market research to discover what customers value in a product or service that current products do not have, then redesigning/modifying the product to deliver the missing/desired benefits, then pricing it at a suitable premium, and advertising and promoting it. During this process, care should be taken to control costs; else the ability to maximize profits will be lost. The investment made in differentiating the product should be recouped as quickly as possible, after which the company will have above-industry-average profits.

In commodity industries, or industries in which the buyer has bargaining power, the secret to getting bargaining power back from customers is to employ a differentiation strategy. But you are not differentiated unless (1) the improvements made are along a dimension that customers really value; and (2) the customers are willing to pay more for the added benefits.

Distribution channels The ways in which your product can reach the market. Choices include through salespeople, sales reps, distributors, wholesalers, retailers (independents, chains, boutiques, mass merchandisers), mail order, and online (the Internet).

Diversification strategy Diversification means entering another industry, which could be related or unrelated to the current business. It could be done either through internal R&D—when a technology or product is developed that has application in another industry—or through acquisition—acquiring a company in another industry, whose managers know that industry very well and already have an established customer base. Calling the broadening or extending of a product line "diversification" is a common mistake.

Economies of scale This refers to lowering unit manufacturing, purchasing, promotion, and distribution costs as manufacturing volume or throughput increases.

Environmental trends Trends occurring in the firm's external environment, consisting of a "task" environment (containing elements with which the company interacts frequently, such as its industry, competitors, markets, creditors, investors, and labor pool) and a "general" environment (subdivided into major categories like economic, technological, political, legislative/regulatory, demographic, sociocultural, and attitudes/lifestyles). The environment is divided into these categories to make it easier to come to grips with all the changes that are happening. For companies, trends that might affect them must be understood and articulated for them to be taken into account in devising alternative strategies. However, if there is not enough time, the following process could be useful (in SAM^{tw}). For each trend, describe the trend, that is, something that may be getting smaller or larger, slower or faster, higher or lower. Then estimate the severity of the impact on the company by choosing either a positive (H, M, or L), neutral, or negative (H, M, or L) impact. The larger the potential impact, either positive or negative, the more data may need to be collected about the trend or change. Trends with positive impacts on the company are potential opportunities, while those with negative impacts are probably threats.

Financial conclusion   For purposes of a strategic analysis, there are basically five types of financial conclusion (that span a continuum) one can draw from an analysis of the past several years of a company's financial statements:

1. The company has been well managed, has been performing well financially, and is in financially sound condition.

2. Same as (1) except for one or possibly two major problems (e.g., high debt, high A/R, one bad year when sales and profits dipped, etc.).

3. Inconclusive, mixed results—can't say it's well managed, and it's not in trouble; it's done some things well and not others.

4. Same as for (5), except for one or possibly two _major_ things done well (e.g., revenue growth, declining debt/equity ratio, etc.).

5. The company is in serious financial trouble, is near bankruptcy, and in perilous financial condition.

Focus strategy   One of three generic strategies (see also _Low-cost leadership strategy_ and _Differentiation strategy_) designed to attain a competitive advantage and achieve above-industry-average returns. It entails competing in a niche within the larger industry and specializing to satisfy and serve a narrow market. Because the act of specialization also serves to differentiate the company, this strategy is sometimes called "focus differentiation." The idea of competing in a niche within the industry, besides enjoying some protection from large competitors, is to eventually dominate it and earn above-industry-average profits.

Fragmented Industry   See _Concentrated industry._

General Electric (GE) Matrix   A two-dimensional plot of the Industry Attractiveness (IA) index against the Competitive Strength (CS) index. Companies with high values of IA and CS should build and invest in improving their position in the industry, while those with low values in both should harvest and consider exiting the industry. See _Industry attractiveness_ and _Competitive strength._

Goal A goal is an end-state that the company would like to achieve, but one that is expressed qualitatively, for example, to become more innovative, to become a stronger competitor, to become known for quality, and so on. By contrast, an objective is measurable and time-dated.

Gross profit margin Calculated by dividing gross profit by total sales (gross profit equals total sales less cost of goods sold). Indicates the total margin available to cover operating expenses and yield a profit.

Industry This is the general name given to the arena in which a company and its competitors compete, such as auto, healthcare, leisure products, entertainment, defense, aerospace, sporting-goods, medical-equipment, and the like. The formal definition is "the collection of competitors that produces similar or substitute products or services to a defined market." Also, take care to specify the appropriate geographic scope of the industry, for example, the worldwide fast-food industry, the U.S. fast-food industry, or the fast-food industry in a particular city or state. Doing so will change the kind of statistics you collect and the competitors you analyze. Sometimes, the label 'industry' is used to denote a segment within it (e.g., the residential-construction industry, which is a segment or part of the larger construction industry). However, whether it is called an industry or a segment, the important thing is to correctly label the arena in which the company competes.

Industry attractiveness (IA) Industry attractiveness (IA) depends on several factors, such as size of market served, industry growth rate, degree of regulation, degree of competition, height of entry barriers (assume company is already a part of the industry), degree of technological innovation, and profitability. With such factors in place, one could then assess the attractiveness of a particular industry by weighting the factors according to their relative importance in your view (allocating 100 points among them), and rating them from your company's point of view (between 0–1.0, 1.0 being highest). The sum of the products of weightings and ratings in the last column yields an IA index (%), later used as one axis of the GE Matrix (see *General Electric matrix*).

Industry concentration See *Concentrated industry*.

Industry driving forces Driving forces are factors that are thought to cause an industry to change. Examples include changes in the industry growth rate, changes in who buys the product, changes in how the product is used, product/marketing innovations, entry or exit of major firms, increasing globalization, buyer preferences for differentiation, changes in regulation or government policies, legislation, changing societal concerns, attitudes, lifestyles, and reductions/increases in uncertainty and risk.

Industry-lifecycle stage Industries have lifecycle curves similar to products, divided into five major lifecycle stages. *Emerging* characterizes an industry before market acceptance of its product (growth rate between 0–5%). Once a market is established, it enters a *growth* period when demand exceeds supply and other competitors enter the industry (growth rates > 5%).

Growth wanes when supply catches up to and exceeds demand, when customers are harder to find (or must be snatched from competitors), and prices drop. Weak competitors fail or are acquired by stronger ones during a period called *shakeout,* as growth transitions to maturity. When growth drops to below 5%, the industry is said to be mature. With negative growth rates year after year (and not just a temporary, cyclical decline), the industry is said to be declining.

Industry profitability This refers to the average profitability of the industry or segment, as measured by net return on sales (NIAT over revenues) expressed as a percentage. Companies in industries with above-average profitability typically have a competitive advantage and bargaining power over their suppliers and customers, while those in industries with low-average profitability do not. Companies in high-profitability industries have highly differentiated products (such as designer perfumes), while the products of those in low-profitability industries are more like commodities (such as fertilizer).

Industry segment A subset of an industry that typically serves a clearly defined market segment. For example, the luxury car segment of the auto industry serves individuals with high incomes and a high need for status. Such a segment has its own set of competitors and unique challenges in competing. Companies in one segment rarely compete with companies in other industry segments unless segment boundaries are changing or blurring, or companies are in multiple segments. Some industries have clearly defined segments, such as insurance, with segments of life, auto, health, marine, workers' compensation, and the like, while others do not. Create a segment label if one is warranted.

Inventory-to-net-working-capital ratio Calculated by dividing inventory by net working capital. Measures the extent to which the firm's working capital is tied up in inventory.

Inventory turnover Calculated by dividing total revenues by inventory. When compared to industry averages, this indicates whether a company has excessive or perhaps inadequate inventory levels.

Joint venture (JV) A form of strategic alliance that requires creating a new company that is jointly owned by the two companies involved in the alliance (often described as two parents "giving birth" to an offspring that is a separate company). Each parent contributes various assets/skills to the "child" in the beginning such as capital, patents, technology, products, management, and so on. Similarly, profits are distributed to the parents (or assets in the case of liquidation) according to what was negotiated when the JV was created. JVs endure as long as the parents benefit from its existence, and can be dismantled at any time.

Key strategic issues A key strategic issue is either one of two things: (1) an external force or impending event that could impact the company dramatically such as an economic downturn, upcoming regulation, or the introduction of a new technology; or (2) a decision the company makes about its future that has a strategic impact on it, for example, merge with or acquire another company, focus on technological development, expand internationally, diversify, and the like. Strategic issues comprise a synthesis of the entire situation-analysis portion of a strategic analysis (weaknesses, opportunities, threats, industry and competitive analysis, market analysis, environmental trends). Think of them also as something that keeps the CEO up at night or that is constantly on his or her mind. Generally, it is not difficult to come up with 12–18 strategic issues, but a list this long should be pared to about 10–12 issues. These should comprise the most critical issues the company needs to address as it develops alternative bundles (options) and chooses a preferred one.

When articulating a strategic issue, it should be phrased as an issue. Either: (a) Should the company: . . . expand into Europe? . . . increase investment in R&D? . . . manufacture offshore? . . . acquire XYZ? Or (b) Whether to expand into Europe, increase investment in R&D, manufacture offshore, acquire XYZ . . . Phrasing them as a question is preferred (the former option). Include only those issues about which the answer to the question is uncertain. For example, if the answer to: "Should the company lower its costs?" is "Yes," then it is not a strategic issue; it is something one would do no matter which option is eventually chosen. But "*How* can the company reduce costs?" is not so clear-cut, and could well be a strategic issue.

Liquidation strategy When a company can no longer continue as a going concern and has debts that are too high for it to service, and a reorganization plan cannot be developed to the satisfaction of the firm's creditors (a condition for seeking bankruptcy protection), it has little choice but to liquidate its assets (i.e., cease to exist) and distribute the resulting proceeds to its creditors (typically cents on the dollar).

Low-cost-leadership strategy One of three generic strategies (see also *Differentiation strategy* and *Focus strategy*) designed to attain a competitive advantage and achieve above-industry-average returns. It entails investing to analyze the company's cost drivers and developing and implementing a plan for reducing costs to the point of being the low-cost leader in the industry. During this process, care should be taken not to reduce prices; else the ability to maximize profits will be lost. The idea is to recoup the investment made in reducing costs as quickly as possible, after which the company will have above-industry-average profits. The power of the strategy derives from being able to withstand any price war initiated by competitors.

Market A market is a group of actual or potential customers or buyers. It could include everyone on the face of the earth (the market for Coca-Cola), or some subset. Markets can comprise consumers (individuals) or businesses. They can be consciously geographically constrained or not—for example, within a 5-mile radius of a store or worldwide. Markets need to be described precisely and concisely, including their geographic scope—for example, not just banks, but banks worldwide or even middle-market banks worldwide. Because some markets are very large, they are often further subdivided into segments, and again into customer groups, which are ultimately clusters of customers.

Market/customer trends Knowing one's market or customers requires knowing what changes are happening to them. Do they now buy differently? Do they use the product differently? Are their needs changing? Are they becoming more price-sensitive?

Market growth This is the rate at which a particular market is growing, not the rate at which the industry serving it is growing. For example, if a particular market consists of U.S. teenagers, then this would allude to the rate at which the population of teenagers in the United States was growing, not the sales of products sold to teenagers. Also, this should not be confused with a company's strategy to "expand its market;" for example, if a company targets teenagers and wishes to expand its market to young adults, it now serves a much larger market, so its market has grown. But the size of the markets in question has not necessarily grown.

Market penetration The proportion of an industry's target market that has purchased the industry's products or services is a measure of the extent to which a market is penetrated. A brand-new market for an industry is 0% penetrated, while a saturated market is 100% penetrated. Thus, the extent to which a market is penetrated determines how much of it is unserved or underserved. If underserved, it presents a growth opportunity for companies in that industry. Estimates of market penetration are often built on assumptions, requiring great care in making or interpreting the estimate. For example, a TV in every household would lead to a conclusion of 100% penetration, assuming that each household would need only one TV. But we all know this is not true, as many households own multiple TVs while others do not even have one. Market penetration is also a concentration strategy.

Market segment See *Industry segment* and *Market.*

Market share Market share is the ratio of a firm's revenues to the total dollar sales in an industry, expressed as a percentage, taking into account not only number of units sold but also their price. Sometimes, market share is calculated on a different basis, for example, number of screens in the movie theater industry, or installed base in the telecommunications-switching industry, or number of beds in hospitals.

Mission statement A mission statement is a concise statement of a company's reason for being, what it actually does, and for whom. It should contain what products or services the company produces for which target market, as well as how it considers itself different or unique. It should not contain statements of values, strategies, or objectives (but often does), but should contain, if possible, the company's customer value proposition. Once formulated, it should guide and constrain the activities and strategies of a company. However, only *after* a thorough strategic analysis of a company is someone able to decide whether an existing mission statement still applies or ought to be changed. If it should be changed, make sure it embraces what the company does now and what it is going to do over the next few years. (Ideally, mission statements should not be changed for several years.) Try not to formulate it too broadly because it will fail to guide or too narrowly because the company might miss out on opportunities. Make it accurate, short, and memorable.

Mobility barrier One or a set of factors that inhibits a company's movement from one strategic group in an industry to another that can include technology, capital, markets served, and so on.

Murphy's Law See *Trigger*.

Net earnings per share Calculated by dividing NIAT by the number of shares outstanding. These are the company's net earnings available (but not paid) to the owners for each share of common stock.

Net return on sales Also called *net profit margin*. Calculated by dividing after-tax profits (NIAT) by total sales, expressed as a percentage. Subpar margins indicate either low prices or high costs or both—and should also be compared to industry averages if available.

Net profit margin See *Net return on sales*.

Operational objectives See *Program objectives*.

Opportunities Opportunities are product-market issues, that is, any combination of current, improved, or new product (or service) for an existing, expanded, or new market. See *Concentration strategy*. Opportunities could also emerge from changes in the environment that affect the company positively or favorably.

Potential entrants Potential entrants include any company (or sometimes an individual) that may enter an industry at any time. Because this happens without warning, they are difficult to identify. However, if the barriers to entering an industry are high, then potential entrants pose no threat; if they are low, then expect new competition to flood the industry.

Pricing strategy Pricing strategy is complex. Major rationales for setting price include: *Low-price leader* (common for companies that have the lowest costs in the industry or that want to gain market share aggressively in a price-elastic market), *pricing to allow for a reasonable profit* (common among mom-and-pops), *pricing to position the company* in the marketplace (e.g., high end), *pricing to force competitors out of business* (a common tactic that instigates price wars), *monopoly pricing* (especially for introducing a first-time product or when one has a captive audience, like concessions at the movies or a stadium), *differentiated pricing* (to affect behavior, such as $1.40 for a small size, $1.60 for medium, and $1.75 for the large—influencing most to ask for a large and few to ask for a small; or different prices for different parts of a theater or stadium, because most people want the best seats and are willing to pay more for them), *discount pricing* (as temporary promotions), or *pricing what the market will bear* (e.g., pay-per-view events and sometimes attributed to airlines, especially first-class seats).

Price-sensitivity Customers are extremely price sensitive if they perceive the industry's products as commodities (i.e., all products are alike), hence go for the lowest price. However, if the industry's products are differentiated, customers will seek the products they want with very little regard to price. Another test to apply is very close to the economic definition of price elasticity of demand: If you lowered your price a little, how many more customers would want to buy your product? If a lot, they are price-sensitive, and the market is said to be price elastic; if very few, they are not, and the market is said to be price-inelastic.

Program These are actual activities the company does to achieve the objectives set for a particular year. In some companies, programs are called "activities," "projects," or "tasks;" as used here, programs encompass all of these. Multiyear programs must be started the very next year, even though they might not be completed that year; some programs will continue from one year to the next, others will start in later years. When first identified, programs are described concisely; details are added during the operational planning stage. Programs for the next year are called "tactics."

Program objective Program objectives refer to objectives of the many operational programs a company is implementing such as an advertising program, PR program, sales-training program, distribution program, R&D program, and so on. It also refers to a partial objective, that is, anything less than a company objective. For example, it could be an objective for one of the company's lines of business, for international or domestic sales, for sales from products that did not exist three years ago, for divisional or sub-unit sales, and the like. Also known as *operational objectives*.

Quick ratio Calculated by dividing current assets less inventories by current liabilities. Measures the ability of the firm to pay off its short-term obligations without having to sell off its inventories. Creditors are pleased if this ratio is greater than 1. Also known as *acid-test ratio*.

Retrenchment strategy In situations where a company's revenues decline appreciably (e.g., in the defense industry as defense spending declines), a company consciously chooses to become smaller (retrenches) by trimming its costs and payroll to fit the lower level of expected revenues. Also, when a business divests itself of a part of the business or some of its assets, it automatically retrenches.

Seeking to be acquired This is another way in which the term *divesting* is used, except here the whole company is being divested or sold. (The term *divesting* is usually reserved for selling some but not all of a company's assets such as a subsidiary or division, a plant, a technology.) When a company is acquired, it could exist with its management and strategies intact and managed more or less at arm's length, or it could be folded completely into the acquiring company, fully integrated, and cease to exist as its former self.

Segment See *Industry segment.*

Served market This is a subset of the target market that can or might want to buy the firm's product or service, for example, if the target market for motorcycles is mainly men aged 18–24 years old, the served market is some subset that both would like to own a bike (not everyone) and can afford one, which reduces the potential market even further.

SPACE Stands for **S**trategic **P**osition and **AC**tion **E**valuation, an analytic tool to help determine the appropriate strategic posture of a firm. *SPACE* involves plotting competitive advantage, industry strength, financial strength, and environmental stability on a two-dimensional graph. Each of these four dimensions itself comprises a number of factors that are evaluated independently and then combined to yield an average score. The resulting plot could end up favoring one of four quadrants (the strategic postures), namely, aggressive, competitive, defensive, and conservative.

Strategic alliances An umbrella term that describes a cooperative strategy with another company, one that stops short of merging with or acquiring a controlling interest in that company. Common ways of cooperating include licensing another company's technology for a fee and ongoing royalties (including the reverse, that is, licensing one's technology to another company), long-term agreements with suppliers or manufacturers, exclusive or cross-distribution agreements (e.g., we will give you exclusive rights to market and sell our products in Germany, and you give us exclusive rights to market and sell your products in the United States), purchasing a noncontrolling interest in another company (for some consideration, like a seat on the board and first rights to its technology when developed), and forming a joint venture with another company (see *Joint venture*).

Strategic alternatives An alternative course of action that an organization should consider. These are called "bundles" in this book and are based on previously identified strategic issues. Bundles contain not only strategies, but also visions, programs, strategic intents, and other components needed to outline a clear direction for the company. Developing them involves strategic thinking and is an art and a creative act. Experience has shown that in order to be in a position to choose the best bundle from among several, the bundles should meet four criteria. They must:

- Be mutually exclusive—doing any one means the company cannot do any other.

- Be feasible—within the current or acquired resources such as capital, know-how, and managerial expertise of the company.

- Lead to a successful outcome as defined by the company.

- Address all the key strategic issues.

Everything one intends to do if adopting a bundle must be in it at this time. To more easily distinguish the bundles, a label should be chosen for each one that captures its essence. Bundles may contain common elements, that is, programs that you feel must be done no matter which bundle is chosen. Bundle elements may be linked together in a narrative description, if desired, to form a business model.

Strategic analysis One person's or group's attempt at arriving at a strategy, objectives, and key programs for a company, or performing an intermediate analytical task. (This definition is presented in Chapter 1.) Examples include comparing the company with its competitors, assessing the attractiveness of an industry, determining which company to acquire, assessing the financial performance and condition of the company, and the like. In doing a strategic analysis of a company, the company is not committed to implement the results of the analysis; however, in good strategic planning, many more people are involved and commitment follows.

Strategic conversation A carefully thought-out but loosely facilitated series of in-depth conversations for key decision makers throughout an organization; viewed as significantly enhancing strategic thinking.

Strategic decision One that affects the company's ability to compete, its position in the industry, or its viability as a going concern. (This definition was presented in Chapter 1.) Typically, operational decisions, such as choosing an ad campaign or financing a venture, are not strategic decisions. Use the definition as criteria for determining whether a decision is strategic.

Strategic group A group of companies in an industry that have similar strategies and that consider each other their primary competitors.

Strategic group map A two-dimensional representation of an industry using unrelated strategic dimensions as axes, and that serves to cluster strategically similar companies together in groups. A company would be most threatened by a competitor in its own strategic group, and may not compete at all with companies in "distant" strategic groups (far away from them on the map).

Strategic intent A statement of what ranking a company would like to aspire to in the industry or what market share it would like to obtain. For example, if it is the market leader, it should want to maintain its leadership position; if not the leader, it might want to overtake the leader, or overtake #4 from #5, or maintain its #2 position, or defend against #8 who is creeping up to challenge, and so on. Note that *maintaining* one's market share means growing at the *same* rate as the industry (rather than not growing at all), and takes fewer resources than increasing share.

Strategic management Encompasses both strategic planning and the implementation of the strategic plan to ensure, ideally, achieving intended results. (This definition is presented in Chapter 1.) It is what CEOs do (or should do) 100% of their time in running their companies.

Strategic planning The process by which a company develops a strategy to achieve certain purposes. (This definition is presented in Chapter 1.) This book is principally about how to do strategic planning.

Strategic thinking Coming up with alternative viable strategies or business models that deliver customer value. (This definition is presented in

Chapter 1.) Strategic thinking drives the strategic-planning process. (See Chapter 2, which discusses strategic thinking.)

Strategy How a company actually competes. (This definition is presented in Chapter 1.)

Strategy, kinds of The most common types include concentration (product development, market penetration, and market development), vertical integration, acquisition or merger, retrenchment, turnaround, strategic alliances, seeking to be acquired, divesting, diversification, liquidation, differentiation, low-cost leadership, and focus. Many of these are growth strategies, although "growth" per se is determined by setting and achieving higher objectives than the previous year.

Strengths Strengths are special capabilities or expertise, things a company does well that has enabled it to be successful to this point, and how it has prepared itself to compete in the future. Comparing a company's strengths against competitors' provides a more realistic assessment of them.

Substitutes An alternative to what is generally offered in an industry that a customer would buy. To help you identify substitutes to an industry's products or services, imagine being a customer and ask, "What are some alternatives to buying the industry's product?" For example, a substitute for eye glasses is contact lenses or laser surgery; a substitute for a live theater experience is going to a concert or the movies.

Substitutes, threat of The competitive threat of substitutes in an industry is high if there is a high likelihood the industry will adopt the substitute such as fiber optics in the cable industry or if substitute sales are increasing, and low if opposite conditions exist.

Target market The particular group of customers or market segment that a company has identified to target and persuade to buy its products (e.g., local people within a one-mile radius of a restaurant or all teenage girls nationally).

Technological innovation An important factor in competing in certain industries, especially high-tech industries. Often, technological innovation is what provides a mature industry with renewed growth. An important facet of a product-development strategy.

Threat A threat is an external force or impending event that may slow or prevent the company from achieving its objectives; it could also be construed as an environmental change or trend that has a negative impact on the company

Times-interest-earned ratio Calculated by dividing earnings before interest and taxes (EBIT) by interest expense. Measures the extent to which earnings can decline until the firm is unable to meet its annual interest costs. This ratio should be greater than 1; if it is less than 1, then the firm does not have enough money to service its debt. Also called *coverage ratio*.

Total assets turnover Calculated by dividing total revenues by total assets. Measures how well the company's assets are utilized. If lower than the industry average, this would indicate the firm is not generating sufficient sales given its investment in assets.

Trigger Murphy's Law ("if anything can go wrong, it will") is alive and well. A trigger is something that might go wrong in the future, such as a key result not being achieved, loss of a key manager, an assumption being proved wrong, and the like. In order to know precisely when the backup plan (contingency) should be invoked, the trigger should be quantitatively expressed. For example, "if revenues slow down, change the advertising campaign" does not tell one when to change the advertising campaign; but "if revenues lag projections by more than 15%" does.

Turnaround strategy Turnarounds are applied only to companies that, to use a medical analogy, are hemorrhaging, that is, they are losing millions of dollars a day and are in serious trouble. The reason the strategy is called turnaround is because the company's revenues and profits decline precipitously, are stabilized when the "bleeding" is staunched, and then rise as a new strategy enables the company to grow again. The strategy is rarely implemented without hiring an experienced turnaround consultant.

Value chain The sequence of stages involved from raw material to finished product to end-user. Each stage is an industry (e.g., a cloth mill being one stage from sheep on a farm, where wool originates, to a finished wool suit that an end-user buys; cloth mills compete with other cloth mills). Because value is added at each stage, the price of the part, component, or product increases; this value-added aspect is how the value chain got its name.

Another meaning of value chain is the sequence of value-added activities within a company, beginning with purchasing and ending with shipping/distribution. Tangential activities that add value are also included such as R&D, human resources, IT, and the like.

Value proposition The entire set of resulting experiences—at some price—that an organization causes its customers to have. (This definition is presented in Chapter 1.) Customers' perceptions of value change as both their needs and competitors' offerings change. Also referred to as *customer value.*

Vertical integration Being vertically integrated means controlling at least two stages of the value chain. Vertical integration also means either making what you used to buy or buying a supplier (backward vertical integration), or competing with or acquiring a customer (forward vertical integration). For example, selling directly to retail outlets instead of through a wholesaler or distributor is an example of forward vertical integration.

Vision statement A vision statement is a concise statement of where you would like to see your company 5–10 years from now, that is, what the company wants to become.

In many ways, a vision statement is more important as a direction setter for a company than a mission statement. It answers the question of where a company aspires to go and what it aspires to become in the future (5–10 years). It embodies the vision articulated by the company's leader. To be more effective, a vision statement should contain numbers that give it greater precision (although some believe it should contain no numbers). Like a mission statement, a vision statement should be short and memorable but, in addition, should be inspiring and achievable. It is the vision that drives the company, not the mission.

Weaknesses Weaknesses are internal. They include problems that need to be corrected, deficiencies recognized through a comparison with competitors, or deficiencies relative to proposed strategies (e.g., not enough resources to grow). Whether or not what is identified is an actual weakness, it is the *perception* of a weakness that counts.

Working capital Defined as current assets minus current liabilities, and indicates the resources available to the firm once its short-term obligations are met. Working capital is *not* cash. When current liabilities exceed current assets, we say that the company has negative working capital, a serious problem if it had to settle its short-term obligations.

Z-Score See *Altman Z-Score.*

Index

Bold numbers signify a table, figure, or sidebar